MW01004595

Anna Akhmatova

Anna Akhmatova

Her Poetry

David N. Wells

BERG

Oxford • Washington, D.C.

First published in 1996 by
Berg
Editorial offices:
150 Cowley Road, Oxford, OX4 1JJ, UK
22883 Quicksilver Drive, Dulles, VA 20166, USA

© David N. Wells 1996

All rights reserved.
No part of this publication may be reproduced in any form
or by any means without the written permission of Berg.

Berg is an imprint of Oxford International Publishers Ltd.

Library of Congress Cataloging-in-Publication Data

A catalogue record for this book is available from the Library of Congress.

British Library Cataloguing-in-Publication Data

A catalogue record for this book is available from the British Library.

ISBN 1 85973 094 9 (Cloth)
1 85973 099 X (Paper)

Typeset by JS Typesetting, Wellingborough, Northants.
Printed in the United Kingdom by WBC Book Manufacturers, Bridgend,
Mid Glamorgan.

Contents

Acknowledgements

A study trip to St Petersburg in early 1994 in connection with this book was assisted by a travel grant from the Australian Academy of the Humanities. In addition many individuals have contributed to it in one way or another. I should like to thank in particular Mikhail Kralin, Kamsar Grigor'yan, Abram Gozenpud, Michael Basker and Sandra Wilson.

Abbreviations

The following abbreviations are used for editions of Akhmatova's works in in-text references and the notes:

I, II, III   *Sochineniya*, 3 vols.: vol. I, 2nd edn, 1967 and vol. II, 1968, both ed. G. P. Struve and B. A. Filippov, Washington; vol. III, 1983, ed. G. P. Struve, N. A. Struve and B. A. Filippov, Paris.

K1, K2   *Stikhotvoreniya v dvukh tomakh*, ed. M. M. Kralin, Moscow, 1990.

SP   *Stikhotvoreniya i poemy* (Biblioteka poeta, bol´shaya seriya, 2nd edn), ed. V. M. Zhirmunskii, Leningrad, 1977.

S1, S2   *Sochineniya v dvukh tomakh*, ed. V. A. Chernykh, Moscow, 1986.

Note

Dates before 1917 are given according to the Julian calendar then in force in Russia. This was twelve days behind the Gregorian calendar used in western Europe during the nineteenth century and thirteen days behind during the twentieth.

The city currently known as St Petersburg is referred to by the various names it has been called at different times, i.e. until 1914, St Petersburg, 1914–24, Petrograd, 1924–90, Leningrad.

Life and Image

Akhmatova has meant widely different things to different people. She is the poet of female love whose lyrics have been avidly read by a mass audience from the 1910s to the present day. She is the courageous documentalist of the Terror of the 1930s whose writing provided secret support for women in the queues outside Stalin's prisons and for inmates of the GULag. For Soviet criticism she was the patriot whose verses inspired Soviet troops during the struggle against Nazi Germany and at the same time the 'decadent' poet left behind by the achievements of the revolution and hostile to the aims of Soviet society. She was a leading figure of the avant-garde at the beginning of the century but in the 1960s became the predominant representative of the literary tradition. Her poetry is accessible to a broad public and at the same time complex enough to sustain a flourishing critical analysis of its subtexts and cultural origins.

These sometimes contradictory positions were embodied by a single life which saw the utter transformation of Russian society, both ideologically and materially, as the result of a succession of revolutions, wars and periods of totalitarian rule. For Akhmatova, short periods of celebrity and official acclaim alternated with years of obscurity, isolation and material hardship. Akhmatova's biography is illuminating in itself as a study of the endurance of human personality, but it is also of interest as a rare example of the life of a creative writer who succeeded in negotiating the transition from tsarism through the traumas of the early Soviet period to the time of Khrushchev without seriously compromising her artistic integrity. Whether obviously or not, Akhmatova's work is substantially informed not only by the details of her private intellectual and emotional development, but also by the broader discourse of Russian and Soviet history.

This is not, of course, to say that Akhmatova's poetry can or should be read only or even principally for what it tells us about her psychology or public role, or for what it reveals about Soviet society in general. The biographical fallacy is one into which Akhmatova's critics have fallen all too easily: her work is important as *literature* through its ability to generalise experience and to move the reader by the power of language. Yet some knowledge of Akhmatova's life is useful even here. It helps us understand the genesis of her poetry: interpretation of her poems can after all be affected by a knowledge of the biographical impetus behind them; textual obscurities can often be resolved by reference to the details of Akhmatova's social activity or domestic routine.

In fact, however, the available sources for a life of Akhmatova are relatively scant. Revolution and war in twentieth-century Russia have caused much of the existing written record to be destroyed. For long periods political conditions made it dangerous to keep records of any kind and letters and other documents were either not written in the first place or deliberately destroyed. Many of those who knew Akhmatova in the earlier part of her life died in the aftermath of the revolution, during the Terror or in the Second World War, and, although there are notable exceptions, the majority of existing memoirs focus principally on her life in the 1950s and 1960s. For long periods Akhmatova was in official disfavour with the communist authorities and lived in relative isolation. These years are particularly invisible to the biographer. The following is therefore by no means a comprehensive account: no biography of Akhmatova will ever be as complete as those that have been written of her western European contemporaries, writers such as George Bernard Shaw or Marcel Proust.

The task, moreover, is complicated by the high degree to which accounts of Akhmatova's life can be seen as 'constructed', either consciously or unconsciously, to serve the polemical purposes of their authors. Akhmatova herself devoted a considerable amount of energy to manipulating the image of herself she presented to others. The lyric 'I' of her early poetry, the prophetic rhetoric of her later verse and the anecdotes which she promoted about her past in later years all tend, often misleadingly, to project Akhmatova's uniqueness as a literary and historical figure and to emphasise her position as representative of her generation and cultural arbiter.[1] Conversely, both émigré and Soviet critics and memoirists, for different reasons, often preferred to ignore Akhmatova's life and poetry after the early 1920s and to cast her either as an innocent victim of the revolution or as its decadent opponent. What follows is partly an attempt to look behind these and other myths, partly an attempt to elucidate their undoubted influence on Akhmatova's life and intellectual development.

Although Akhmatova is often thought of as pre-eminently a poet of

1. See C. Kelly, *A History of Russian Women's Writing, 1820–1992*, Oxford, 1994, pp. 207–23.

St Petersburg, she was born, on 11 June 1889, in the Black Sea resort of Bolshoi Fontan, now a suburb of Odessa. Akhmatova's original surname, Gorenko, is of Ukrainian derivation, and there were southern connections on both sides of the family: her father, Andrei Antonovich Gorenko, was born in Sevastopol, and her mother, Inna Erazmovna, née Stogova, had strong family links with Kiev. Akhmatova's association with Odessa, however, was short-lived since her parents moved to Pavlovsk and then Tsarskoe Selo, both outside St Petersburg, in the year after her birth. There were brief visits during the summers of 1904 and 1909, but while Akhmatova was growing up the family's usual holiday destination was the Crimea. Between 1896 and 1903 the Gorenkos returned regularly to a house on Streletskaya Bay, just west of Sevastopol. Akhmatova seems to have come to know the area extremely well, exploring not only its coastline but also the extensive remains of the ancient Greek settlement of Chersonesus and the traces left by the Crimean War. Her memoirs of these childhood summers by the Black Sea suggest a holiday life of complete freedom and unconventional behaviour. One fragment reads: 'A pagan childhood. [. . .] I was given the nickname 'the wild girl' because I went around barefoot and without a hat, dived from a boat into the open sea, swam during storms and was sunburned till my skin peeled, and all this shocked the provincial young ladies of Sevastopol' (S2, 243).

Akhmatova's winter life in Tsarskoe Selo was outwardly more formal and marked by the usual concerns of a young woman of the educated classes. She attended the Mariinskaya *gimnaziya* (high school), went to church, visited St Petersburg from time to time to go to the opera and to the museums, made excursions to Pavlovsk to the famous railway station concerts.[2] There were long walks through the parks with their follies and neoclassical statues, and much time spent reading, particularly the fashionable literature of the day, from the novels of Knut Hamsun to the works of the Russian decadent poets. At the same time Akhmatova remained to some extent the 'wild girl' of the Crimea, running off to St Petersburg without permission, for example, and liking to shock occasionally by her speech and behaviour.[3]

Both Anna and her older sister Inna wrote poetry from an early age, imitating the 'new style' they found in their reading. Though none of this *juvenilia* has survived, it is described by one school friend who remembered hearing it as 'vague and allusive' in the Symbolist

2. See R. D. Timenchik (ed.), *Anna Akhmatova: desyatye gody*, Moscow, 1989, p. 13.
3. See O. A. Fedotova, 'Anya Gorenko', in M. M. Kralin (ed.), *Ob Anne Akhmatovoi: stikhi, esse, vospominaniya*, Leningrad, 1990, pp. 29–32.

manner.[4] Inna married soon after completing the *gimnaziya* and with her husband, Sergei Vladimirovich von Stein, presided over artistic soirées which, notwithstanding her father's opposition, the young Anna sometimes also contrived to attend.[5]

It was during this period in Tsarskoe Selo that Akhmatova first attracted the attention of her future husband, the poet Nikolai Gumilev. The pair first met on Christmas Eve 1903, and in spite of Akhmatova's initial indifference Gumilev continued to seek her out, making use of his friendship with Akhmatova's older brother, Andrei, to give him access to the Gorenko house. He was to pester Anna with innumerable proposals of marriage from 1905 onwards.

After Akhmatova's parents separated in 1905, Inna Erazmovna moved with the younger children to Evpatoriya, further up the Crimean coast from Sevastopol, and Akhmatova lived there until the autumn of 1906 while preparing for her final year of school in Kiev. She spent the summers of 1907 and 1908 at or near Sevastopol, but afterwards did not return to the Crimea until the summer of 1916.

Most of the period 1906–10 was spent in Kiev. After completing her studies at the Fundukleevskaya *gimnaziya* there in 1907, Akhmatova enrolled in the Law Faculty of Kiev University (the Higher Women's Courses), where she studied for two years, taking particular interest in Latin and the history of the law. She had many relatives in Kiev, and while there lived with the family of her mother's sister, Iya Erazmovna Zmunchilla. Akhmatova's letters from this period to Sergei von Stein, which have against all the odds survived, refer to several aunts and cousins with whom she was in regular contact. The young Akhmatova must have felt keenly the untimely death of her sister Inna in 1906, and found that she had little in common with most of her Kiev relatives. She remarked many years later:

> I did not like pre-revolutionary Kiev. A city of vulgar women. There were many rich people and owners of sugar factories. They threw themselves in their thousands on the latest fashions, they and their wives. . . My twenty-stone cousin, waiting to try on a new dress at Schweitzer's, the famous tailor's, used to kiss an icon of St Nicholas: 'Please let it hang nicely'. . .[6]

Some idea of the resentment felt by Akhmatova at the restrictions of provincial life after the glamour of the capital can be seen in her letters to Stein. As Anatolii Naiman suggests, such expressions as 'The only

4. Ibid., p. 34.

5. V. K. Luknitskaya, *Nikolai Gumilev: zhizn' poeta po materialam domashnego arkhiva sem'i Luknitskikh*, Leningrad, 1990, p. 34.

6. L. K. Chukovskaya, *Zapiski ob Anne Akhmatovoi*, vol. 1, Paris, 1976, p. 47.

good moments are when everybody goes to have dinner at the pub', or 'This summer Fedorov kissed me a lot again, and swore that he loved me, and he smelled of his lunch', or 'Of course, I shall never study again, except perhaps at cooking classes' recall the oppressive narrow world of Chekhov's frustrated provincial heroines.[7]

Further brief insights into Akhmatova's life in Kiev are provided by the memoirs of her classmate V.A. Beer. On one occasion Beer portrays the poet as a sensitive and diffident young woman absorbed in her thoughts in the cathedral of St Sophia, and on another as an alert reader, familiar as no one else in her circle with the romantic early work of the Symbolist poet Valerii Bryusov.[8] It seems too that Akhmatova attracted many admirers in Kiev. Valeriya Sreznevskaya recalls that her friend received numerous proposals of marriage which, however, she treated with little seriousness. Akhmatova herself was infatuated for a while with a certain Vladimir Golenishchev-Kutuzov, whom she had known in St Petersburg, and whose photograph she insistently requested from Stein.

Gumilev, however, still persisted in his attentions in spite of numerous refusals and contrived to visit Akhmatova in Kiev and elsewhere regularly, even during the time he was studying in Paris. Her rejections led him to attempt suicide at least once, but Akhmatova finally accepted him, though clearly not without misgivings, after they met at an artistic event in November 1909. The wedding took place in Kiev on 25 April 1910.

After honeymooning in Paris, where Akhmatova became aware for the first time of the international culture of the Russian emigration – the art of Chagall, the music of Stravinsky, Diaghilev's *ballets russes* – she returned with Gumilev to Tsarskoe Selo. At first she found that she had lost all contact with her previous schoolgirl life there and her life was relatively quiet. In September 1910 Gumilev left on a long trip to Abyssinia, returning only in March 1911. While he was away Akhmatova attended the Raev historical and literary courses in Petersburg and spent a good deal of time writing.[9]

The first poem of Akhmatova's to be published had appeared in a minor literary magazine edited by Gumilev in Paris in 1907. It was only in 1910, however, that she began to take the matter of publishing her verse seriously. It has sometimes been asserted that Akhmatova emerged fully formed as a mature poet. Certainly the poems which she

7. See A. Naiman, *Rasskazy o Anne Akhmatovoi*, Moscow, 1989, pp. 40–2.

8. Timenchik, *Desyatye gody*, pp. 39–41.

9. S2, 237. A. Haight, *Anna Akhmatova: A Poetic Pilgrimage*, New York, 1976, p. 17.

first presented to a public literary audience show remarkable confidence and technical skill, but Akhmatova had been refining her technique and honing her vision for many years before she thought of publishing. The vast majority of her very early works have not survived. Writing later about her first poems Akhmatova remarks on her strict selectivity: of the two hundred poems she had written by September 1911, only thirty-five were included in her first book.[10]

A major influence on Akhmatova at this time was Innokentii Annenskii's second collection of poems *Kiparisovyi larets (The Cypress Chest)*, with its penetrating psychological subtlety and its insistence on the poetic possibilities of the mundane. In her later memoirs she confirmed its importance for her own writing: 'I read (in the Bryullov hall of the Russian Museum) the proofs of *The Cypress Chest* (when I came to Petersburg at the beginning of 1910) and suddenly understood something about poetry.'[11] It seems reasonably clear too that Akhmatova's move from provincial Kiev to Tsarskoe Selo, where she had access to the cultural resources and literary contacts of the capital, her first trip to Paris, and no doubt the guidance and example of Gumilev, who by 1910 had already published three books of verse, contributed much to her maturity as a poet. Nevertheless, it is also notable that it was precisely during Gumilev's absence that the critical moment occurred. Akhmatova later recorded that when she read her poetry to him at the railway station in St Petersburg on his return from Africa he was struck by a qualitative difference: 'You are a poet; you should put out a book.'[12]

To complete her new self-identification as a poet, in 1910 Anna Gorenko first adopted the literary pseudonym Anna Akhmatova.[13] The name is that of her great-grandmother, Praskov'ya Fedoseevna Akhmatova, who according to Akhmatova's note on the matter was descended from the Mongol khan Akhmat and ultimately from Genghis Khan.[14] Akhmatova began to appear in prominent literary circles in St Petersburg: she attended, for example, the Monday gatherings at the house of the prominent Symbolist poet and theoretician Vyacheslav

10. S1, 386–7.
11. A. A. Akhmatova, 'Avtobiograficheskaya proza', *Literaturnoe obozrenie*, no. 5, 1989, p. 11. On the significance of Annenskii for the development of Akhmatova's poetry see A. Ariev, '"The Splendid Darkness of a Strange Garden": Tsarskoe Selo in the Russian Poetic Tradition and Akhmatova's "Ode to Tsarskoe Selo"', in L. Loseff and B. Scherr (eds), *A Sense of Place: Tsarskoe Selo and its Poets: Papers from the 1989 Dartmouth Conference Dedicated to the Centennial of Anna Akhmatova*, Columbus, Ohio, 1993, pp. 64–8.
12. S1, 386.
13. Ibid.
14. S2, 240.

Ivanov.[15] She began too to publish in the literary journals of the capital, notably in *Apollon (Apollo)*, one of the most influential publications of the younger generation of writers.

Most of the spring and summer of 1911 were taken up with travelling. Akhmatova spent two months in Paris without her husband, and then divided the summer mostly between Kiev and Slepnevo, Gumilev's mother's estate to the north of Moscow in the province of Tver'.[16] Akhmatova was to spend a good deal of time at Slepnevo during the next few years and reacted to it ambiguously. On the one hand she found it dull after the excitements of Paris and St Petersburg and felt to some extent stifled by her husband's relatives. She describes it as 'an unpicturesque place: fields ploughed in equal squares on the slopes, windmills, quagmires, drained swampland, gates, wheat and more wheat. . .'[17] But at the same time she could be sensitive to Slepnevo's rural charm and the months she spent there proved very productive for her poetry: many of the poems of *Chetki (Rosary)* and *Belaya staya (White Flock)*, her second and third collections, were written at Slepnevo, as was the long poem *U samogo morya (By the Sea Shore)*.[18]

Akhmatova's début on the literary stage came at a significant transitional point in the history of Russian literature. Up until 1910 the dominant literary aesthetic had been that of Symbolism. This movement had itself been a reaction against the utilitarian and realist tendency in literature which had dominated from the mid-nineteenth century, and it had brought new life to Russian poetry at a time when the favoured mode of expression was prose. The Symbolists, in brief, sought to look beyond the realities of this world towards a higher reality that was accessible through the power of language, by means of the magic of words. This search naturally took many forms in the work of different writers, but was characterised by an essential mysticism and by an allusive use of language which at its best was exhilarating, but which often slipped into absurdity. By 1910, the year of the so-called 'crisis of Symbolism', the movement had reached a dead end, and the time was ripe for a re-evaluation of its role.

By 1911, moreover, Gumilev in particular was becoming increasingly frustrated with the proprietorial role over literature that was being exercised by Vyacheslav Ivanov and the rift was exacerbated when,

15. Luknitskaya, *Nikolai Gumilev*, p. 115; L. Ivanova, *Vospominaniya: kniga ob ottse*, Moscow, 1992, p. 33.

16. See Luknitskaya, *Nikolai Gumilev*, p. 117 for details of Akhmatova's and Gumilev's hectic travel schedules.

17. S2, 238.

18. See SP, 510–11.

for example, he published a damning review of the latter's book, *Cor ardens*, in *Apollo*. In the autumn, together with a group of younger writers including Akhmatova, Osip Mandelstam and Sergei Gorodetskii, he formed a literary discussion group called the 'Guild of Poets' ('Tsekh poetov'). This group, as suggested by its name, consciously promoted the idea of poetry as a craft in opposition to Ivanov's view of it as essentially an esoteric mystery. The 'Guild of Poets' did not itself attack Symbolism directly – indeed, its first meeting was attended by one of the movement's leading representatives, Aleksandr Blok. However, a group within the 'Guild', consisting of Gumilev, Akhmatova, Mandelstam, Gorodetskii, Vladimir Narbut and Mikhail Zenkevich, gradually formulated the anti-Symbolist doctrine which became known as Acmeism.

Acmeism may well have been more important in providing a literary-political platform for its adherents than in its attempts to enunciate a clear aesthetic position.[19] The manifestos issued rather belatedly by Gumilev and Gorodetskii in early 1913 are on close examination contradictory and obscure. Nevertheless, their main focus can be represented as a call for clarity, for an emphasis on the objects of this world for their own sake and not on their potential value as symbols. As Gorodetskii wrote in his manifesto: 'For the Acmeists the rose has again become beautiful for itself alone, for its petals, scent and colour, and not for its supposed likeness to mystical love or anything else.'[20] Akhmatova's early verse embodied this ideal of clarity and concreteness to a high degree and, because these qualities were unusual in the poetry of the period, this was no doubt an important cause of its instant success.

In March 1912 the 'Guild of Poets' published Akhmatova's first book, *Vecher (Evening)*, in a modest edition of 500. It was quickly sold out and received about a dozen encouraging notices in the literary press. According to her later memoirs, however, Akhmatova herself was less satisfied with her work and resented the loss of privacy which her new-found fame brought with it. She writes of herself in the third person:

These poor verses of an empty-headed little girl were for some reason reprinted thirteen times. [. . .] The little girl herself (so far as I can remember) did not foresee any such fate for them and hid the issues of the journals in which they appeared under the cushions of the sofa 'so as not to upset herself'. Out of distress that *Evening* had been published, she even

19. For a detailed discussion of Acmeist aesthetics see J. Doherty, *The Acmeist Movement in Russian Poetry: Culture and the Word*, Oxford, 1995. The literary history of the movement is treated here in ch. 2, pp. 60–102.
20. Quoted in C. Brown, *Mandelstam*, Cambridge, 1973, p. 142.

went to Italy (spring 1912) and, sitting in the tram, she would look at her neighbours and think 'How lucky they are – they haven't got a book coming out.' (S2, 245–6)

Be this as it may, during the next few years Akhmatova gradually threw off her early shyness. Her second book, *Rosary*, appeared in March 1914 in an edition of 1,000 and established Akhmatova definitively as one of the most popular poets of the day, and as one of the most prominent and sought-after figures in literary and artistic St Petersburg.

From the winter of 1911–12 Akhmatova was reading her work regularly in public. One fashionable venue which she frequented until the First World War was the 'Brodyachaya sobaka' ('Stray Dog') cabaret, a major focal point for the literary bohemia of its day. Akhmatova gave particular attention to the performance aspect of her readings, rehearsing them with meticulous care, and contemporary memoirs indicate that she impressed as much by her physical presence as by her literary talents. The following passages suggest something of the impact she made on her audiences:

Anna Akhmatova, a shy and elegantly insouciant beauty with her 'straight fringe' covering her forehead, with her rare grace in half-movements and half-gestures, read her early poems, almost singing them. I cannot remember anyone else who read so well or with such musical subtlety as Akhmatova.[21]

Anna Akhmatova struck me by her appearance. Now, in memoirs about her she is sometimes called a beauty – no, she was not a beauty. But she was more than a beauty, better than a beauty. I have never seen a woman whose face and whole appearance stood out wherever she was, in the midst of any beauties, with such expressiveness, such genuine animation, something that immediately attracted attention.[22]

Akhmatova's early audiences were also struck by the narrative point of view of her verse and her manipulation of current patterns of poetic discourse. Her poems regularly take a female perspective on what had hitherto been largely a male domain. Akhmatova's version of the Hamlet story, for example, is told from the point of view of Ophelia ('Chitaya Gamleta' ('Reading Hamlet', S1, 21–2)). More importantly so far as the creation of the Akhmatova mythology is concerned, her poetic scenarios frequently provide a mouthpiece for such elusive and

21. Yu. Annenkov, *Dnevnik moikh vstrech: tsikl tragedii*, Leningrad, 1991, vol. 1, p. 107.
22. G. Adamovich, 'Moi vstrechi s Annoi Akhmatovoi', in Kralin, *Ob Anne Akhmatovoi*, p. 90.

mysterious female figures of Symbolist poetry as Blok's 'Stranger', defined as they are in terms of male experience.[23] The impact of such rewritings of existing texts is strengthened by Akhmatova's near exclusive use of a first-person narrator, and the success of her literary strategy is reflected in the persistent (and untrue) rumours that circulated in the 1910s that she was having a real-life affair with Blok.

The St Petersburg season lasted only from September to May, and Akhmatova continued to travel extensively during the summer months. In the early spring of 1912 she was in Kiev; in April she left Tsarskoe Selo for Switzerland and Northern Italy, returning to Kiev by early summer via Vienna and Cracow. Now pregnant, she divided the summer between Slepnevo and the Zmunchilla estate in south-west Russia. Akhmatova's son, Lev, was born on 18 September 1912 in St Petersburg. The next few years followed essentially the same pattern: winters in Tsarskoe Selo and St Petersburg and summers spent partly in Slepnevo, partly with Akhmatova's relatives in Kiev or in the Crimea.

The routine was broken, however, by the outbreak of war with Germany on 19 July 1914 (by the Russian calendar, 1 August in western Europe). The activities of artistic Petersburg were naturally to some extent curtailed; Gumilev, among others, enlisted in the army. Moreover, the circumstances of Akhmatova's personal life also kept her for a while out of the public eye. In August 1915 her father died. Earlier that year she had contracted severe bronchitis and was showing the first symptoms of tuberculosis, an illness from which she did not fully recover until late the following year. As a result she spent the autumn of 1915 partly at a sanatorium in Finland and almost all the second half of 1916 in the Crimea.

By 1914 Akhmatova's marriage to Gumilev had begun to break down. They had always spent long periods apart because of Gumilev's trips to Africa and because their families lived in different places. Gumilev had been seeing other women since at least the previous year and Akhmatova too began to form intimate friendships with other men. Among these friendships was that with Nikolai Nedobrovo, a minor Symbolist writer and critic, to whom Akhmatova dedicated several poems between 1913 and 1916. Nedobrovo was responsible for one of the earliest sustained pieces of criticism on Akhmatova, an article which she considered particularly perceptive and remembered with affection many years later.[24] Another close friendship was formed with the artist

---

23. On Akhmatova's exploitation also of the conventions of women's writing see Kelly, *History*, pp. 211–17.

24. N. Nedobrovo, 'Anna Akhmatova', *Russkaya mysl'*, vol. 7, pt. 2, 1915, pp. 50–65.

Boris Anrep, to whom many of the poems of Akhmatova's third collection, *White Flock* (1917), are addressed. Both men were to pass out
of Akhmatova's life within a few years. Nedobrovo, whom she last saw
during the autumn of 1916 in the Crimea, was to die there of tuberculosis in 1919. Anrep left Russia for England in 1916 and after the
revolution did not return.

In 1918 Akhmatova and Gumilev were finally divorced, more or less
amicably. In August Akhmatova married Vladimir Kazimirovich Shileiko, a prominent Middle East scholar and poet whom she had known
for some time. The match was very widely seen by Akhmatova's friends
as a mistake. Gumilev at first refused to believe that it was true. Valeriya
Sreznevskaya, with whom Akhmatova had lived in St Petersburg since
1916, also found the alliance improbable. She considered Shileiko
self-absorbed and capricious, and although impressed by his scholarship wondered after a first meeting how long Akhmatova could remain
devoted to him.[25]

Notwithstanding the misgivings of her friends, Akhmatova stayed
with Shileiko for three years during the increasingly difficult times
following the October revolution. At first little had changed for
Akhmatova — she was still able to travel to Bezhetsk, the town near
Slepnevo where her son was now living with his grandmother, during
the summer of 1918. But under War Communism communications
rapidly deteriorated; food and fuel became increasingly difficult to
obtain. The city of Akhmatova's early literary successes had, as she
noted in her memoir of Mandelstam, turned into its opposite: 'All the
old Petersburg signboards were still in place, but behind them there was
nothing but dust, darkness and yawning emptiness. Typhus, hunger,
executions, darkness in the flats, damp firewood, people so swollen as
to be unrecognizable.'[26] Akhmatova earned her living for a while by
working in the library of the Institute of Agronomy. Not surprisingly,
she wrote very little poetry in 1918 and 1919, and apparently none at
all in 1920.

The year 1921, however, was a particularly important one for
Akhmatova as in many ways it marked a definitive transition between
the person and poet of the pre-revolutionary avant-garde and the role
Akhmatova was to play in the new Soviet state. The year 1921 saw the
break with Shileiko; Akhmatova later commented that he was impossible to live with and remarked: 'If I had lived any longer with [him] I
should [. . .] have forgotten how to write poetry.'[27] Once she had left

25. Timenchik, *Desyatye gody*, pp. 213–14.
26. II, 172, quoted in Haight, *Anna Akhmatova*, p. 57.
27. V. M. Zhirmunskii, *Tvorchestvo Anny Akhmatovoi*, Leningrad, 1973, p. 182.

Shileiko and moved in with her friends the actress Ol´ga Sudeikina and the composer Arthur Lourié, she did in fact rediscover her poetic voice. Akhmatova published two books in 1921. The first, *Podorozhnik (Plantain)*, which appeared in April, was a small volume containing mostly work written between 1917 and 1919. The second, *Anno Domini MCMXXI*, came out in November, and contained, apart from the reprinted *Plantain*, chiefly poems of 1921.[28] The second edition of this book, issued in 1923, was to be the last major publication of Akhmatova's verse until 1940.

In 1921 Akhmatova's life was also affected by the deaths of several people who had provided a continuity with her youth. In July, Gumilev, who had recently been in the Crimea, where he had seen Akhmatova's mother and sister, brought news of the death by suicide the previous year of her brother Andrei. (Because of the general breakdown in communications Akhmatova herself had lost contact with her family in 1918.)[29] In August, Petrograd was shocked by the untimely death of Aleksandr Blok, by then the pre-eminent representative of the literary establishment. At Blok's funeral Akhmatova first heard the news that Gumilev had been arrested: he was accused of complicity in a pro-monarchist plot, the so-called Tagantsev conspiracy. As later emerged, he was summarily executed shortly after his arrest.

Akhmatova's life was changing in many ways, but throughout the early 1920s she was still writing and publishing, and still reading her verse at public meetings. In April 1924 she travelled as far as Moscow and Khar´kov in order to recite her poetry. Several articles and even books were written about her work, but as the decade went on she found herself becoming in various ways more and more isolated. Akhmatova's sister Iya died of tuberculosis in 1922, and many of her close friends, including both Lourié and Sudeikina, emigrated to western Europe. Akhmatova also found it increasingly difficult to publish. The Communist Party was by this time striving to bring all cultural activity under its control, and Bolshevik criticism tended to see Akhmatova as belonging to the old regime, and to dismiss the dominant theme of love in her work as a decadent bourgeois preoccupation irrelevant to the concerns of the progressive citizens of an emerging Soviet state. Grigorii Lelevich, for example, wrote in 1923: 'The circle of emotions open to the poet is exceptionally limited. She has responded to social upheavals, basically the most important phenomena of our time, in a

28. S1, 405; SP, 470 gives publication date as 1922. The verso of the title page notes that the book was printed in October 1921.
29. Luknitskaya, *Nikolai Gumilev*, pp. 254–5; P. N. Luknitskii, *Acumiana: vstrechi s Annoi Akhmatovoi*, vol. 1, Paris, 1991, pp. 161–3, 165.

feeble and hostile manner.'[30] These sentiments were echoed by figures as prominent as Mayakovskii and Trotskii. The religious elements in Akhmatova's verse also attracted official disfavour, and in 1925 the Central Committee of the Communist Party appears to have issued a resolution that Akhmatova should not be allowed to continue publishing her poetry. This resolution was never made public and Akhmatova only found out about it two years later. Nevertheless a two-volume collection of her poetry which had been scheduled to appear in 1925 and had already been printed was suddenly prohibited from sale.[31]

Akhmatova's life in the mid-1920s was marked by considerable material hardship. The interdiction on her poetry had effectively deprived her of the ability to earn her living, and although the state had by way of compensation awarded her a small pension, this was by no means sufficient even for food. Furthermore, Akhmatova attempted to send what money she could to her son and mother-in-law in Bezhetsk and to her own mother.[32] She was therefore to a large extent dependent on the support of her friends in Leningrad, particularly since at this time she was also often ill.

In the mid-1920s Akhmatova began to draw close to the art historian Nikolai Punin. Eventually she moved into his flat in Fontannyi Dom, one of several St Petersburg palaces that had belonged to the Counts Sheremetev. This domestic arrangement was problematic because of the chronic housing shortage of the period: Punin's first wife, Anna Arens, and their young daughter continued to live with them. The situation cannot have become easier when Akhmatova's son also arrived from Bezhetsk in 1928 in order to continue his education in Leningrad. Akhmatova's relationship with Punin was not always an easy one for other reasons as well: there were many disagreements and she tried at least once to leave him. They nevertheless remained together until 1938.[33]

Akhmatova wrote relatively little poetry in the late 1920s and during the 1930s, but turned her energies to other areas of intellectual endeavour. She devoted much effort to preserving the memory of Gumilev, and spent many hours clarifying detailed points concerning his life and work with the researcher Pavel Luknitskii, who was compiling a biography. Akhmatova herself was studying Gumilev's poetry,

30. G. Lelevich, 'Anna Akhmatova', *Na postu*, nos. 2–3. 1923, p. 202, quoted in R. Reeder, *Anna Akhmatova: Poet and Prophet*, New York, 1994, p. 171.

31. See Akhmatova, 'Avtobiograficheskaya proza', pp. 8, 14; Luknitskii, *Acumiana*, vol. 1, p. 22.

32. Luknitskii, *Acumiana*, vol. 1, p. 217.

33. See Haight, *Anna Akhmatova*, pp. 81–2, 88, 91, 97; Reeder, *Anna Akhmatova*, pp. 192–3; L. Zykov, 'Nikolai Punin – adresat i geroi liriki Anny Akhmatovoi', *Zvezda*, no. 1, 1995, p. 90.

tracing, in particular, the influence on him of other writers, notably Baudelaire and Annenskii. She planned to write a series of articles on this theme as her tribute to Gumilev's memory.[34]

After she went to live with Punin, Akhmatova spent a good deal of time helping him with his work, sometimes even preparing whole lectures on topics in art history. It was in the 1920s too that Akhmatova began to study seriously the history of St Petersburg and the life and work of Pushkin, which were to become a major preoccupation for the rest of her life. Akhmatova's earliest scholarly work on Pushkin is, like her study of Gumilev's poetry, textual in focus: Luknitskii has left a comprehensive account of her investigations (1925–7) on Pushkin's use of sources from the eighteenth-century French poet André Chénier.[35] By the early 1930s, Akhmatova was well established as a Pushkinist. An article on the literary and satirical origins of Pushkin's *Skazka o zolotom petushke (The Tale of the Golden Cockerel)* was published in 1933 and acclaimed by the leading Pushkin scholars of the day.[36]

Akhmatova's second article, on the role of Benjamin Constant's *Adolphe* in the development of Pushkin's writing, appeared in 1936. Akhmatova worked too on many projects which were either not completed or have been lost – there are known, for example, to have been essays on 'Pushkin and Mickiewicz', 'Pushkin and Dostoevskii' and 'Mozart and Salieri'[37] – and it is clear that Akhmatova's work on Pushkin provided her with a creative outlet that was no longer easily available to her through her poetry.

A further such outlet, and one which also provided her with much needed income, was translation. Although at this time Akhmatova was reluctant to translate verse, believing that to do so would interfere with her own poetic creativity, she responded differently to the translation of prose. She provided versions of the French texts for the Academy edition of Pushkin that was being prepared for the centenary of his death in 1937, and in 1933 published a translation of the letters of Rubens. Notwithstanding her scruples on the matter, she is also known to have worked in the 1930s on translations from Armenian poets and on

34. Luknitskii, *Acumiana*, vol. 1, p. 303.
35. V. K. Luknitskaya (ed.), 'Rannie pushkinskie shtudii Anny Akhmatovoi (po materialam arkhiva P. Luknitskogo)', *Voprosy literatury*, no. 1, 1978, pp. 185–228.
36. II, 422.
37. E. G. Gershtein, 'Posleslovie', in A. Akhmatova, *O Pushkine*, Leningrad, 1977, pp. 278, 281–2.

versions of Shakespeare's *Macbeth* and Shelley's *The Cenci*, though neither of these latter two projects was completed.[38]

Although Akhmatova herself did not become a direct victim of the Stalinist Terror of the 1930s, many of those who were close to her did. Her son, Lev, was detained briefly in the wave of arrests which followed the murder of the Leningrad Communist Party First Secretary, Sergei Kirov, in December 1934. Punin and Lev were both held under arrest for a short period the following year. In May 1934 Mandelstam had been arrested in Moscow in Akhmatova's presence, partly because of a poem he had written satirising Stalin. He was sentenced to exile in Cherdyn´ in the Urals and later in the southern Russian town of Voronezh, where Akhmatova was able to visit him in February 1936. After three years he was allowed to return to Moscow, but was arrested again at the beginning of May 1938, and this time did not return from the prison system, dying in a transit camp somewhere in the Far East towards the end of the year.[39]

Shortly before this, on 10 March 1938, Lev had again been arrested in Leningrad and held there for seventeen months before being sent into exile.[40] Queuing outside prisons with countless others in an attempt to find out first where exactly her son was being held and later to deliver parcels of food and clothing, doing what little she could to intervene with the authorities on his behalf, Akhmatova acquired her most direct experience of the mechanisms of the Terror. This experience was to be reflected most poignantly in the tragic cycle *Rekviem (Requiem)*. The impact of repression on Akhmatova's circle of acquaintances was so great that in 1935, when she went to the railway station to see a friend off into exile, she found herself greeting people she knew at every step: so many representatives of cultural and intellectual St Petersburg were being deported from the city on the same train.[41]

The poverty of Akhmatova's domestic environment in the late 1930s is indicated by her friend Lidiya Chukovskaya, who visited her in

38. See Anna Akhmatova, 'Otryvok iz perevoda "Makbeta"', *Literaturnoe obozrenie*, no. 5, 1989, pp. 18–21; S. Dedyulin, 'Maloizvestnoe interv´yu Anny Akhmatovoi', *Voprosy literatury*, no. 7, 1978, p. 314. A poem by D. Varuzhan in Akhmatova's translation appeared in *Zvezda*, no. 7, 1936, pp. 3–4, and a poem by E. Chrenets was published in *Literaturnyi Leningrad* in September 1936 (see Reeder, *Anna Akhmatova*, p. 224).
39. See M. N. Bazhenov, 'Anna Akhmatova – Osip Mandel´shtam: Biobibliografiya', *Sovetskaya bibliografiya*, no. 2, 1991, pp. 86–100, for a summary of Akhmatova's relationship with Mandelstam.
40. See Haight, *Anna Akhmatova*, p. 97.
41. R. D. Timenchik (ed.), *Anna Akhmatova: Requiem*, Moscow, 1989, p. 18.

Fontannyi Dom in late 1938:

> The room's overall impression is one of neglect and disorganisation. Near the stove there is a tattered armchair without a leg, its springs sticking through the upholstery. The floor is unswept. The good pieces – a carved chair, a mirror with a plain bronze frame, the woodblocks on the walls – don't brighten the room so much as underline its poverty still further.[42]

However, Akhmatova benefited, along with many other literary figures, from the brief thaw that took place in official cultural policy between late 1939 and September 1940.[43] For reasons which have not yet been satisfactorily explained, the unofficial Central Committee ban of 1925 against Akhmatova was apparently lifted. Her poetry began to appear again in journals, and in the early summer of 1940 she was able to publish a book, *Iz shesti knig (From Six Books)*, which contained not only a substantial selection from her earlier work, but also thirty-eight pages of poems which had not been published before.[44] Akhmatova was able to approach her writing with renewed confidence, and 1940 is arguably the most productive year of her career, seeing not only the completion of many short pieces, but also the beginning of work on the long and complex *Poema bez geroya (Poem Without a Hero)*.

Although the thaw of 1939 and 1940 was shortlived and *From Six Books* was withdrawn from circulation a few months after publication, Akhmatova's position was once more improved by the outbreak of war with Germany on 22 June 1941, as the Party allowed itself to subordinate internal ideological warfare to the more pressing need to defend the country from invasion. All citizens were rallied to the patriotic cause, and in August Akhmatova was even invited as a prominent public figure to speak to the citizens of Leningrad on the radio.[45] In the early days of the Leningrad siege she also took on more prosaic war work: standing on air raid duty outside Fontannyi Dom, sewing sandbags for use in the shelter trenches.[46] However, she was not to have to endure the full horrors of the 900-day blockade of the city. She was evacuated at the end of September 1941, first to Chistopol' in Tatarstan, and then to Tashkent, the capital of Uzbekistan, where she remained until May 1944.

42. Chukovskaya, *Zapiski*, vol. 1, pp. 14–15.
43. On this phenomenon, see A. Metcalf and J. Neville, '1940: Not So Much a Thaw – More a Change in the Air', in M. Pavlyshyn (ed.), *Glasnost' in Context: On the Recurrence of Liberalizations in East European Literatures and Cultures*, New York, 1990, pp. 117–26.
44. According to the publication information contained in the book it was typeset on 4 April 1940 and released by the censor for printing in an edition of 10,000 on 8 May.
45. V. K. Luknitskaya, *Pered toboi – zemlya*, Leningrad, 1990, p. 220. The broadcast took place in September. For the text see II, 289–90.
46. A. I. Pavlovskii, *Anna Akhmatova: zhizn' i tvorchestvo*, Moscow, 1991, p. 131.

Akhmatova's experience of Tashkent was perhaps on balance a positive one even though it contained a large measure of physical discomfort. She spent most of her time there living in a cramped room at the top of a former hotel which had been given over to the use of refugee writers.[47] The summers were unbearably hot for those unaccustomed to the Central Asian climate, there were difficulties with food supply and there was much sickness. In 1942 Akhmatova fell seriously ill with typhus and was forced to spend a period during the summer at a convalescent home outside the city.

At the same time, exile in Central Asia had its advantages: above all of course it allowed many residents from the war zone in European Russia to survive the war in relative safety. Tashkent, moreover, may have been a foreign Asian city far from the European civilisation of Leningrad, but even during the war years it had charms of its own for those who were prepared to look for them. As one of Akhmatova's fellow evacuees wrote: 'She likes Tashkent, loves to walk along its streets lined with poplars and elms and flanked by irrigation canals. There are many green spaces, gardens, squares, courtyards — everywhere there are gardens, but there are relatively few flowers, apart from the tea roses which brave the winter in every Uzbek courtyard.'[48]

Because so many writers and intellectuals had been evacuated from Moscow and Leningrad to Tashkent, the cultural environment in the city was surprisingly lively. Akhmatova was in close contact with prominent literary figures like Aleksei Tolstoi and Nikolai Tikhonov. Like other poets, she regularly read her poetry in military hospitals.[49] During the war years Akhmatova's poetry brought consolation to a very wide range of people, from those struggling to survive far away from the actual fighting to troops in the front line.[50] In 1943 the demand for a new edition of her work was partly met by a small volume of poems, *Izbrannoe (Selected Poems)*, which was published in Tashkent, partly through the agency of Tolstoi. Although this book contained only 114 pages, it included poems written under the influence of the war as well as selections from earlier collections. The 10,000 copies that were printed rapidly sold out.[51]

47. Haight, *Anna Akhmatova*, p. 124.
48. V. A. Merkur´eva, 'Iz pis´ma k E.Ya. Arkhipovu', in Timenchik, *Requiem*, p. 168.
49. S2, 238.
50. See I. Berlin, *Personal Impressions*, London, 1980, p. 160; L. Shilov, *Anna Akhmatova (100 let so dnya rozhdeniya)*, Moscow, 1989, p. 33.
51. Cf. I. Bakhterev, 'Tot mesyats v Tashkente', in Kralin, *Ob Anne Akhmatovoi*, p. 222.

The renewal of poetic inspiration that Akhmatova first felt during the 1939–40 thaw continued throughout the time she spent in Tashkent. Not only did she write lyric poems about her Asian experience and nostalgic pieces about Leningrad, she also felt increasingly drawn towards longer forms. She continued to work on *Poem Without a Hero* and completed a long dramatic piece *Enuma Elish*.

Akhmatova's personal life was enlivened during her years in Central Asia by an erratic correspondence with Vladimir Georgievich Garshin, a doctor who had remained in besieged Leningrad whom she had agreed to marry after she left Punin in 1938. Although Akhmatova eagerly awaited Garshin's letters, she seems to have found it difficult to allow for the strain wrought on him by the blockade.[52] However, even though in the end she did not marry him, Akhmatova remained on good terms with Garshin until after the war. A different form of consolation was provided by Akhmatova's friendship with Jozef Czapski, a Polish army officer working on the staff of General Anders, who was at that time based outside Tashkent. Czapski had been educated in St Petersburg before the revolution and was the first foreigner whom Akhmatova had met for many years. She felt drawn to him doubtless partly because she saw him as a representative of European civilisation. As Czapski relates in his memoir of their meetings, the two immediately found a mutual respect and trust, and spent much time in conversation and discussion of Russian and Polish poetry.[53]

Akhmatova left Tashkent on 15 May 1944, by which time it was already clear that the Germans would be driven out of Russia, and after two weeks in Moscow returned to Leningrad. The city had changed almost beyond recognition: Akhmatova calls it in one of her autobiographical sketches 'a terrible ghost, pretending to be my city' (S2, 239). But in spite of this, and in spite of the sudden and unexplained split with Garshin which occurred shortly after her return to Leningrad, Akhmatova continued, for the next two years, to ride the wave of her wartime popularity and acceptability to the authorities.[54] There were, for example, poetry readings to troops in the front line, which remained for a while not far distant from Leningrad, and similar events took place in the city itself.[55] Perhaps the most successful such readings were those in Moscow in April 1946. Akhmatova travelled to the capital as part of

52. L. Zhukova, 'Iz knigi "Epilog"', in Timenchik, *Requiem*, p. 187; Haight, *Anna Akhmatova*, p. 127.

53. See Haight, *Anna Akhmatova*, p. 130; J. Czapski, 'Iz knigi "Na zhestokoi zemle"', in Timenchik, *Requiem*, pp. 170–4.

54. On the relationship with Garshin, see O. I. Rybakova, 'Grustnaya pravda', in Kralin, *Ob Anne Akhmatovoi*, pp. 224–30.

55. See S2, 239.

a delegation of Leningrad writers, and read her poems to large audiences at several different venues. One of her appearances was described as follows: 'It was a real triumph. For a long time she was not able to start reading her poems, so deafening was the applause.'[56] Akhmatova was now publishing in the literary journals and alongside her poetry she turned cautiously to prose in order to record her impressions of post-war Leningrad.[57] In 1946 two collections of Akhmatova's poetry were printed, one a substantial volume of 340 pages in an edition of 10,000, the other a smaller book of 48 pages in an edition of 100,000.

However, on 14 August 1946, the bubble burst. The Communist Party had decided to take back the ideological control over the arts which it had temporarily ceded during the war years. The decisive instrument of this policy was a Central Committee resolution attacking the journals *Zvezda (Star)* and *Leningrad*, and condemning their contributors Akhmatova and the prose writer Mikhail Zoshchenko by name. Shortly after the resolution, Andrei Zhdanov, Stalin's henchman and Central Committee secretary with responsibility for cultural affairs, made reports to the Party and writers' organisations in Leningrad, confirming the Central Committee's decision and reiterating its condemnation of Akhmatova. Ignoring the patriotic role which Akhmatova had adopted during the war, and in which she had been sponsored by the authorities, Zhdanov castigated her as a relic of the pre-revolutionary past, and her work as a pernicious influence on Soviet youth: 'What is there in common between this poetry and the interests of our people, our government? Absolutely nothing. Akhmatova's work belongs to the distant past; it is alien to modern Soviet reality and cannot be tolerated on the pages of our magazines.'[58] Akhmatova was expelled from the Union of Writers; the two volumes of her poetry, which had not yet been distributed, were pulped; and she was plunged into personal and professional isolation as former friends and colleagues avoided her for fear of calling down the Party's wrath on their own heads.

It has been suggested that one reason that Akhmatova and Zoshchenko were singled out for condemnation was their very popularity – and the repressive measures taken more generally in 1946 certainly show an extreme intolerance of any cultural activity that might side-step rigid Party control.[59] Akhmatova herself, though, firmly believed that a strong contributory reason for her persecution, and indeed for the Cold

56. N. Chulkova, 'Iz vospominanii', in Timenchik, *Requiem*, p. 226.

57. S2, 239; cf. A. V. Lyubimova, 'Zapisi o vstrechakh', in Kralin, *Ob Anne Akhmatovoi*, p. 236. Unfortunately these prose sketches were destroyed in 1949.

58. Quoted in Haight, *Anna Akhmatova*, p. 145.

59. Ibid.

War which was unleashed more or less simultaneously, was her clandestine meetings with the British scholar and diplomat Isaiah Berlin in 1945. Berlin was attached to the British embassy in Moscow, and while on a brief visit to Leningrad contrived to make Akhmatova's acquaintance and to spend many hours in conversation with her. Berlin visited her again in January 1946 shortly before his return to England.[60]

For Akhmatova, as with her meetings with Czapski in Tashkent, this was a rare opportunity to commune with a representative of the western cultural world, all the more welcome since Berlin knew personally many people with whom Akhmatova had lost contact since the 1920s and was able to provide her with news of them. However, in Stalin's Russia contact with foreigners was regarded with deep suspicion by the authorities, and by seeing Berlin on several occasions, Akhmatova was running a considerable risk, especially since on his first visit he was conspicuously followed by Randolph Churchill, the son of the British prime minister, then in Russia in a journalistic capacity. Akhmatova herself was already being kept under surveillance before the Zhdanov resolution, and became aware that electronic bugging devices had been installed in her flat not long after Berlin's visit.[61]

In consequence of the Central Committee ban on her work, Akhmatova was once again deprived of the means of making a living. As in the 1920s she was awarded a small pension, but again became largely dependent on the generosity of friends.[62] As in the 1920s too, she turned to Pushkin for consolation and intellectual stimulation. An essay on the psychological impetus behind *The Stone Guest* was completed in 1947 and Akhmatova began to study the theme of 'Pushkin and Dostoevskii' and the circumstances surrounding the poet's fatal duel.[63] Her health continued to suffer from her impoverished circumstances. In a sense this may have worked to her advantage: in February 1948, for example, the Moscow Litfond, or writers' benevolent society, offered her money and a place in a rest-home.[64]

Materially, Akhmatova's situation improved considerably in 1949 when she was given a commission to translate the letters (written in French) of the eighteenth-century radical Aleksandr Radishchev. Further translation work followed rapidly, notably of works by Victor Hugo and the classical Chinese poets, which she rendered into verse from literal prose versions. Activity of this type was to provide

60. For Berlin's account see his *Personal Impressions*, pp. 189–200.
61. See N. Mandel'shtam, *Kniga tret'ya*, Paris, 1987, p. 114; L. V. Yakovleva-Shaporina, 'Iz dnevnika', in Timenchik, *Requiem*, p. 264.
62. N. Roskina, *Chetyre glavy: iz literaturnykh vospominanii*, Paris, 1980, p. 15.
63. See Akhmatova, 'Avtobiograficheskaya proza', pp. 14–15.
64. Yakovleva-Shaporina in Timenchik, *Requiem*, p. 264.

Akhmatova with her main source of income for the rest of her life. In the late 1940s and early 1950s, moreover, it gave her official recognition as a translator even if she remained unacceptable to the authorities as a poet.

On the other hand, the Communist Party launched another attack on the intelligentsia in 1949. In November Lev was again arrested (he had been released from his earlier exile to fight in the war and had returned to Leningrad in November 1945) and much of Akhmatova's activity for the next few years was directed towards trying to secure his release. To this end in 1950 she published a cycle of overtly propagandistic poems praising Stalin and the Soviet regime in the mass-circulation Moscow monthly magazine *Ogonek*. For all the painful searching of conscience that publishing this cycle must have caused – and Akhmatova never acknowledged it as belonging to the genuine corpus of her works – Lev remained in the camps until 1956. Akhmatova was, however, readmitted to the Union of Writers in February 1951. By this time, she was spending more and more time in Moscow, where she stayed with her numerous friends sometimes for months at a stretch, and where she was perhaps better placed to influence officialdom concerning the fate of her son. Although probably the main catalyst for Lev's release was Khrushchev's Secret Speech of 1956 in which he condemned the excesses of Stalinism, Akhmatova's numerous attempts to petition the authorities may at least have ensured that his case was reconsidered as soon as possible after this.[65]

Akhmatova's full reinstatement in the Soviet literary world began soon after the death of Stalin in 1953. She was allowed to attend the Second Congress of Soviet Writers in 1954 and her name gradually began to appear in print in contexts which were no longer derogatory: Chukovskaya notes, for example, how excited Akhmatova was to see a translation of hers praised in a review in 1955.[66] In 1956 her own poems began to appear again in gradually increasing numbers, and in 1958 her status was secured by the publication of a book, *Stikhotvoreniya (Poems)*, which contained a careful selection of poems and thirty pages of translations. This was followed in 1961 by a much fuller collection, *Stikhotvoreniya (1909–1960) (Poems (1909–1960))*, and in 1965 by the

65. See E. G. Gershtein, 'Memuary i fakty (ob osvobozhdenii L'va Gumileva)', *Russian Literature Triquarterly*, no. 13, 1976, pp. 645–57. The surviving correspondence between Akhmatova and her son during his imprisonment also sheds light on her efforts to secure his release: A. M. Panchenko and N. V. Gumileva (eds), 'Perepiska A. A. Akhmatovoi s L. N. Gumilevym', *Zvezda*, no. 4, 1994, pp. 170–88.
66. L. K. Chukovskaya, *Zapiski ob Anne Akhmatovoi*, vol. 2, Paris, 1980, pp. 103–4.

most complete volume to appear in Akhmatova's lifetime, *Beg vremeni (The Flight of Time)*.

In her last ten years Akhmatova's life was perhaps more stable than at any other time. In Leningrad she continued to live with the Punin family, though they were obliged to move out of Fontannyi Dom in 1952. Eventually she was given a summer dacha at Komarovo in the 'writers' colony' outside Leningrad. Although she suffered from a heart condition she maintained an active literary life. As well as continuing with her voluminous translation work, she found time to write many new poems of her own, and to continue with her researches on Pushkin. In her last years too, she was especially concerned to set down in writing an authorised version of her past – particularly those aspects of it which had perforce been ignored or suppressed by the changing demands of Soviet ideology. She attempted to reconstruct works such as *Enuma Elish* which had been destroyed for reasons of expediency on the arrest of her son in 1949. She turned to the genre of prose memoir in order to record her version of the literary politics of her youth, and her youthful friendships with figures such as the Italian artist Amedeo Modigliani and Mandelstam. She continued to work on *Poem Without a Hero*, attempting to make the portrait it painted of the Soviet era both fuller and more accessible to the contemporary reader and to the reader of the future. There were even plans for the writing of a novel.

In all of Akhmatova's later literary activity there is a careful and complex 'writing between the lines', a balancing of her need to express the circumstances of the human condition in Stalin's Russia against the limitations on public expression under a regime of strict government censorship. Like many writers in the Soviet Union she frequently says one thing while seeking to convey something else to those who have ears to hear it. The mechanics of this strategy will be examined in later chapters.

Even though it sometimes led to textual obscurities, in terms of literary politics, this practice was highly successful. On the one hand, by the early 1960s Akhmatova was being actively claimed by the authorities as a Soviet poet. In 1964 she was permitted to represent her country abroad by travelling to Sicily to accept a literary prize from the Italian government. The following year she received an honorary doctorate from Oxford University and was afforded the opportunity also to visit London and Paris. By the time of Akhmatova's death on 5 March 1966 she was as celebrated in the Soviet Union as she had ever been in tsarist Russia. Yet at the same time that Akhmatova was being promoted officially, she was also establishing herself as an unofficial leader of the dissident movement. The continuing prominence of the lyric 'I' in Akhmatova's verse, its frequently prophetic tone and the direct attacks on totalitarianism which appeared in unpublished works such as *Requiem*, circulated surreptitiously by hand, all served to enhance her authority as the spokesman, *par excellence*, of her generation.

When Isaiah Berlin visited Russia in 1956 Akhmatova had refused to see him, fearing that a meeting with someone so ideologically suspect might lead to the rearrest of her son. But in the thaw years she was able to find intellectual companionship not only among those who had shared her experiences, but also among the new post-Stalin generation of writers and intellectuals. In particular she gathered around her a group of young poets, notably Iosif Brodskii, Anatolii Naiman, Evgenii Rein and Dmitrii Bobyshev, whose work fell outside the Soviet mainstream and is only now being incorporated fully into the development of Russian poetry. In the 1960s, as the last remaining major representative of the Silver Age of Russian letters, Akhmatova became an important source of inspiration and advice for a very large number of aspiring writers.

Since her death Akhmatova's reputation has only continued to grow. Her life and writing have attracted detailed attention from professional critics and general readers alike. The centenary of her birth in 1989 produced conferences on her work all over the world and inspired the accelerated publication of at least part of the scattered memoir and archival material associated with her name. At least three museums dedicated to her memory have opened in recent years in and around St Petersburg and the new political culture is allowing a fuller picture to emerge of Akhmatova both as a person and as a writer than ever before. Her status as one of the most significant cultural figures of twentieth-century Russia is now unassailable.

–2–

The Early Poetry: Form and the
Expansion of Meaning

The hiatus in Akhmatova's publishing career caused by the unofficial ban which was placed on her work in 1925 marks a major division for the purposes of the periodisation of her poetry. Before it Akhmatova was very largely in control of her own work: the influence of the tsarist censorship was negligible and she retained a high degree of editorial control over her collections *Evening* (1912), *Rosary* (1914) and *White Flock* (1917).[1] The post-revolutionary books *Plantain* (1921) and *Anno Domini* (1921 and 1923) were also mostly free of extra-literary intervention. By the mid-1920s, however, Akhmatova was dependent on the Communist Party authorities to publish at all, and on those occasions when the opportunity did arise she had far less control over exactly what appeared in print.

Although Akhmatova continued to write, she in fact produced very little poetry in the late 1920s and early 1930s. She notes that by the time she began to write again in earnest in the mid-1930s a definite change had come over her work: 'but my handwriting had changed, my voice sounded different [. . .] There could be no return to the earlier manner' (S2, 251). The new departure in her poetry that Akhmatova notes here in impressionistic terms has been confirmed by later scholarship in respect of a wide variety of features, including thematic and stylistic content, verse structure and epigraph use.[2]

This is not of course to say that Akhmatova's poetry from *Evening* to *Anno Domini* is uniform in nature. On the contrary, it contains considerable variety and explores with increasing confidence many different thematic and stylistic paths. In particular, from *White Flock* onwards there is an ever greater concern with the public sphere as the

1. But see L. Genin, 'Akhmatova i tsarskaya tsenzura', *Zvezda*, no. 4, 1967, pp. 203–4.
2. See D. N. Wells, 'The Function of the Epigraph in Akhmatova's Poetry', in S. I. Ketchian (ed.), *Anna Akhmatova, 1889–1989: Papers from the Akhmatova Centennial Conference, Bellagio Study and Conference Center, June 1989*, Oakland, Calif., 1993, pp. 267–8.

inner turmoil of the lyric heroine is seen first against the background of the First World War and later alongside the events of the Revolution and its aftermath. Yet the period up to 1925 is worth considering as a unit because from many points of view the similarities among poems written in this period are greater than the differences. Moreover, although Akhmatova destroyed the larger part of her *juvenilia*, we are clearly in possession of everything or almost everything which she wrote between about 1911 and 1923, and are therefore in a position to make an assessment of her poetry as a whole. This is not true for the later period, since, during the 1930s and late 1940s particularly, Akhmatova either destroyed or chose not to commit to paper in the first place numerous works which cannot now be reconstructed or which can be reconstructed only partially.

The Early Love Poetry: Content and Style

The thematic range of Akhmatova's early books, and particularly of *Evening* and *Rosary*, is relatively narrow and must have seemed especially so to readers accustomed to the broad philosophical sweep of much Symbolist writing.[3] The dominant focus is the emotional state of the lyric heroine in her search for a beloved worthy of her affections. The poems illuminate as if with a spotlight a specific instant in the heroine's quest for love. Sometimes this is a moment of elation:

> Solntse komnatu napolnilo
> Pyl'yu zheltoi i skvoznoi.
> Ya prosnulas' i pripomnila:
> Milyi, nynche prazdnik tvoi.
> Ottogo i osnezhennaya
> Dal' za oknami tepla,
> Ottogo i ya, bessonnaya,
> Kak prichastnitsa spala.
>
> (S1, 66)

> The sun filled the room
> With yellow transparent dust.
> I woke and remembered:
> Darling, today is your name-day.
> That is why even the snowy distance
> Outside the windows is warm;
> That is why even I, who do not sleep,
> Slept like a communicant.

---

3. B. Eikhenbaum, *Anna Akhmatova: opyt analiza*, Petrograd, 1922, p. 28.

More often, though, the scene is one of sadness, and especially the bitter-sweet sadness which combines unhappiness at the breakdown of a relationship or the separation of the two parties for reasons beyond their control with the memory of the hopeful beginnings of a romance or with thoughts of how events might have turned out differently:

> Vchera eshche, vlyublennyi,
> Molil: 'Ne pozabud''.
> A nynche tol'ko vetry
> Da kriki pastukhov
>
> (S1, 89)

> As late as yesterday, in love,
> He begged 'Do not forget me'.
> But today there is only the wind,
> And the cries of the shepherds

> Ne budem pit' iz odnogo stakana
> Ni vodu my, ni sladkogo vina,
> Ne potseluemsya my utrom rano,
> A vvecheru ne poglyadim v okno.
> Ty dyshesh' solntsem, ya dyshu lunoyu,
> No zhivy my lyuboviyu odnoyu.
>
> (S1, 56)

> We shall not drink water or sweet wine
> From the same glass;
> We shall not kiss in the early morning
> And look out of the window together in the evening.
> You breathe the sun and I breathe the moon
> Though we live through a single love.

Paradoxically, it is often the heroine herself who pulls back from final commitment: her overpowering need to love and to be loved is matched by an inability to accept the partial surrender of will that this implies.[4] The idea is examined explicitly in a poem of 1915 addressed to Nikolai Nedobrovo:

> Est' v blizosti lyudei zavetnaya cherta,
> Ee ne pereiti vlyublennosti i strasti [. . .]

4. See W. A. Rosslyn, *The Prince, the Fool*, and *the Nunnery: The Religious Theme in the Early Poetry of Anna Akhmatova*, Amersham, 1984, p. 210.

Stremyashchiesya k nei bezumny, a ee
Dostigshee – porazheny toskoyu. . .
Teper´ ty ponyal, otchego moe
Ne b´etsya serdtse pod tvoei rukoyu.

(S1, 83)

In closeness between people there is a hidden border-line.
It cannot be crossed by love or passion [. . .]

Those who strive for it are mad, but those who
Reach it are struck down by grief. . .
Now you understand why my heart
Does not beat faster under your hand.

In her early books Akhmatova investigates the theme of the heroine's quest for love in considerable detail. Within this general framework, moreover, she offers a significantly broader view of the world than is apparent at first sight. She achieves this both through her choice of the thematic material which accompanies and supports the theme of love, and through the use of certain stylistic features which combine to extend the meaning of her work beyond the confines of individual poems. This principle of 'extratextuality' is one that Akhmatova was to employ and develop throughout her career, adapting it according to the needs of both inspiration and literary politics.

The most salient example of the principle in action is the complex picture of the heroine herself, glimpsed partially and enigmatically in individual poems.[5] The reader is led inevitably, because of the superficial narrowness of the thematic range, to attempt to explain the heroine of one poem by reference to the heroines of the others, to try to construct an organic whole from the fragments which the poet offers. In particular, critics have sometimes been tempted to read Akhmatova's poems as if the heroines were identical with the author herself. Yet while there is doubtless a high degree of biographical impetus behind many of the early poems, it is dangerous to posit the self-identification of the poet and her subject, if only because of the different aesthetic purposes of poetry and biography. The heroines of *Evening* may have much in common with, for example, the Akhmatova of the letters of 1906–8 addressed to Stein – 'an isolated and solitary girl, dependent

---

5. On the use of the poetic persona more generally by Acmeist poets see Doherty, *The Acmeist Movement*, pp. 170–200.

for sympathetic understanding on one or two distant correspondents'[6] – but they are also separate. Indeed, they are multiple, not just the sensitive upper-class young woman but also among other things a water nymph, a tightrope walker and a peasant woman; occasionally the principal lyric voice is male. Although in general terms the heroines may derive partly from Akhmatova's own experience they are essentially a romanticisation of it, an extrapolation from it in the interests of investigating the broader psychology of love.

Lidiya Ginzburg goes so far as to suggest that Akhmatova's heroines are entirely the product of her poetic method: 'In life Anna Andreevna was not like her heroines. But Akhmatova, with her sober, observant, rather rationalistic mind, was somehow like her poetic method. [. . .] Akhmatova created a lyric system – one of the most remarkable in the history of poetry, but she never conceived of poetry as the spontaneous outpouring of the soul.'[7] This caveat is necessary because of the ways in which the rhetorical structure of Akhmatova's poetry actually encourages a biographical interpretation. Its most striking feature in this respect is the predominance of first-person narration. As has often been remarked, this insistence on the lyric 'I' gives the impression of an intimate diary and more particularly a confession.[8] The view of the poetry as confession is, of course, encouraged by the intimate nature of the amatory themes, and the reader is placed in the role of confidant to the rejoicing or sadness of the lyric heroine. We find, for example, such confidences as:

> Zhdala ego naprasno mnogo let.
> Pokhozhe eto vremya na dremotu.
> (S1, 133)

> I waited many years for him in vain.
> That time now seems a dream.

> Skazal, chto u menya sopernits net.
> Ya dlya nego ne zhenshchina zemnaya.
> (S1, 138)

> He said that I had no rivals.
> For him I was not a woman of this earth.

---

6. Rosslyn, *Prince*, p. 77.
7. L. Ya. Ginzburg, *O starom i novom: stat'i i ocherki*, Leningrad, 1982, p. 329.
8. E.g. Eikhenbaum, *Anna Akhmatova*, p. 29.

Very often the heroine addresses her lover directly. The reader thus gets the impression of overhearing a delicate conversation as in 'Zdravstvui! Legkii shelest slyshish'' ('Hello. Do you hear a light rustling', S1, 58), in which the speaker pleads for her companion's attention.

Akhmatova's work is further personalised by the general avoidance of high rhetorical or overtly 'poetic' language and the use instead of a broadly conversational style. The use of metrical schemes based on the dol'nik and the relative unobtrusiveness of Akhmatova's rhymes work to similar effect.[9] An impression is created of the simple acceptance of what may be a complex situation, the response of an ordinary person with whom the reader can identify rather than that of a poet. For example, in the lines

> Budem vmeste, milyi, vmeste,
> Znayut vse, chto my rodnye
> (S1, 109)

> We will be together, darling, together.
> Everybody knows that we are kindred spirits,

the straightforward expression of feeling combines with a simplicity of syntax and the use of everyday vocabulary to amplify the impression that the reader is being addressed by an intimate companion. (The striking effects that Akhmatova occasionally achieves by the use of unusual vocabulary or combinations of words are only possible against this background of conversational style.[10])

If the language of Akhmatova's poetry can be linked specifically with the everyday spoken style of the educated classes, the sense of place which informs it is also calculated to bring her readers within the ambit of her poems. As Kees Verheul has pointed out, fixity and continuity of place in Akhmatova's poems are often used to emphasise the changeability of the heroines' emotional moods and the blurring of time frames which occurs in her memories of love and its decay.[11] The details

---

9. *Dol'nik*: a metre characterised by a fixed number of stresses separated by variable intervals of either one or two unstressed syllables.

10. See V. Vinogradov, *O poezii Anny Akhmatovoi (stilisticheskie nabroski)*, Leningrad, 1925, pp. 36–59.

11. K. Verheul, *The Theme of Time in the Poetry of Anna Axmatova*, The Hague, 1971, pp. 8–17.

provided are typically very specific, whether they are of St Petersburg:

> Ottogo, chto stali ryadom
> My v blazhennyi mig chudes,
> V mig, kogda nad Letnim sadom
> Mesyats rozovyi voskres
> (S1, 72)

> Because we stood together
> In the blessed moment of wonders,
> In the moment when the pink moon
> Rose over the Summer Garden

or Tsarskoe Selo:

> Po allee provodyat loshadok.
> Dlinny volny raschesannykh griv.
> O, plenitel´nyi gorod zagadok,
> Ya pechal´na, tebya polyubiv.
> (S1, 23)

> They are leading ponies along the avenues.
> How long the waves of their groomed manes are.
> Oh, captivating town of mysteries,
> I have fallen in love with you and am sad.

or Kiev:

> Drevnii gorod slovno vymer,
> Stranen moi priezd.
> Nad rekoi svoei Vladimir
> Podnyal chernyi krest.
> (S1, 87)

> It is as if the ancient town had died.
> My arrival feels strange.
> Above his river St Vladimir
> Has raised a black cross.

This specificity of place is accompanied by a remarkable attention to precise details of the heroine's surroundings and attire, of such accessories as fans or riding crops, and also occasionally by exact statements of the time or date at which an important event occurred. Thus:

Ya soshla s uma, o mal´chik strannyi,
V sredu, v tri chasa!

(S1, 29)

I lost my mind, strange boy,
On Wednesday at three o'clock!

One other principal feature of Akhmatova's verse produces a similar
result. The use of reminiscence as one of the most important building
blocks of the poetry gives the reader a historical perspective on a supposed knowledge of the lyric heroine in the present, and this historical
perspective is further widened by the insistence on the affective
function of memory. This can be seen clearly, for example, in 'Stikhi o
Peterburge' ('Poems about Petersburg'):

Serdtse b´etsya rovno, merno.
Chto mne dolgie goda!
Ved´ pod arkoi na Galernoi
Nashi teni navsegda.

(S1, 72)

My heart beats evenly, steadily.
What are the long years to me!
For our shadows are for ever
On the arch over Galernaya Street.

In being admitted to the heroine's private material world by this
accumulation of concrete detail, the reader is seduced into thinking that
equal access has genuinely been granted to the world of her emotional
relationships. In fact this is not exactly the case since the details provided concerning these relationships are generally extremely vague and
are presented through hints and evasions rather than directly.[12] The
overwhelming focus on the figure of the heroine herself paradoxically
makes her unknowable, as the reader is given no alternative models of
social interaction against which her behaviour can be measured.

The narrowness of the lyric situation may be seen in terms of the
mythologisation of the poetic experience. For poetry to acquire the
status of myth the range of themes has to be limited because this makes
it simpler to achieve a larger identity of experience between the reader
and the writer, an identity which is in some measure created by this
repetition of images and themes. Particular words and concepts acquire,

---

12. See Vinogradov, *O poezii Anny Akhmatovoi*, pp. 137–49.

in the course of repetition from one poem to another, values that in isolation they would not have had. Jerzy Faryno has written in terms of Akhmatova's 'code': 'Akhmatova uses a certain language (known only to her), which is not identical to the ethnic Russian language, but has a high degree of homonymity with it. For the reader of Akhmatova's texts this means the following: "reading Akhmatova's discourse" = "mastering the language of this discourse (learning its language)".'[13] Sometimes this code has its origins in earlier poetic traditions, as when Akhmatova takes the long-standing elegiac metaphor of autumn and emphasises over a whole series of poems its association with parting and death. For example:

> Tragicheskoi oseni skudny ubranstva.
> (S1, 76)

Tragic autumn is meanly arrayed.

> Chtoby pesn´ proshchal´noi boli
> Dol´she v pamyati zhila,
> Osen´ smuglaya [. . .]
> (S1, 97)

So that a song of the pain of parting
Should live longer in the memory,
Dark-complexioned autumn [. . .]

> Zaplakannaya osen´, kak vdova
> V odezhdakh chernykh, vse serdtsa tumanit. . .
> (S1, 168)

Tear-stained autumn, like a widow
In black, clouds every heart. . .

More often, though, Akhmatova invests items of vocabulary with meanings wholly her own. This is the case, for example, with the term 'smuglyi' ('dark-complexioned'), which acquires an association with poetic creativity through allusion to the part-African extraction of Aleksandr Pushkin and to the Russian south, which often appears in Akhmatova's work as the scene of encounters with the Muse and the origins of her own poetry. A similar phenomenon can be observed with other adjectives describing colour: white, for example, becomes associated with death.[14]

---

13. J. Faryno, 'Kod Akhmatovoi', *Russian Literature*, vols. 7/8, 1974, p. 83.
14. E.g. 'Chem khuzhe etot vek predshestvuyushchikh?' (S1, 131).

The External Text

The linguistic structures of Akhmatova's verse, then, act in such a way as to compel the reader to take her work as one continuous text, to search for the meanings of individual poems in those that surround them. At the same time, the poems frequently contain references to systems of discourse which lie outside them and which widen their perspective from private to general.[15] The cumulative effect of the various literary, historical, religious, musical and visual associations is to give the sentiments of the lyric heroine a resonance far beyond the purely personal. This is a feature of Akhmatova's poetry which becomes increasingly important as her career progresses. In broad terms it is more central to her late poetry than to her earlier work, but even within the earlier books it clearly plays a greater role in *White Flock* and *Anno Domini* than it does in *Evening*.

Akhmatova avoids the set poetic forms borrowed from Renaissance France – triolets, villanelles, etc. – which attracted many of her contemporaries in the 1910s.[16] However, in some other respects she does make use of stylisations which were characteristic of her day. Most noticeably she draws occasionally on the contemporary cult of the masquerade and the *commedia dell'arte*. In 'Maskarad v parke' ('Masquerade in the Park'), for example, she restates her constant theme of conquest and disappointment in love using the abstracted, symbolic figures of the masked ball. The triangle of Prince–Marquise–Pierrot has an archetypal value:

> I blednyi, s buketom azalii,
> Ikh smekhom vstrechaet P'ero:
> 'Moi prints! O, ne vy li slomali
> Na shlyape markizy pero?'
> (S1, 41)

> And pale, with a bouquet of azaleas,
> Pierrot meets them with a laugh:
> 'My prince! Was it not you who broke
> The feather on the marquise's hat?'

More frequently Akhmatova draws on the traditions of Russian folklore to similar effect. The lyric hero, for whom the heroine is waiting, becomes identified with the folkloric 'tsarevich' or prince. In 'Ty

---

15. This practice was shared by other Acmeists: see Doherty, *The Acmeist Movement*, pp. 200–10.
16. But cf. 'Segodnya mne pis'ma ne prinesli' (S1, 43).

pover´, ne zmeinoe ostroe zhalo' ('Believe me, it is not the sharp sting of a snake', S1, 37), for example, the heroine is excluded from the castle where the tsarevich lives for reasons that are not explained, but continues to live only in her love for him. In 'Seroglazyi korol´' ('The Grey-Eyed King', S1, 42), the heroine is shown to be secretly in love with her king though married to somebody else. 'Net, tsarevich, ya ne ta' ('No, tsarevich, I am not she', S1, 114) presents a more complex situation in which the heroine warns the prince that only grief will result for him from further contact with her. In these poems the heroine often ascribes to herself magical powers, and the motif of the magic ring which will give her power over her beloved occurs in several poems (S1, 29, 38, 125). Perhaps the most striking example is the treatment found in 'Skazka o chernom kol´tse' ('Tale of the Black Ring', S1, 150–1, 409–10), where the ring given to the heroine by her pagan grandmother accords her the power to make anyone she chooses fall in love with her. Other folkloric motifs, such as the dragon which keeps the heroine in thrall, also occur (S1, 155–6).

Sometimes the heroine is identified with specific characters from the folk-tale tradition. In one poem, for example, she is the Snow-Maiden (*Snegurka*), whose body will melt in the spring (S1, 26). In another she is Cinderella at the moment she has returned secretly from the prince's ball leaving her slipper behind. She tries to conceal the three carnations he has given her, and is waiting for him to search her out with a mixture of longing and trepidation (S1, 53).

Just as important as these *topoi* taken from folk literature are Akhmatova's use and adaptation of the *forms* of folk poetry. There are, for example, poems which imitate the folk genres of song (*pesenka*) (S1, 34, 150), lament (*prichitanie*) (S1, 149), lullaby (*kolybel´naya*) (S1, 168) and humorous ditty *(chastushka)* (S1, 120–1). Several poems consciously imitate the ballad tradition, notably 'The Grey-Eyed King' with its couplet structure and four-stress dol´nik verse, 'Ya prishla tebya smenit´, sestra' ('I have come to take your place, sister', S1, 71–2), which combines the same folkloric couplet with more literary six- and four-line stanzas, and 'Novogodnyaya ballada' ('New Year's Ballad', S1, 169), where a folkloric dol´nik line is found in conjunction with a structural parallelism organised around a series of three toasts. Patterns of repetition characteristic of folk poetry are found even quite independently of direct thematic links with the folkloric tradition. We find, for example:

> Tak glyadyat koshek ili ptits,
> Tak na naezdnits smotryat stroinykh. . .
> (S1, 52)

This is how they stroke cats or birds;
This is how they look at slender horsewomen. . .

Vse ravno, chto ty naglyi i zloi,
Vse ravno, chto ty lyubish´ drugikh
(S1, 56)

It doesn't matter that you are insolent and bad;
It doesn't matter that you love others.

And in this way the 'horizons of meaning' contained within the folkloric tradition are projected on to the relations between Akhmatova's
heroines and heroes as well.

Akhmatova's treatment of the figure of the Muse in her early poems
links the latter very firmly with the folkloric tradition. In *By the Sea
Shore* the classical Muse appears in peasant dress, but is nonetheless
identifiable by her flute:

Devushka stala mne chasto snit´sya
V uzkikh brasletakh, v korotkom plat´e,
S dudochkoi beloi v rukakh prokhladnykh.
(S1, 265)

I began to dream often of a girl
In narrow bracelets and a short skirt,
With a white flute in her cool hands.

It is this figure who instills the heroine with the power to invent a song
with which to welcome the tsarevich when he arrives. In an earlier
poem, 'Muze' ('To the Muse', S1, 38), the Muse is seen taking back the
gift of song which had been vouchsafed through the medium of a magic
ring. In later poems about the Muse, in which the folkloric coloration is
generally lost, she remains in a sense the heroine's sister, an intimate if
unreliable companion on whom she is dependent.[17]

Another important way in which Akhmatova extends the applic-
ability of her lyric situations is by reference to other works of literature.
As early as 1909 she wrote a poem, 'Chitaya Gamleta' ('Reading
Hamlet'), which is a dramatisation of a literary work and a projection

17. On Akhmatova's treatment of the Muse see M. Graf-Schneider, '"Musa" dans
l'œuvre d'Anna Akhmatova', *Slavica Helvetiva*, vol. 16, 1981, pp. 187–203; G.
Spendel, 'Anna Akhmatova e la Musa', in M. L. Dodero Costa (ed.), *Anna Akhmatova
(1889–1966): Atti del Convegno nel centenario della nascita, Torino, Villa Gualino,
12–13 dicembre 1989*, Allessandria, 1992, pp. 41–50.

of it on to the concerns of her own poetry. It is written from the point of view of Ophelia, but in Akhmatova's own idiom of emotional disappointment:

Ty skazal mne: 'Nu chto zh, idi v monastyr´
Ili zamuzh za duraka. . .'
Printsy tol´ko takoe vsegda govoryat,
No ya etu zapomnila rech´

(S1, 21)

You said to me, 'Well now, go into a convent,
Or marry a fool. . .'
Princes always speak like this,
But I remembered these words.

In later poems of Akhmatova's early period this type of transformation of the plot of another literary work is unusual, although it does occur with literary forms of European folk stories, such as Cinderella and Blue Beard (S1, 144), and with the biblical stories of Rachel, Lot's wife and Michal. It is a technique, however, which Akhmatova was to use with great effect in some key poems of her second period, as will be seen later.

A related device which Akhmatova also uses extensively in her later verse, but which is present in lesser measure from the beginnings of her poetry, is the less direct evocation of other works of literature through quotation and allusion. One of the first poems of *Evening*, the third poem of the cycle 'V Tsarskom Sele' ('In Tsarskoe Selo'), makes the importance of the literary tradition for Akhmatova clear:

Smuglyi otrok brodil po alleyam,
U ozernykh brodil beregov,
I stoletie my leleem
Ele slyshnyi shelest shagov.

Igly sosen gusto i kolko
Ustilayut nizkie pni. . .
Zdes´ lezhalo ego treugol´ka
I rastrepannyi tom Parni.

(S1, 24)

A dark youth wandered along these avenues
And grieved beside these lakes,
And for a hundred years we have cherished
The faint rustle of his footsteps.

The low stumps are covered with
A thick layer of prickly pine needles. . .
This is where his three-cornered hat lay
And his tattered copy of Parny.

Here Akhmatova is describing the young Aleksandr Pushkin in the park at Tsarskoe Selo. Although he is not named directly, Pushkin is easily identified by the epithet 'smuglyi' referring to his dark complexion, and by allusion to the dress and literary fashions of the period. For Akhmatova the poetic past manifests itself clearly in the present. The link between present and past is conveyed not only by the statement 'And for a hundred years we have cherished the faint rustle of his footsteps', but also by the juxtaposition of past and present tenses in each of the two quatrains of the poem. In each case a statement about the present day is linked with a statement about the time of Pushkin. This thematic link is reinforced by sound patterning – the repetition of o, e, i within the poem – which, as Timenchik has shown, again binds the two time frames closely together. Furthermore, Akhmatova's use of the word 'otrok' with its eighteenth-century tone evokes the image of Pushkin deferring to Derzhavin, who encouraged him at an early stage of his career, and suggests a similar deference on the part of Akhmatova towards Pushkin.[18]

Elsewhere Akhmatova also draws on specific works by Pushkin either as models or in order to offer her own treatment of particular themes which the earlier poet had addressed. 'The Tale of the Black Ring', for example, is on one level a polemic against Pushkin's poems 'Khrani menya, moi talisman' ('Preserve me, my talisman') and 'Talisman', both of which describe the powers of a magical object to protect its owner against love.[19]

An example of the way in which reference to folklore and to the

18. See E. V. Dzhandzhakova, 'Smuglyi otrok brodil po alleyam', *Russkaya rech'*, no. 5, 1976, pp. 16–19; R. D. Timenchik, 'Akhmatova i Pushkin: razbor stikhotvoreniya "Smuglyi otrok brodil po alleyam"', *Pushkinskii sbornik*, Riga, 1968, pp. 124–31; I. M. Landsman and E. B. Naumov, 'Iz nablyudenii nad yazykom A. Akhmatovoi', *Voprosy russkogo i obshchego yazykoznaniya* (Sbornik nauchnykh trudov, (Tashkentskii un-t), 580), 1979, pp. 75–82.

19. See D. N. Wells, 'Akhmatova and Pushkin: The Genres of Elegy and Ballad', *Slavonic and East European Review*, vol. 71, no. 4, 1993, pp. 643–5.

literary tradition can be combined in Akhmatova's work in order to increase the impact of her own themes can be found in the long poem *By the Sea Shore*. The essentially folkloric situation of a young girl waiting expectantly for her prince combines with Akhmatova's use of anaphora and other forms of repetition within relatively simple stylistic constructions in the same way as in folk poetry. The use of animal imagery also has much in common with folkloric models. For example, the heroine's unselfconscious identification with the natural world is conveyed using a traditional pattern of repetition in the lines:

Ko mne priplyvala zelenaya ryba,
Ko mne priletala belaya chaika,
A ya byla derzkoi, zloi i veseloi
I vovse ne znala, chto eto – schast'e.
(S1, 262)

A green fish would swim up to me,
A white gull would fly up to me,
But I was daring, wild and cheerful
And quite unaware that this was happiness.

Akhmatova's use of religious motifs and colour imagery is also close to that found in folklore.[20]

Although the degree to which Akhmatova was directly influenced by folk forms should not be underestimated, her borrowing from Pushkin for her first narrative poem is also considerable. As Zhirmunskii has pointed out, the poem relies on Pushkin's *Skazka o rybake i rybke* (*Tale of the Fisherman and the Fish*) for its title, its particular adaptation of folkloric verse metre, and its vocabulary and syntax.[21] Akhmatova's title is taken from the first lines of Pushkin's tale:

Zhil starik so svoeyu starukhoi
U samogo sinego morya.[22]

There lived an old man and his wife
On the edge of the blue sea.

---

20. For a comprehensive account of the influence of folkloric patterns on *By the Sea Shore* see N. Ecker, 'Elemente der Volksdichtung in der Lyrik Anna Achmatovas', unpublished D.Phil. thesis, University of Vienna, 1973, pp. 103–11.

21. Zhirmunskii, *Tvorchestvo Anny Akhmatovoi*, pp. 127–8.

22. A. S. Pushkin, *Polnoe sobranie sochinenii v desyati tomakh*, 3rd edn, Moscow, 1962–6 (hereafter Pushkin, *PSS*), vol. 4, p. 460.

This reference contributes to the image of the sea as the source of ful-filment which is central to *By the Sea Shore*. Just as the sea is the magical source of power for the fisherman and his wife, and also the source of their downfall, it is similarly the element of freedom for the heroine of *By the Sea Shore* and the source of both fulfilment and grief simultaneously. The long-awaited tsarevich comes, eventually, from the sea, but he is dead. From Pushkin too Akhmatova takes the four-stress dol'nik of her verse line. Although Zhirmunskii has suggested that Akhmatova adapts this line to conform with her own use of the dol'nik in lyric poems,[23] her use of unrhymed feminine endings follows Push-kin rather than the epic folk tradition, which characteristically employs dactylic endings.[24]

The subject matter of *By the Sea Shore*, beyond the broad symbolic outline, is, of course, remote from both Pushkin and the folkloric trad-ition, and has much more in common with the themes of Akhmatova's own lyric poetry written during the same period.[25] Both components are borrowed to provide a formal framework, in terms of vocabulary and symbolic structure, on which the theme of the search for fulfilment in love, central to the lyrics of *Rosary*, is developed within wider than usual dimensions.

Pushkin is not by any means the only author to whom Akhmatova responds in this way, though overall he is certainly the single most important source of external texts in her work. There are, for example, poems which reflect the early importance of Annenskii in helping to form Akhmatova's poetic method. Thus the second poem of the cycle 'In Tsarskoe Selo', '. . . A tam moi mramornyi dvoinik' ('. . . And there my marble double') is a response to Annenskii's 'Pace'.[26] Both poems describe a damaged and neglected classical statue in the park and both express admiration at the dignity which the goddess is able to maintain in spite of her degradation. Whereas Annenskii, however, is content to admire the goddess from the psychological distance of his different age and gender, for Akhmatova the proud and elegant woman is a double,

23. Zhirmunskii, *Tvorchestvo Anny Akhmatovoi*, p. 128.

24. Akhmatova's use of the dol'nik in *By the Sea Shore* is the first time in Russian literature that the metre is used in a literary poema. See A. J. Hartman, 'The Metrical Typology of Anna Akhmatova', in L. Leighton (ed.), *Studies in Honor of Xenia Gasio-rowska*, Columbus, Ohio, 1982, p. 116. For a discussion of the dol'nik in Akhmatova's poetry, see A. N. Kolmogorov and A. V. Prokhorov, 'O dol'nike sovremennoi russkoi poezii', *Voprosy yazykoznaniya*, no. 6, 1963, pp. 84–95 and no. 1, 1964, pp. 75–94; R. D. B. Thompson, 'The Anapaestic Dol'nik in the Poetry of Axmatova and Gumilev', in D. Mickiewicz (ed.), *Toward a Definition of Acmeism, (Russian Language Journal Supplementary Issue)*, East Lansing, Mich., 1975, pp. 42–58.

25. Rosslyn, *Prince*, p. 114.

26. I. F. Annenskii, *Stikhotvoreniya i tragedii*, ed. A. V. Fedorov, Leningrad, 1990, p. 122.

a figure with whom she identifies. Compare the endings of the two poems:

Annenskii:

> O daite vechnost' mne, – i vechnost' ya otdam
> Za ravnodushie k obidam i godam.

> Oh, give me eternity – and I will give away eternity
> For indifference to insults and to years.

Akhmatova:

> Kholodnyi, belyi, podozhdi,
> Ya tozhe mramornoyu stanu.
> (S1, 24)

> Wait, cold and white one,
> I will become marble too.

The title of another early poem, 'Podrazhanie I. F. Annenskomu' ('Imitation of I. F. Annenskii'), makes the debt to the older poet explicit. However, as Catriona Kelly has shown, this poem is far from a straightforward imitation. Although there are textual allusions to Annenskii's work, and the melancholy of the scene in which a male hero reflects on the unsatisfactory ending of a romantic episode is broadly similar to the situation in several of Annenskii's poems, Akhmatova deliberately avoids the Symbolist rhetoric and high style of Annenskii's writing in this genre, preferring to emphasise the overwhelming sense of loss by the use of deliberately prosaic imagery and dialogue.[27]

Apart from literature and folklore there are several other types of external text which are found in Akhmatova's early work. She refers first of all to other types of artistic expression, and particularly to the visual arts. That the architecture of St Petersburg features prominently in her poetry has already been mentioned; there are also references to specific sculptures and paintings which are evoked to give additional emotional coloration to Akhmatova's poems. For example, a poem of 1910, dedicated to the artist Aleksandra Ekster, describes in detail the

---

27. See C. Kelly, 'The Impossibility of Imitation: Anna Akhmatova and Innokentii Annenskii', in W. A. Rosslyn (ed.), *The Speech of Unknown Eyes: Akhmatova's Readers on her Poetry*, Nottingham, 1990, vol. 2, pp. 238–43.

canvas of an unnamed old master: a proud and sensuous woman sits in enigmatic splendour attended by a black servant (S1, 305–6). The subject of this poem is described in similar terms to the heroines of other poems of the period as a *femme fatale*, and thereby becomes an archetypal image of them:

> I dlya kogo eti zhutkie guby
> Stali smertel'noi otravoi?

> And for whom did these terrifying lips
> Become a deadly poison?

Similarly, in a poem of 1924, 'Khudozhniku' ('To an Artist'), Akhmatova describes the work of an unnamed artist, seeing it as an illustration of the power of art to transcend time and nature. The painting thus becomes in Akhmatova's poem a symbol of how her affection for the artist has survived the passing of the years (S1, 174).

Related effects are occasionally produced through auditory Symbolism, as notably in several of the poems Akhmatova wrote in Kiev, where the ringing of bells provides a link between the present and the historical and religious traditions of the city, and leads the heroine to reflections on duty or on a change that has taken place in her view of the world (S1, 317, 108–9).

The discourse of Akhmatova's poetry is often supported by imagery taken from the lexicon of Orthodox Christianity – words like 'stole', 'communicant', 'psalmist' occur with some frequency, particularly in *White Flock*. Although different critical opinions exist as to the exact status of the religious theme in Akhmatova's work, it is clear that when ecclesiastical motifs are used in poems where love is the predominant concern, as in 'The sun filled the room', quoted above, resonances are produced which would otherwise not be present.[28]

Several of the poems which Akhmatova wrote in Kiev are particularly imbued with a religious sensibility and are concerned above all with duty. Thus in 'I v Kievskom khrame Premudrosti Boga' ('In the Kiev church of the Divine Wisdom') the heroine insists that the icon of St Sophia and the sound of the cathedral bells will remind her of the vows she has made to her beloved (S1, 317). In 'Budu chernye gryadki kholit'' ('I will tend the black flower-beds') the distinction is made between wild flowers which grow spontaneously and flowers which are cultivated with great care and effort. It is only the latter which can be taken to St Sophia as a sign of repentance, because, like the faith

---

28. For a discussion of religion in Akhmatova criticism see Rosslyn, *Prince*, pp. 5–13.

necessary for salvation, they require diligent attention and self-sacrifice to ensure that they flourish (S1, 168–9). The poem implies that natural instincts must be overcome in the interests of duty, but at the same time implicitly expresses the wish that this were not so.[29]

The comparison between the heroine's situation and the archetypal stories of biblical or ecclesiastical history is also stated explicitly. In 'Goryat tvoi ladoni' ('Your hands are burning'), for example, the torments of the hero are compared to those of St Antony, and the importuning of memories is likened to the persistence of Mary Magdalene (S1, 55).

The cycle of 'Bibleiskie stikhi' ('Biblical Poems', S1, 146–9) takes three episodes from the Old Testament and retells them from the perspective of the usual concerns of Akhmatova's poetry. Thus 'Rakhil'' ('Rachel') relates how Jacob was tricked into marriage with Leah and emphasises the emotional trauma of his forced separation from Rachel and the latter's smouldering resentment of her sister. 'Lotova zhena' ('Lot's Wife') stresses the memories of domestic happiness associated with the city of Sodom which make it impossible for Lot's wife not to turn back. The third poem, 'Melkhola' ('Michal'), investigates the contradictory feelings of Saul's daughter Michal, who finds herself attracted to her father's protégé David even though she despises him for his lowly origins.[30]

A similar expansion of meaning is achieved through Akhmatova's use of material from Russian and Ukrainian history. In the Kiev poems the significance of the city is, of course, stressed by the references to St Vladimir and St Sophia, but there are also allusions to the Mongol invasion (through the icon in St Sophia which survived it), to Mazeppa and to Prince Yaroslav. In 'Plotno somknuty guby sukhie' ('The dry lips are tightly closed') Akhmatova describes the funeral of the Russian Saint Evdokiya (widow of Dmitrii Donskoi, died 1407) and likens the scene to an unexplained event in the life of the lyric heroine (S1, 65). In a poem about Novgorod her characterisation of the town mentions not only its natural and architectural features, but also its historical destiny by referring metonymically to the popular leadership of Marfa Boretskaya in the fifteenth century and to the tyrannical discipline of Aleksei Arakcheev in the nineteenth (S1, 99).[31]

The incorporation of historical and political themes into the framework of Akhmatova's early love poetry, as we shall see in the following

29. Ibid., p. 203.
30. This poem was not completed until 1961, but it was apparently conceived and begun in the early 1920s.
31. See R. Reeder (ed.), *The Complete Poems of Anna Akhmatova*, trans. Judith Hemschemeyer, Somerville, Mass., 1990, vol. 1, p. 635.

chapter, becomes increasingly insistent in the work she produced after the First World War. It is, moreover, the fusion of public and private themes that begins here, the explanation of the personal fate of the heroine in terms of the historical context of her times, and conversely the examination of the epoch through the feelings and reactions of the individual which underlie not only Akhmatova's poetry of 1917–25, but also the work she produced in her later, 'Soviet' period.

From *Evening* to *Anno Domini*: Akhmatova and the Poetic Book

The close attention which Akhmatova gave to the internal structuring of individual poems and to their oral presentation at public readings is also found in her organisation of the verse contained within specific collections. One feature of her early books that stands out is that although their poems frequently appear to represent portions of an implicit narrative, their ordering normally eschews the linear progression that would make this narrative explicit. For all their appearance of 'lyric diary', Akhmatova's sequences of poems sidestep the logic of cause and effect, and avoid a straightforward construction of the personality of the lyric narrator in a historical perspective. Such an approach, in which the inner biography of the poet was paramount, had been characteristic of Symbolist poetics, and, as Justin Doherty has noted, was rejected by Acmeist practice in general.[1] Instead, the early Akhmatova offers series of poems linked thematically and connected by the principles of fragmentation and reflection. These are often arranged around particular key poems which function as focal points for the ideas expressed in neighbouring verses.[2] The hierarchical connections are not always rigorous since Akhmatova's sequences regularly contain poems of different dates and composed under widely different circumstances, yet they do provide a link which allows them to be read not simply as random agglomerations of discrete poetic units.

Akhmatova's concern with sequences of poems has been more obvious in her poetry after 1925, in which she shows an increasing tendency to group poems together in explicit cycles, but it is clearly present from her earliest published work.[3] The original architectonics of her first five books has generally been obscured, in later publications of

---

1. Doherty, *The Acmeist Movement*, pp. 210–27.
2. See S. Shwartzband, 'Anna Akhmatova's Second Book, *Chetki*', in Rosslyn, *The Speech of Unknown Eyes*, vol. 1, p. 123.
3. See S. Driver, 'Anna Akhmatova and the Poetic Sequence', in Ketchian, *Anna Akhmatova, 1889–1989*, p. 65.; A. Kushner, *Apollon v snegu: zametki na polyakh*, Leningrad, 1991, pp. 41–3.

her work, by editorial interventions and, of course, Akhmatova's own revisions. The collections themselves, are, however, quite subtle instruments which allow Akhmatova an additional mode of expression to that available through individual poems. Their structures develop together with the thematic and stylistic concerns of Akhmatova's poetry, both conditioning these and being influenced by them. The organisation of *Anno Domini*, for example, is thus not only more complex than that of *Evening*, but is designed to emphasise its different preoccupations in content.

Evening and *Rosary*

S. Shwartzband has gone some way towards investigating the issue as it affects Akhmatova's second collection, *Rosary*. His analysis of the book shows that its five sections are orchestrated around poems which contain combinations of themes explored individually in series of 'micro-narratives' which precede and follow them in a symmetrical arrangement. Shwartzband's elucidation of the underlying pattern is most convincing for the first section. The key poem here is 'Pokorno mne voobrazhen´e' ('My imagination obeys me', DG, 97–8, S1, 54).[4] This contains both an account of a broken love affair in which the heroine is rejected by her lover and a suggestion of rivalry between the man and the woman in poetic as well as emotional endeavour. The two spheres of activity, indeed, are closely intertwined:

Vy, prikazavshii mne: dovol´no,
Podi, ubei svoyu lyubov´!
I vot ya tayu, ya bezvol´na,
No vse sil´nei skuchaet krov'.

I esli ya umru, to kto zhe
Moi stikhi napishet Vam,
Kto stat´ zvenyashchimi pomozhet
Eshche ne skazannym slovam?

You, who ordered me: enough,
Try and kill your love!
And now I am languishing, I am weak willed,
But my blood is yearning all the more strongly.

4. In the discussion which follows, poems from *Evening*, *Rosary* and *White Flock* are cited from Timenchik, *Desyatye gody* (DG), which reproduces the original texts of these collections. For the convenience of readers the reference to DG is followed by a further reference to S1.

And if I die, then who
Will write my poems to you,
Who will help my as yet unspoken words
To ring out?

'My imagination obeys me' is preceded by two triplets of poems on the theme of disappointment in love. In the first of these the obstacle is caused by the failure of one party to respond to the advances of the other. The second takes a different tack and contrasts a past where the heroine both loved and was loved in return with a present in which she has been abandoned by the lyric hero. Akhmatova follows 'My imagination obeys me' with a further pair of triplets of poems, where the emphasis turns to writing as a surrogate for love. The first of these triplets contrasts alienation in a personal relationship with an intimacy which is still possible on the level of poetic collaboration. The second records a failure in love which coincides (and is attendant upon) a success in poetic achievement. The tension between the two modes of expression – love and poetry – is reinforced by the single poem with which the first section of *Rosary* closes, 'Zdravstvui! Legkii shelest slyshish'' ('Hello. Do you hear a light rustling', DG, 101, S1, 58). This again suggests that poetry and love are incompatible:

Etikh strochek ne dopishesh' –
Ya k tebe prishla.
Neuzheli ti obidish'
Tak, kak v proshlyi raz

You will not finish these lines –
I have come to you.
Surely you won't hurt my feelings
As you did last time.

The end of this poem, with its hint at possible suicide, underlines the notion that rivalry in both areas is a major source of grievance for the lyric heroine.

Basing his argument on a series of allusions to the poetry of Gumilev which he identifies in *Rosary*, Shwartzband sees Akhmatova's book as a reflection of the complex relationship – with its separate psychology of personal and professional interaction – which existed between her and her first husband. This is perhaps an oversimplification, given the more general difficulties at the time facing a woman who wished to compete on terms of equality with men in the literary arena. Moreover, although *Rosary* was certainly for the most part written during the years when Akhmatova's and Gumilev's marriage was already under considerable strain (1912–14), Akhmatova was in fact on terms of intimacy with many people of artistic Petersburg during this period, notably Nikolai Nedobrovo, and an exclusive psychological link with Gumilev is by no means proved.

Nevertheless, the use of the principle of reflection to group poems and provide them with at least a loose thematic framework is certainly found throughout *Rosary*. The second section thus pivots around the central poem 'Golos pamyati' ('The Voice of Memory', DG, 105, S1, 61) in the form of two sequences devoted to the memory of a love affair on the one hand and a creative partnership on the other. The third section focuses on two issues relating to literary fame linked together by the poem 'Umiraya, tomlyus´ o bessmert´i' ('Dying, I am tormented by immortality', DG, 112, S1, 67), with its evocation of both corporeal and literary death, while the fourth section functions as a link between the first three and the selection of poems from *Evening* with which *Rosary* concludes. In this context the poems of *Evening* serve as prototypes for the more sophisticated treatment of the themes of love and art which appear in the later book.

Much work still needs to be done to establish the full hierarchy of poems and poetic themes within *Rosary*: Shwartzband's short study remains unconvincing in some of its details, and is perhaps unnecessarily reductive in its psychoanalytical interpretations. Nevertheless, the identification of a hierarchical principle of organisation at the heart of Akhmatova's early collections is a compelling one. Similar patterns can indeed also be detected in *Evening* and *White Flock*, both of which share the division found in *Rosary* into roughly equal sections each prefaced with a Roman numeral.

Like *Rosary*, its precursor, *Evening*, avoids chronological perspective and groups poems on thematic lines.[5] The three sections of the collection, although they are equally devoted to the tormented loves of the narrator, are thus nevertheless distinct and complementary in emphasis. For each section the first poem can be taken as emblematic of the poems which follow. The poem 'Lyubov´' ('Love', DG, 53, S1, 23), with which *Evening* and its first section begin, suggests love in a positive aspect, stressing its attractions for the lyric heroine regardless of any suffering it may incidentally cause. Love steals unpredictably up

---

5. This has also been noted, in slightly different terms from what follows, by Doherty, *The Acmeist Movement*, pp. 213–15. Doherty sees section I of *Evening* as an exploration of emotional involvement and section II as focusing on the loss of innocence.

to its victims and is irresistible even as it frightens:

> Umeet tak sladko rydat'
> V molitve toskuyushchei skripki,
> I strashno ee ugadat'
> V eshche neznakomoi ulybke.

> It knows how to sob so sweetly
> In the prayer of a melancholy violin,
> And it's terrifying to guess its presence
> In a still unfamiliar smile.

The poems which follow in section I echo this bitter-sweetness with particular attention to the heroine's enjoyment of it. Love is nearly always in the past and it has been the heroine herself who has ended it. She continues, however, to relish its memory as, for example, in 'Lyubov'' pokoryaet obmanno' ('Love conquers by deceit', DG, 55, S1, 25) with its recourse to the pathetic fallacy to describe a radiant moment in the past:

> Ved' zvezdy byli krupnee,
> Ved' pakhli inache travy

> And the stars were bigger,
> And the grass smelt different.

She also dwells on the pathos of the moment of parting or of realisation that her love is doomed in poems such as 'Szhala ruki pod temnoi vual'yu' ('I clenched my fists under my dark veil', DG, 55–6, S1, 25) or 'Khochesh' znat', kak vse eto bylo' ('Do you want to know how it all was', DG, 57, S1, 28), both of which contain a tormented dialogue between the two players of the love drama, oscillating between mutual incomprehension and mutual sympathy. Yet the heroine keeps the initiative, and the dispassionate independence suggested earlier by the comparison of the heroine to a marble statue in '. . .A tam moi mramornyi dvoinik' ('And there my marble double', DG, 54, S1, 24) is confirmed by the concluding poem of the section, 'Mne bol'she nog moikh ne nado' ('I don't need my legs any more', DG, 59, S1, 29–30), in which she becomes a mermaid and swims off in freedom while her companion stands, pale, by the side of the water.

The second section of *Evening* is dominated, on the other hand, by the negative aspect of love, signalled by the imagery of the first poem of the cycle 'Obman' ('Betrayal', DG, 60–2, S1, 32–4) with which it begins. Here, reading love poetry addressed to her grandmother, the narrator is drawn from the contemplation of love's charms to an implicit recognition of its darker aspects:

> O, serdtse lyubit sladostno i slepo!
> I raduyut izyskannye klumby,
> I rezkii krik vorony v nebe chernoi,
> I v glubine allei arka sklepa.
>   (DG, 60, S1, 32)

> Oh, the heart loves sweetly and blindly,
> And the manicured flowerbeds rejoice,
> And the harsh cry of the crow is in the sky,
> And in the depths of the avenue is the arch of the crypt.

The 'Betrayal' cycle itself contains only a very understated indication of betrayal, which is immediately contradicted by the heroine's wishful thinking:

> Milym prostila gubam
> Ya ikh zhestokuyu shutku. . .
> O, vy priedete k nam
> Zavtra po pervoputku.
>   (DG, 62, S1, 33)

> I have forgiven your dear lips
> Their cruel joke. . .
> Oh, tomorrow you will come to us
> Over the first snow.

In the poems which follow, however, the heroine's prospects for fulfilled romance become progressively bleaker. Three poems which hint at the complications of infidelity are followed by three in which the dominant motif is the abandonment of the heroine by her lover. The consequences of such an abandonment are then translated into concrete terms in 'Pod navesom temnoi rigi zharko' ('It is hot under the awning of the dark threshing barn', DG, 65, S1, 36), with its admonition 'Akh pusty dorozhnye kotomki, / A na zavtra golod i nenast´e!' ('Ah, our knapsacks are empty and tomorrow will bring hunger and bad weather!'), and in 'Khoroni, khoroni menya, veter!' ('Bury me, bury me, wind!', DG, 65–6, S1, 36–7), in which the heroine speaks from the grave. The section concludes with a restatement of the theme of abandonment in 'Ty pover´, ne zmeinoe ostroe zhalo' ('Believe me, it is not the serpent's sharp sting', DG, 66, S1, 37), which adopts the folkloric topos of the humble maiden's love for the Prince in order to underline the themes of rejection and betrayal. Throughout all the poems of section II, in contrast to section I, the heroine is seen as powerless, responding to events rather than able to control them. As she complains in the final poem:

Vorozhu, chtob tsarevichu noch´yu prisnit´sya,
No bessil´na moya vorozhba.

My magic tries to make the tsarevich dream of me,
But my spells are powerless.

The literary stylisation of 'Believe me, it is not the serpent's sharp sting' becomes a primary concern of the third and final section of *Evening*. This is introduced by the only poem in the collection directly addressed to the Muse. In 'Muze' ('To the Muse', DG, 67, S1, 38) the heroine situates her failure in love in a broader human context: 'Dolzhen na etoi zemle ispytat´ / Kazhdyi lyubovnuyu pytku' ('Everyone on this earth must suffer the torments of love'), and at the same time suggests the possibility of a relationship outside the framework of love and rejection, a creative relationship with her 'sister' the Muse.[6] By way of demonstration of this realisation, the third section of *Evening* is made up of reworkings of the themes of the two previous sections, which are now treated in an overtly and consciously literary fashion. Thus the grammar of the assignation is presented in 'Maskarad v parke' ('Masquerade in the Park', DG, 69–70, S1, 40–1) through the stylised evocation of the masked ball in a manner reminiscent of the paintings of Konstantin Somov. A folkloric model is used as a framework for the exploration of infidelity in 'Seroglazyi korol´' ('The Grey-Eyed King', DG, 70–1, S1, 42). Fishermen and shepherds are used as correlatives of the heroine's unrequited love or delirium in 'Rybak' ('The Fisherman', DG, 71, S1, 42–3) and 'Nad vodoi' ('On the Water', DG, 76–7, S1, 45–6). 'Segodnya mne pis´ma ne prinesli' ('They brought me no letter today', DG, 72, S1, 43) is a rare example of Akhmatova using a fixed poetic form involving the repetition of lines, and the theme of abandonment is also placed within external formal constraints – in this case through the evocation of another artistic genre – in 'Nadpis´ na neokonchennom portrete' ('Inscription on an Unfinished Portrait', DG, 72–3, S1, 44).

The final poem of *Evening*, 'Tri raza pytat´ prikhodila' ('Three times it came to torment me', DG, 77, S1, 38–9) stands at first sight as something of a contrast to what has preceded it, both in section III and in the

---

6. See Rosslyn, *Prince*, p. 69.

book as a whole, because it foregrounds the theme of guilt. This theme, of course, has been present below the surface in poems such as 'Pesenka' ('Song', DG, 63–4, S1, 34–5) and 'Tumanom legkim park napolnilsya' ('The park was filled with a light mist', DG, 74, S1, 47),[7] but it is now brought out into the open. The heroine is haunted by a night-time voice which accuses her of treating her love affairs as a game and of living a lie. The accusation hits home, as the final lines of the poem indicate:

O, ty nenaprasno smeyalas´,
Moya neproshchennaya lozh´!

Oh, you didn't laugh in vain,
My unforgiven lie!

In the light of section III, the heroine's own life as reflected in the earlier parts of the book is itself seen here as a form of literary stylis- ation at odds with the demands of genuine human communication, and her failure to find long-term satisfaction in love is rooted firmly within her own psyche.

White Flock

In *White Flock* the urgent descriptions of specific episodes in the love drama and the minutely registered details which characterise Akhmatova's first two books in large measure give way to an elegiac mode of discourse in which the heroine remembers events clearly constructed as having taken place in the past. On occasion, indeed, the poems become entirely abstract, devoid of any *realia* at all from the heroine's biography. This is the case, for example, in the well-known 'In closeness between people there is a hidden border-line', which justifies in rigorously theoretical terms the heroine's failure to respond to the addressee's declaration of love.

As was early pointed out by contemporary critics, the reflective mode is underlined by an increased formality in the linguistic and metrical structures of *White Flock* as compared to the earlier collections. The conversational vocabulary and syntax of *Rosary* is replaced by a diction which makes widespread use of Church Slavonic forms and religious imagery. The dol´nik tends to yield to the iamb, and the rhymes become more exact.[8] Moreover, still greater weight is now

---

7. Ibid., pp. 41–5.
8. See V. M. Zhirmunskii, *Voprosy teorii literatury*, Leningrad, 1928, pp. 322–6.

placed on the overall architectonics of the book. The dependence on reflective 'micro-narratives' is reduced and greater emphasis is given to the relationship between sections, which has now developed into a sophisticated play of light and dark. In the first four of the five numbered parts, examination of private factors affecting the heroine's psychological state alternates with wider explorations of the role of experience. The fifth part, the long poem *By the Sea Shore*, provides a synthesis of both aspects, and in allegorical terms a rounded summary of the heroine's journey towards maturity.

The first section is devoted principally to the transformation of experience into art. At its centre is a poem to the Muse, 'Muza ushla po doroge' ('The Muse left along the road', DG, 140, S1, 8), which brings out the heroine's reliance on her – 'Ya lyubila ee odnu' ('I loved only her'), she declares – at the same time as stressing the Muse's inconstancy. The duality of art as represented here is a recurrent theme throughout the section. Love and suffering are identified as the raw material of poetry, which indeed replaces them as the focus of the heroine's attention: poetry lasts after love is forgotten. On the other hand, poetry brings with it its own complications. The public rehearsal of the passion and disappointment which produce it lead to further suffering in the form of public humiliation. Yet like love itself, the preservation of its memory in the form of verse is an irresistible avocation.

Akhmatova's most succinct exposition of this entire cycle – memory of lost love, poetry, humiliation – is found in the short poem 'Ya ulybat´sya perestala' ('I have stopped smiling'):

> Odnoi nadezhdoi men´she stalo,
> Odnoyu pesnei bol´she budet.
> I etu pesnyu ya nevol´no
> Otdam na smekh i porugan´e.
> (DG, 140, S1, 82)

> One hope less will become
> One hope more,
> And this song, against my will,
> I will give over to laughter and profanation.

Section III is dedicated to interpretation of the First World War. Its central point is a prayer for the safety of Russia, 'Molitva' ('Prayer', DG, 161, S1, 102), in which the heroine offers all that is dear to her –

her child, her lover and her poetic gift:

> Chtoby tucha nad temnoi Rossiei
> Stala oblakom v slave luchei.

> So that the storm-cloud over darkened Russia
> May become a cloud bathed in the glory of light.

This statement of nationalism is preceded by a sequence in which the main motifs are war itself and the death and anguish at parting which it inevitably causes and an apocalyptic sense of unease, which sees the war as potentially presaging the end of civilisation itself. This last theme is particularly clear in poems such as the famous 'Iyul´ 1914' ('July 1914', DG, 158–9, S1, 100) and 'Tot golos, s tishinoi velikoi sporya' ('That voice arguing with the great silence', DG, 159–60, S1, 101), which looks back at the innocence of the time immediately before the beginning of the war.

The poems which follow 'Prayer' are a litany of illness, loss separation and death, not explicitly connected with the war, but reinforcing at the level of private experience the sense of catastrophe with which Akhmatova's depiction of the war is embued. The concluding poem of the section, 'Pamyati 19 iyulya 1914' ('In Memory of 19 July 1914', DG, 168, S1, 109–10), refers to the day of Germany's declaration of war on Russia and provides a link with the metapoetical text of section I. The collective suffering of the heroine and her contemporaries has provided a new and urgent subject for her art, the recording not only of personal memory, but also of history:

> Iz pamyati, kak gruz otnyne lishnii,
> Ischezli teni pesen i strastei.
> Ei – opustevshei – prikazal Vsevyshnii
> Stat´ strashnoi knigoi grozovykh vestei.

> The shadows of songs and passions disappeared
> From my memory like a burden no longer required.
> The Almighty ordered it, emptied,
> To become a grim book of fearful news.

The public themes of poetry and war alternate, in sections II and IV of *White Flock*, with the more private concerns of the heroine. In section II, memory has become the most important influence on her thoughts as experience leads her into a deeper understanding of her feelings. She is able to accept her fate with a certain philosophical detachment, whether it is loss, as in the central poem of the section 'Vse obeshchalo mne ego' ('Everything promised him to me', DG, 149, S1, 91), or anticipated happiness as in the poems which begin and end it. The last words of the section sound a particular note of hope, based on an implied memory of past happiness:

> Ya schastliva. No mne vsego milei
> Lesnaya i pologaya doroga,
> Ubogii most, skrivivshiisya nemnogo
> I to, chto zhdat' ostalos' malo dnei.
> (DG, 156, S1, 98)

> I am happy. But dearest of all to me
> Are the sloping path through the forest,
> The broken-down, crooked bridge,
> And the fact that there are only a few more days to wait.

If section II is concerned chiefly with mature reflection on the past, section IV is focused rather on the future. The dominant motif here is one of waiting and searching. The mood of anticipation which informs the poems of the first half of the section is signalled in the opening poem:

> A pesnyu tu, chto prezhde nadoelo,
> Kak novuyu, s volneniem poesh'.
> (DG, 169, S1, 110)

> And the song which you found boring before,
> You now sing with excitement as if it was a new one.

This mood gradually gives way to a waiting without hope as in 'Nebo melkii dozhdik seet' (The sky sows a light rain', DG, 176, S1, 116–17), where the return of the hero is long overdue, and in 'Milomu' ('To my Beloved', DG, 177–8, S1, 118), where the hero continues to wait for his bride though, unknown to him, she is already dead. A coda to the section is provided by its final poems, which reconfirm the power of memory to preserve the past. 'Pervyi luch – blagosloven'e Boga' ('The sun's first ray, God's blessing', DG, 179–80, S1, 120) recapitulates the metapoetic theme and celebrates the transposition of memory into poetry. 'Ne ottogo l', uidya ot legkosti proklyatoi' ('Is this not why, escaping from accursed frivolity', DG, 180, S1, 167) shows the negative aspect of the ability of memory to preserve the past, the insistent suspicion that the heroine is to blame for the death of the hero.[9]

The fifth and final section of *White Flock* consists of the long poem *By the Sea Shore*. This offers a formal contrast to the preceding short lyrics, and at the same time provides a sustained restatement of its main themes. The poem is dominated, of course, by the topos of the heroine waiting for her prince, and by the sentimental education of the heroine as her expectation turns into mourning for the figure who is eventually washed up dying on the shore. Into this underlying plot-line is woven a strong metapoetical theme describing the heroine's meetings with the Muse, and the song that she will sing in order for the prince to recognise her. The foreboding of Akhmatova's First World War poetry of section III is reflected too in references at the beginning of *By the Sea Shore* to the Crimean War of sixty years earlier, which can be seen as presaging the eventual violent death of the prince. Akhmatova's long poem thus functions as a conclusion of *White Flock* as a whole by restating and combining the messages of its individual sections.

Anno Domini

To some extent the thematic principle of organisation seen in *Evening*, *Rosary* and *White Flock* was maintained in *Anno Domini* as it appeared in 1921. The first of its three sections, 'Anno Domini MCMXXI', although it offers an occasional moment of consolation in the contemplation of nature or in communion with the Muse,[10] contains poems where the dominant motifs are separation, fear and death. The heroine thus variously appeals for help in escaping from a dragon which is imprisoning her (AD1, 8–9, S1, 163),[11] lies awake at night anticipating disaster (AD1, 12–13, S1, 157) and inadvertently causes by her poetry the death of her friends (AD1, 27, S1, 163). Her relationship with the figure of the hero is defined in terms of mutual incompatibility (AD1, 11, 18–19, S1, 156–7, 159). The section contains an elegy to Aleksandr Blok written on the occasion of his funeral (AD1, 24–5, S1, 160–1). A contrasting note is sounded in the opening poem, which acknowledges

---

9. This poem lost its prominent position at the end of the section when extra poems were added in some later editions of *White Flock*. From *Iz shesti knig* it was transferred to *Anno Domini*.

10. 'Vse raskhishcheno, predano, prodano', 'Koe-kak udalos' razluchit'sya', 'Pust' golosa organa snova gryanut' (AD1, 7, 16–17, 20–1; S1, 155, 158–9, 159–60).

11. References will be given to *Anno Domini MCMXXI*, Petrograd, 1921 (AD1) and *Anno Domini*, 2nd edn, Petrograd, 1923 (AD2) as appropriate, and also to S1.

a moment of hope amid the prevailing mood of destruction:

Vse raskhishcheno, predano, prodano,
Chernoi smerti mel'kalo krylo,
Vse golodnoi toskoyu izglodano,
Otchego zhe nam stalo svetlo?
(AD1, 7, S1, 155)

Everything has been plundered, betrayed, sold.
The wing of black death has flashed by.
Everything has been devoured by starving anguish.
Why then do we find it so bright?

The optimism found here in the contemplation of nature finds little reflection in the poems of 'Anno Domini MCMXXI', but looks forward rather to the second section, 'Golos pamyati' ('The Voice of Memory').[12] The focus here is on the moment of recognition, of revelation, of change in a variety of different contexts. The section begins, for example, with a poem, 'Shiroko raspakhnuty vorota' ('The doors are thrown wide open', AD1, 31, S1, 164–5), which describes a moment of understanding occasioned by the sound of church bells. It ends by recording a moment of shelter from the emotional vicissitudes of the heroine's life:

Teper' vo mne spokoistvie i schast'e.
Proshchai moi tikhii, ty mne vechno mil
Za to, chto v dom svoi strannitsu pustil.
(AD1, 52, S1, 142)

Now I am calm and happy.
Goodbye my quiet one, you will always be dear to me
For allowing a wanderer into your home.

Other poems find comfort in nature, or in the act of contrition, or in the expectation of forgiveness before death.[13] The lost innocence of Akhmatova's earlier art is also celebrated in, for example, 'Pokinuv roshchi rodiny svyashchennoi' ('Leaving the groves of my sacred homeland', AD1, 48–9, S1, 153–4), where the muses of her youth are

12. On the pathetic fallacy in Akhmatova's early civic poetry, see K. Verheul, 'Public Themes in the Poetry of Anna Axmatova', in J. van der Eng-Liedmeier and K. Verheul (eds), *Tale Without a Hero and Twenty-Two Poems by Anna Axmatova*, The Hague, 1973, pp. 36–9.
13. 'Pochernel, iskrivilsya', 'Smerkaetsya', 'Budu chernye gryadki kholit'', 'Poka ne svalyus' pod zaborom', 'Na poroge belom raya' (AD1, 32–3, 50–1, 45–6, 40–1, 42; S1, 165, 154–5, 168–9, 162).

compared to 'girls who have not yet known love'. And a new function for art is revealed in 'Tot avgust, kak zheltoe plamya' ('That August, like a yellow flame', AD1, 34–5, S1, 165–6), in the context of the First World War. Just as the face of the capital is changing as a result of the war, so too the warrior and the poet must both adopt new roles:

> I brat mne skazal: nastali
> Dlya menya velikie dni.
> Teper' ty nashi pechali
> I radost' odna khrani.

> And my brother said to me:
> Great days have arrived for me.
> Now you alone must preserve
> Our sorrows and our happiness.

The social role which Akhmatova had begun to explore in *White Flock* asserts itself here with even greater force.[14]

The third and final section of *Anno Domini* in its original form consisted of the collection *Plantain* reprinted from its separate publication earlier in 1921. It represents perhaps the final stage of development of the 'biographical' themes of *Rosary* and *White Flock*,[15] and contains a familiar mixture of scenes from the cycle of the heroine's exaltation and despair. In the context of *Anno Domini* it represents a combination of the motifs of revelation and parting which dominate the two sections which precede it.

The thematic arrangement of *Anno Domini* is, however, overlaid with a strong chronological perspective. The title of the first edition, *Anno Domini MCMXXI*, with its echoes of medieval chronicles, announces from the outset that the work is to be a record of the times in which it is written. This particular connotation is partially lost by the change in the title which was made for the second edition (it became *Anno Domini* alone with no year specified), but regained by the addition of a fourth section, 'Novye stikhi' ('New poems'), at the beginning of the collection to provide a continuation of the chronicle from 1921 up to the time of publication.[16]

The time sequence, in reverse chronological order implied by the titles of the sections of *Anno Domini* – 'New Poems', 'Anno Domini

14. On the ethical component in Acmeist thinking more generally see Doherty, *The Acmeist Movement*, pp. 264–86.

15. SP, 468.

16. The following remarks about the chronological structure of *Anno Domini* refer to the second edition.

MCMXXI', 'The Voice of Memory', 'Plantain' – is confirmed by the dates attached to individual poems. In Akhmatova's earlier collections poems from different years had been freely intermingled; in *Anno Domini* the provision of dates has been much more carefully considered. The poems of 'Plantain', all but two of which are dated in the second edition of *Anno Domini*, are predominantly from 1917, though these are interspersed with small numbers of works from the periods 1918–19 and 1913–16. These dates mark 'Plantain' off as belonging to the period before the central concern of *Anno Domini*. 'The Voice of Memory', which contains nine undated poems, one from 1919 (added in the second edition) and five from 1921, marks a transition in chronological terms from the poems of 'Plantain' which precede it to those of 'Anno Domini MCMXXI' which follow. All fourteen poems of this latter section bear the date 1921, thus emphasising its especial historical significance. 'New Poems' contains mostly undated poems, but a transition from 1921 into the future is suggested by the date of its first poem, 26 December 1921, and by two later poems, both of which are dated 1922.

From this point of view too it is clearly the year 1921 around which everything revolves, and the reader is willy-nilly obliged to see the events of this year as forming a watershed. For Akhmatova, 1921 was indeed a year vested with particular significance on several different planes. It was the year of the breakdown of her marriage with Shileiko, the year in which Blok died and Gumilev was killed, the first year after the end of the Civil War, in which the peace-time cynicism of the new order began to be felt.[17] It is hard therefore not to read the emphasis in 'Anno Domini MCMXXI' on separation and death as a more or less direct reflection of Akhmatova's experience at this specific point in time. The entrapment expressed in the epigraph to the section from Ovid's *Amores*, 'Nec sine te, nec tecum vivere possum' ('I can live neither with you nor without you'),[18] applies not only to the obsessive love-hate relationship described in 'O, zhizn´ bez zavtrashnego dnya' ('Oh, life without a yesterday', AD2, 36, S1, 158), but more broadly to the heroine's ambiguous place in early Soviet society.

By contrast, the poems of 'The Voice of Memory', with their generally more optimistic flavour, are constructed as belonging to the past. So too is the 'Plantain' section, which was, of course, already familiar to Akhmatova's readers by the time *Anno Domini* came to be published. The epigraphs to both of these sections draw attention to this

17. See V. N. Toporov, 'Ob istorizme Akhmatovoi', *Russian Literature*, vol. 28, 1990, pp. 319–20.
18. *Amores*, III, xi.

chronological element. The lines 'Mir – lish' luch ot lika druga, / Vse inoe ten' ego' ('The world is only a ray from the face of a friend, / Everything else is its shadow'), which preface 'The Voice of Memory', are taken from Gumilev's 'P' yanyi dervish' ('The Drunk Dervish') and epitomise the dervish's disillusionment and despair.[19] 'Plantain' is preceded (for the first time in its republication as a section of *Anno Domini*) by two lines from Pushkin's dedication to *Poltava* in which the speaker hopes to move the feelings of a woman who had loved him at an earlier time: 'Uznai, po krainei mere, zvuki, / Byvalo, milye tebe' ('Recognise, at least, the sounds / Once dear to you').[20]

The epigraph to 'New Poems', which later came to be applied to the whole volume, sets the entire collection in the past. The line 'V te basnoslovnye goda' ('In those days of fable'), from Tyutchev's poem 'Ya znal ee eshche togda' ('I knew her even then'), in itself suggests a nostalgic look at the past as well as evoking Tyutchev's portrait of a beautiful woman whose perfection has been overcome by death.[21] The poems which the section contains suggest a new start after the tribulations of 'Anno Domini MCMXXI'. The opening poem, 'Bezhetsk' (AD2, 9, S1, 136–7), combines a powerful evocation of Christmas in the Russian countryside with a refusal to accept the invitation of memory to examine the past. In this poem, as Wendy Rosslyn has noted, 'the mundane is exalted and endowed with spiritual significance'.[22]

Something similar is found in many other poems of the section which have recourse to absolute and religious values as a source of strength. Akhmatova, for example, describes the constancy of the love between Jacob and Rachel in the biblical story in spite of the former's marriage by trickery to her sister Leah (AD2, 23–4, S1, 146–7). In 'Prichitanie' ('Lamentation'), she describes the congregation leaving a church in terms of saints from the orthodox canon: their everyday simplicity is saintly in its mundane determination (AD2, 25, S1, 149).[23] A similar search for durable values is found in, for example, 'Slukh chudovishchnyi brodit po gorodu' ('A monstrous rumour wanders through the town', AD2, 19, S1, 144), where the comforting conclusion of the tale of Blue Beard is suspected of not meeting the heroine's present circumstances, and in the political nationalism of 'Ne s temi ya,

19. N. S. Gumilev, *Stikhotvoreniya i poemy*, ed. M. D. El'zon, Leningrad, 1988, p. 335.
20. Pushkin, *PSS*, vol. 4, 253.
21. F. I. Tyutchev, *Polnoe sobranie sochinenii*, ed. A. A. Nikolaev, Leningrad, 1987, pp. 205–6.
22. Rosslyn, *Prince*, p. 198.
23. Ibid.

kto brosil zemlyu' ('I am not with those who threw away the land', AD2, 14, S1, 139).

One effect of the chronological framework which underpins *Anno Domini* is to increase the impact of the political poems which it contains. In *White Flock*, Akhmatova's treatment of the First World War had been largely confined to a single section. Now political poems are spread throughout the collection in recognition that the private and public worlds of the heroine are no longer distinct, and in conformity with the civic role of the poet announced in 'That August like a yellow flame'. The essence of Akhmatova's politics in *Anno Domini* is a fervent nationalism combined with a profound uneasiness about the changes in society which were taking place around her, and particularly the harsh methods being used by the Bolsheviks to consolidate their power. These two factors combine in an ambivalence in the heroine's attitude towards the society in which she lives, which forms an exact counterpart to the tormented personal relationship between heroine and hero.

The nationalist stance is evident in poems which celebrate the traditional way of life of rural Russia such as 'Bezhetsk' and a poem of the war-torn year 1917, which opens with the following description of the Russian countryside:

> Techet reka nespeshno po doline,
> Mnogookonnyi na prigorke dom,
> I my zhivem, kak pri Ekaterine,
> Molebny sluzhim, urozhaya zhdem.
> (AD2, 96, S1, 134)

> The river flows unhurriedly down the valley,
> The house on the hill has many windows,
> And we live as we did under Catherine,
> Going to church and waiting for the harvest.

There are also more reasoned statements of the poet's position with regard to her country. In 'Kogda v toske samoubiistva' ('When in a suicidal yearning', AD2, 100, cf. S1, 135, 405), for example, which concludes 'Plantain' as it appeared in the second edition of *Anno Domini*, she rejects the idea of exchanging her part in her country's suffering for the life of an exile. In the later 'I am not with those who threw away the land', she rejects both the temptations of exile and the blandishments of the new political masters whose actions had surrendered Russia to war: 'Ikh gruboi lesti ya ne vnemlyu, / Im pesen ya svoikh ne dam' ('I pay no attention to their crude flattery, I will not give them my songs').[24] Instead she prefers to retain her moral independence at whatever cost it may bring:

> My ni edinogo udara
> Ne otklonili ot sebya.
>
> I znaem, chto v otsenke pozdnei
> Opravdan budet kazhdyi chas;
> No v mire net lyudei bessleznei,
> Nadmenee i proshche nas.
>
> We did not deflect
> A single blow from ourselves.
>
> And we know that in the appraisal of future generations,
> Every hour will be justified,
> But the world has no people
> More tearless, prouder, and simpler than us.

The fear which is the counterpoint of the heroine's nationalism has already been mentioned in the context of the section 'Anno Domini MCMXXI'. The same theme of foreboding is found in other sections as well, for example, in 'Za ozerom luna ostanovilas'' ('The moon stopped behind the lake') from 'New Poems', which is full of images of death and decay beyond the control of the protagonist:

> Strashnuyu bedu
> Pochuvstvovav, my srazu zamolchali.
> Zaupokoino filiny krichali,
> I dushnyi veter buistvoval v sadu.
> (AD2, 21, S1, 146)
>
> Sensing
> A terrible misfortune, we at once fell silent.
> The owls shrieked a requiem,
> And a stifling wind raged in the garden.

It seems likely, moreover, that Akhmatova intended at least some of the love poetry of *Anno Domini* to be read as an allegory of the political

---

24. On the political stance of 'Kogda v toske samoubiistva' and 'Ne s temi ya, kto brosil zemlyu', see D. Bobyshev, 'Akhmatova i emigratsiya', *Zvezda*, no. 2, 1991, pp. 177–80.

situation. The parallel between the heroine's private and public lives and the juxtaposition of clearly political poems and apparently personal ones seem to be too deliberate to be purely coincidental. Poems such as 'Ty vsegda tainstvennyi i novyi' ('You are always mysterious and new', AD2, 77, S1, 140) and 'Putnik milyi, ty daleche' ('Traveller dear, you are far away', AD2, 32, S1, 155–6), which talk of enthralment and forced humility before a pitiless master, are certainly susceptible of interpretation in terms of current events.[25] Moreover, at least two of the epigraphs to the four sections of *Anno Domini* have political subtexts. The broader context of the quotation from Gumilev's 'The Drunk Dervish' which precedes 'The Voice of Memory' presents a clear parallel with Akhmatova's own position in 1921 as she searched in vain for Gumilev's grave:

Vot idu ya po mogilam, gde lezhat moi druz'ya.
O lyubvi sprosit' u mertvykh neuzheli mne nel'zya?
I krichit iz yamy cherep tainu groba svoego:
'Mir lish' luch ot lika druga, vse inoe ten' ego!'

I am walking among the graves where my friends lie.
Surely I may ask the dead about love?
And a skull cries from the pit the secret of its tomb:
'The world is only a ray of light from the face of a friend,
Everything else is its shadow!'

Here too is a reflection of the motif made explicit in 'That August like a yellow flame' of the ability of the dead to speak through the poetry of those they have left behind, and it is perhaps not surprising, in view of these associations, that the Gumilev epigraph was dropped in all republications of *Anno Domini* after 1923.

The 'Plantain' epigraph also has political implications. In writing the dedication to *Poltava* it seems that Pushkin had in mind Mariya Volkonskaya (Raevskaya), who followed her Decembrist husband into exile. The connection with the Decembrist movement, which attempted to overthrow the tsarist autocracy in 1825, gives the heroine's feelings for Russia as expressed in the more nationalist poems of the section a more specifically anti-establishment coloration than might otherwise be the case. As will become clear, Akhmatova regularly draws on the history of the Decembrist movement in both her poetry and her prose as a metaphor for the political persecutions of the Soviet period.

25. See C. M. Bowra, *Poetry and Politics, 1900–1960*, Cambridge, 1966, pp. 26–7.

After *Anno Domini* the poetic book ceased to be the main organis-ational vehicle for Akhmatova's poetic thought. The external constraints placed on the publication of her verse and the instability of her material position in the late 1920s and early 1930s discouraged the elaboration of such large-scale structures and focused her attention more on individual poems or shorter sequences. As will be seen in the next chapter, during this period poetry's function as comment on the historical situation in Russia continued to provide a major driving force behind Akhmatova's writing.

−4−

Stalinism and War: Works of the 1930s and 1940s

The Voice of Dissent

When Akhmatova returned to writing poetry in the mid-1930s it was at a time which was hardly conducive to the free expression of ideas. And indeed the number of surviving poems from before the 'change in the air' which took place in late 1939 is very small. Nevertheless, Akhmatova remained keenly aware of her responsibility as a poet, in the long tradition of Russian poetry, to speak out on social, moral and political issues. By the 1930s she felt more than ever that she was one of the few people still able and willing to chronicle the era through which she was living, and to keep alive the literary and social traditions of the past. In 1924 Akhmatova had written a poem which had identified her muse with that of Dante and implied that her task in describing contemporary Russia was parallel to the Italian poet's in portraying the Inferno:

> Ei govoryu: 'Ty l' Dantu diktovala
> Stranitsy Ada?' Otvechaet: 'Ya'.
> (S1, 174)

> I say to her, 'Was it you who dictated
> The pages of Hell?' She answers, 'It was I'.

Later, in the introduction (added in 1957) to the cycle *Requiem*, which describes in penetrating detail the experiences of a generation of women in the queues outside Stalin's prisons, Akhmatova echoes these lines and notes with pride the duty which has fallen on her shoulders:

> 'Can you describe this?'
> And I said,
> 'I can'.
> Then something like a smile briefly lit up what had once been her face. (I, 361)

The notion implicit in these two passages that poetry arises independently of the poet's will from the experience of the poet is found also in three poems on creativity written between 1936 and 1940 which eventually became part of a cycle entitled 'Tainy remesla' ('The Secrets of the Craft'). The earliest of these, 'Tvorchestvo' ('Creativity'), speaks of the birth of a poem in terms of a sound gradually detaching itself from a background of undifferentiated groans, complaints and whispers, and repeats the imagery of dictation:

> Togda ya nachinayu ponimat',
> I prosto prodiktovannye strochki
> Lozhatsya v belosnezhnuyu tetrad'.
> (S1, 190)

> Then I begin to understand,
> And the simply dictated lines
> Fall into place in my snow-white notebook.

The other two poems both emphasise that poetry can emerge from negative phenomena, or from objects normally held in disregard. Thus 'Mne ni k chemu odicheskie rati' ('I have no need for odic regiments') stresses that there is poetry in weeds:

> Kogda b vy znali, iz kakogo sora
> Rastut stikhi, ne vedaya styda.
> (S1, 191)

> If you only knew from what rubbish
> Poems grow, knowing no shame.

And 'Pro stikhi' ('On Poetry') provides a list of poetic subjects recalling Pasternak's 'Opredelenie poezii' ('Definition of Poetry') in its structure and comprehensiveness but, unlike Pasternak's poem, ending on a distinctly sombre note:

> Eto – pchely, eto – donnik,
> Eto – pyl', i mrak, i znoi.
> (S1, 193)[1]

---

1. Cf. B. Pasternak, *Stikhotvoreniya i poemy v dvukh tomakh*, ed. V. S. Baevskii and E. B. Pasternak, Leningrad, 1990, vol. 1, pp. 133–4.

It is bees, it is clover,
It is dust and darkness and stifling heat.

Other poems of the same period spell out with greater or lesser clarity the public role of the poet. In a poem written in memory of the writer Mikhail Bulgakov, who died in 1940, Akhmatova writes of herself as the sole remaining voice prepared to speak out:

> I net tebya, i vse vokrug molchit
> O skorbnoi i vysokoi zhizni,
> Lish' golos moi, kak fleita, prozvuchit
> I na tvoei bezmolvnoi trizne.
>
> (S1, 244)

> You are no more, and everything around is silent
> About your sorrowful and noble life.
> Only my voice, like a flute, will sound out
> At your silent funeral feast.

The image of the flute, or reed, the conventional accessory of the lyrical muse, is found again in a poem addressed to Mikhail Lozinskii. Akhmatova, echoing Pushkin's celebration of creativity in his 1828 poem 'Muza' ('The Muse'), records the return of poetic inspiration that led to the particularly fruitful year of 1940:

> I nad zadumchivoyu Letoi
> Trostnik ozhivshii zazvuchal.
>
> (S1, 173)

> And above thoughtful Lethe
> The reed will come to life and sing.

The opening lines of this poem, however, make it clear that an important cause of Akhmatova's inspiration is not the calm process of poetic apprenticeship which is recorded in Pushkin's poem, but rather the turbulence of the times in which the poem is written: 'V tot chas, kak rushatsya miry' ('In an hour when worlds are falling apart').[2]

Of course, direct and open comment on Stalinist society was inconceivable for Akhmatova in the 1930s: she remembered only too clearly the repercussions for Mandelstam of his 1933 poem to Stalin. There

---

2. See D. N. Wells, *Akhmatova and Pushkin: The Pushkin Contexts of Akhmatova's Poetry*, Birmingham, 1994, pp. 46–7.

were, however, strategies which could be used to maximise the chances of a poetic message surviving until such time as the political situation had changed, in the hope that it would at least provide a record of its times for the reader of the future. One such method was to avoid committing sensitive lyrics to paper and to restrict their dissemination to oral circulation among a narrow circle of friends. Chukovskaya, for example, describes how poems would be written out for a moment, memorised by Akhmatova's visitor, and then burnt in the stove.[3] In this way, politically sensitive writing could avoid coming to the attention of the authorities, but would nevertheless be preserved until it could be written down and distributed more widely.

It seems likely that not all the poems compiled in this way have survived. Those that do remain, however, bear witness to a courageous attempt to keep alive the traditions of free speech in a political climate of ever-increasing despotism. Thus Akhmatova succinctly expresses the fears that prevailed at all levels of society during the Terror:

> A delo v tom,
> Chto suzhdeno nam vsem uznat',
> Chto znachit: tretii god ne spat',
> Chto znachit: utrom uznavat'
> O tekh, kto v noch' pogib.
> (III, 57)

> But the point is
> That we are all condemned to know
> What it means not to sleep for three years,
> What it means to find out in the morning
> About those who have perished in the night.

Some of the overtly political verses are epigrammatic in nature like this extract or like the self-contained admission of the danger involved in writing them contained in:

> Za takuyu skomoroshinu,
> Otkrovenno govorya,
> Mne svintsovuyu goroshinu
> Zhdat' by ot sekretarya.
> (III, 48)

---

3. Chukovskaya, *Zapiski*, vol. 1, p. 65; cf. Haight, *Anna Akhmatova*, p. 98.

For this buffoonery,
To be frank,
I should expect lead pellets
From the secretary.

The reference to Stalin here as First Secretary of the Communist Party is unmistakable. Other poems are more complex in design, drawing on a variety of external discourses in order to amplify their themes. Thus the 1933 poem 'Privol´em pakhnet dikii med' ('Wild honey smells of freedom', S1, 180) characterises the scent of various objects and concludes that blood smells only of itself. This statement is then made into a metaphor for the impossibility of hiding responsibility for the deaths of others: Akhmatova invokes the examples of Pontius Pilate attempting to absolve himself of the blood of Jesus by symbolically washing his hands, and of Lady Macbeth frenziedly trying to rub from her hands the blood of the murdered Duncan. In 'Nemnogo geografii' ('Some Geography'), a poem dedicated to Mandelstam and written during his visit to Leningrad in 1937, Akhmatova sees the city not as the European capital of Pushkin and other writers, but as a transit point to the network of camps and places of exile in the Asian parts of the Soviet Union, listing half a dozen place names in a parody of an exotic travelogue (III, 47–8).[4] 'Podrazhanie armyanskomu' ('Imitation of the Armenian') spuriously adopts the form of a literary imitation in order to present a picture of Stalin as a despotic monster who has devoured the author's child (III, 48–9).

Akhmatova also draws on episodes in medieval Russian history for metaphors to describe the situation in the 1930s. She compares herself, for example, to the noblewoman Feodosiya Morozova who was persecuted for her religious beliefs at the time of the Great Schism in the Russian church in the seventeenth century. Referring to the famous painting by Vasilii Surikov which depicts Morozova being dragged off into captivity, the poem's speaker asks what artist would be so foolhardy as to document her own last journey into the Stalinist prison system (III, 49). In another poem, 'Stansy' ('Stanzas', III, 52), Akhmatova evokes Moscow at the time of Peter the Great's bloody and merciless suppression of the Strel´tsy rebellion at the end of the seventeenth century. Peter's brutality is likened to the worst excesses of earlier princes of Muscovy, and because of the present tense which is used to describe the persistence of terror and arbitrary rule in Moscow, a par-

---

4. For the circumstances surrounding the writing of this poem see N. Ya. Mandel´shtam, *Vospominaniya*, 3rd edn, Paris, 1982, p. 337.

allel is implied with Russia at the time the poem was written (1940):

> V Kremle ne nado zhit', – Preobrazhenets prav, –
> Tam drevnei yarosti eshche kishat mikroby:
> Borisa dikii strakh i vsekh Ivanov zloby
> I Samozvantsa spes' – vzamen narodnykh prav.

> Don't live in the Kremlin – Peter the Great was right –
> The germs of ancient fury swarm there still:
> Boris' wild fear and the spite of all the Ivans,
> And the Pretender's conceit – but not the people's rights.

That Russian readers would have no trouble in identifying their own leader in the composite portrait of Russian rulers contained in the last two lines is suggested by Chukovskaya's comment on the poem made in the context of its possible publication in 1956: 'but in the last two lines there is a full and accurate portrait of Stalin'.[5]

Requiem

Akhmatova's most sustained piece of overtly oppositional writing in the 1930s is the cycle *Requiem* (I, 359–70).[6] Although the epigraph and prose introduction to the cycle were both added later, the cycle as such was put together in 1940.[7] The poems which make it up appear to have been inspired by several different episodes in Akhmatova's biography. Although the most immediate impetus is clearly Akhmatova's experience, following her son's arrest in 1938, in the queues of women waiting outside prisons attempting to receive news of their imprisoned menfolk, there are also additional sources. The first of the ten numbered poems, 'Uvodili tebya na rassvete' ('They took you away at dawn', I, 363) is dated 1935, and according to Akhmatova's memoir of Mandelstam, refers to the arrest that year of Nikolai Punin (II, 181). Mandelstam, it appears, took this poem to refer to his own arrest. But the exact biographical referents are perhaps not important. Akhmatova, by combining them in her cycle has produced what is, in its own way, a comprehensive social history of the Terror, what Haight has called 'an

5. Chukovskaya, *Zapiski*, vol. 2, p. 153. On this poem and a possible subtext in Pushkin see S. I. Ketchian, 'Akhmatova's Civic Poem "Stansy" and its Pushkinian Antecedent', *Slavic and East European Journal*, vol. 37, no. 2, 1993, pp. 194–210.
6. The work has also, with some reason, been called a narrative poem (*poema*). For a discussion of its genre see E. Etkind, 'Bessmertie pamyati. Poema Anna Akhmatovoi *Rekviem*', *Studia Slavica Finlandensia*, vol. 8, 1991, pp. 100–3.
7. One poem, 'Eto bylo, kogda ulybalsya', although written in 1940, was not included in the cycle until 1962, see Chukovskaya, *Zapiski*, vol. 1, p. 65.

organic unit documenting a precise progression through all the stages of suffering'.[8]

Although *Requiem* has no plot in any conventional sense, the ten numbered poems which form its centre do represent a process of emotional change. They do this through a lyrical examination of a series of emotional states presented in a chronological sequence which is rendered coherent by the two unnumbered introductory poems entitled 'Posvyashchenie' ('Dedication') and 'Vstuplenie' ('Introduction'). 'Dedication' in particular not only makes it clear that the poems which follow are written in the name of a large and anonymous group of women, but also specifies the time frame of the cycle:

> Gde teper' nevol'nye podrugi
> Dvukh moikh osatanelykh let?

> Where now are the chance friends
> Of those two demoniacal years?

'Introduction', on the other hand, focuses rather on place:

> I nenuzhnym priveskom boltalsya
> Vozle tyurem svoikh Leningrad.

> And Leningrad dangled around its prisons
> Like a useless appendage.

By later referring more broadly to the sufferings of 'Rus'', it affirms that the description of Leningrad is meant to stand also for the entire country.

The central section of the poem begins with an arrest, laconically described in the first line of poem No. 1: 'They took you away at dawn.' The scene is likened to a funeral, but a note of defiance is implied by the heroine's comparison of herself to the wives of the Strel'tsy in the last two lines:

> Budu ya, kak streletskie zhenki,
> Pod kremlevskimi bashnyami vyt'.

> Like the wives of the Strel'tsy
> I shall howl under the Kremlin towers.

8. Haight, *Anna Akhmatova*, p. 100.

In the poems which follow, however, this defiance gives way to passivity and to a gradual breakdown of personality. In the second poem the speaker sees herself partly as someone else:

Eta zhenshchina bol´na,
Eta zhenshchina odna,
Muzh v mogile, syn v tyur´me,
Pomolites´ obo mne.

This woman is ill,
This woman is alone,
Son in prison, husband in the grave,
Pray for me.

And in the third poem the gap between mental processes that predate the arrest and the current reality is rendered explicit. The speaker is unable to believe that it is indeed her own actions that she is watching:

Net, eto ne ya, eto kto-to drugoi stradaet.
Ya by tak ne mogla

No, it is not I, it is somebody else who is suffering
I should not have been able to bear it.

The fourth poem marks a particular stage in the history of individual prisoners – their mothers and wives queuing outside the Kresty prison in Leningrad in order to hand over parcels, and shows the speaker, more resignedly now, contrasting her present fate with her life in earlier years. The fifth, explicitly situated seventeen months after the arrest, shows increasing disorientation:

Vse pereputalos´ navek,
I mne ne razobrat´
Teper´, kto zver´, kto chelovek

Everything has been muddled for ever,
And now I cannot work out
Who is a beast and who is a human being.

This is also reflected in the sixth poem. The seventh, entitled 'Prigovor' ('Sentence'), initiates a further new stage. Notification that her son has been sentenced – presumably to death – throws the speaker back into despair:

> I upalo kamennoe slovo
> Na moyu eshche zhivuyu grud'.

> And the word fell like a stone
> On my still living breast.

She is led into another round of denial and suppression of her emotions:

> U menya segodnya mnogo dela:
> Nado pamyat' do kontsa ubit',
> Nado, chtob dusha okamenela,
> Nado snova nauchit'sya zhit'

> Today I have many things to do:
> I must kill my memory off completely,
> My heart must turn to stone,
> I must relearn how to live.

The next two poems deal with different and more extreme manifestations of despair: in the first (No. 8) the speaker invites death to come to her to release her from her torments; in the second (No. 9) it is insanity which is seen as the only possible form of consolation even though it will remove all memories of the past, the welcome as well as the terrible.

Up to this point the numbered poems of the narrative sequence had been written almost entirely in the first person. (The exceptions are No. 2, which is written partly in the third person, and No. 4, which is written as a second-person address by the speaker to herself.) The tenth and final poem of the inner narrative, which represents the carrying out of the sentence passed in the seventh poem, that is the execution of the heroine's son, switches to the third person, discursively reflecting her inability to speak after this latest shock. In order to describe this culmination of the narrative, Akhmatova has recourse to Biblical history and finds a model in the crucifixion of Jesus, and particularly in the responses of female figures – Mary Magdalene and Mary the Mother of Jesus – to the crucifixion:

> Magdalina bilas' i rydala,
> Uchenik lyubimyi kamenel,
> A tuda, gde molcha Mat' stoyala,
> Tak nikto vzglyanut' i ne posmel.

Mary Magdelene beat her breast and sobbed,
The beloved disciple turned to stone,
But no one even dared to look
At where the Mother stood in silence.

Haight has suggested that the three figures here represent three different stages of suffering: Mary Magdalene the defiance of poem No. 1, John the beloved disciple the paralysis of, for example, No. 7, and Mary the Mother a deep understanding arrived at by passing through all stages.[9] The silence of Mary the Mother at the moment of the crucifixion, however, may represent not so much wisdom as a state of catatonia induced in her, as in the first-person heroine of the narrative, by the finality of her son's death.

However, invoking the crucifixion is not merely a method for projecting the sufferings of women in Russia in the late 1930s on to a universal plane. In theological terms the crucifixion implies the resurrection, and the memorialising function of the *Requiem* cycle foreshadowed in 'Dedication' (and affirmed in the introductory prose passage added in 1957) is rendered explicit in the two poems which form its 'Epilogue'. Having passed through the Terror documented in the ten poems of the narrative, the speaker finds she has survived and is able to record the experience of her sisters:

I ya molyus´ ne o sebe odnoi,
A obo vsekh, kto tam stoyal so mnoyu,
I v lyutyi kholod, i v iyul´skii znoi,
Pod krasnoyu oslepsheyu stenoyu.

And I pray not for myself alone,
But for all those who stood there with me
In the bitter cold and in the heat of July
Under that blind red wall.

The final poem contains an affirmation of the power of words to recall the female, indirect victims of Stalinism and also an assertion that the act of recalling has its own therapeutic and protective effect:

Dlya nikh sotkala ya shirokii pokrov
Iz bednykh, u nikh zhe podslushannykh slov.

For them I have woven a broad shroud
From poor words, overheard from them.

9. Ibid., p. 105.

Having established the power of such a monument, Akhmatova then, secure in the knowledge of its durability, turns to the question of a sculptural monument to herself as the author of *Requiem*. In considering where such a monument should be placed, Akhmatova rejects locations that have associations with her life and poetry before *Requiem* – the Black Sea coast and the park at Tsarskoe Selo – and insists that it should be outside the prison walls in Leningrad, so that even in death she should not forget the events of the 1930s. This choice too marks a partial rejection of the poetry of Akhmatova's youth now that her pen has found its vocation as public chronicler of the Terror.

The superficial clarity and simplicity of the *Requiem* cycle belie a considerable underlying complexity of imagery, allusion and compositional technique. As Michael Basker has argued, the disorientation of the heroine is mirrored stylistically in the cycle in many ways.[10] Most obviously, there is no unequivocal link between the various poems that make up *Requiem*: they vary greatly in length, metrical format and rhyme scheme; they do not maintain unity of place – some are clearly set in Leningrad, while others are on the river Don (No. 2) or in Biblical Palestine (No. 10); they do not contain a consistent narrative viewpoint, changing abruptly, for example, between the first and third person ('Dedication', No. 2). Much of the imagery is similarly dislocated, even verging on the surreal, as in the opening lines of 'Dedication':

> Pered etim gorem gnutsya gory,
> Ne techet velikaya reka.

> Mountains bend down before this grief,
> The great river does not flow.

or the description of prisoners in 'Introduction':

> Shli uzhe osuzhdennykh polki,
> I korotkuyu pesnyu razluki
> Parovoznye peli gudki.

> Regiments of the already condemned were marching
> And the whistles of steam engines
> Sang brief songs of farewell.

---

10. M. Basker, 'Dislocation and Relocation in Akhmatova's *Rekviem*', in Rosslyn, *The Speech of Unknown Eyes*, vol. 1, pp. 5–25.

This is much more nearly the Leningrad of Nikolai Zabolotskii than of Akhmatova's early poems. Expressions from different semantic registers are placed in juxtaposition. Thus 'Rus'' ('Russia') is made to rhyme with 'chernykh marus'' ('black marias'); in No. 8 ('To Death') terms of Soviet *realia* – 'verkh shapki goluboi' ('the top of a pale blue cap', alluding to the NKVD uniform), and 'upravdom' ('house manager') – appear in the middle of an otherwise broadly abstract invocation of death. The religious metaphors which abound in the cycle serve to highlight the enormity of events by their incongruity: 'Kresty' ('Crosses') is the name of a prison (No. 4); the scene of arrest is compared to a funeral (No. 1). Even the title of the work, *Requiem*, with its associations above all with Catholic Christianity and the civilisation of western Europe, sits uneasily with the Orthodox tradition evoked in the poems themselves by references, for example, to icons (No. 1), to the 'pominal'nye dni' ('remembrance days') of the Orthodox funeral ritual ('Epilogue') and to the language of the Church Slavonic Bible: 'Ottsu skazal: "Pochto Menya ostavil!" / A Materi: "O, ne rydai Mene..."' ('To the Father he said, "Why hast thou forsaken me", but to his Mother, "Oh, do not weep for me...", No. 10). The numerous allusions to Old Russia further serve to set the work in an Orthodox historical context rather than in a more broadly European one.

At the same time, as with the early books discussed in chapter three, the architectonics of the cycle are calculated with deliberate rhetorical precision. Various schemes have been devised to show a symmetry of themes and images around a central poem operating as a pivot.[11] While these are apt to overstate their case, at the very least it can be said that the ten 'narrative' poems are situated within a symmetrical framework of two introductory and two concluding poems which emphasise the courage and persistence of Russian women outside the prisons of the 1930s and lay great weight on the power of poetry to record their sufferings and to transcend them. The 'narrative' sequence is organised around three points of transformation, beginning with an arrest (No. 1), ending with an execution (No. 10) and articulating itself around the seventh poem, in which the sentence is pronounced.

As might be expected from a knowledge of Akhmatova's early poems, the superficially limpid poetry of *Requiem* is rich in evocations of other literary works. Allusions have been detected to a very wide range of authors from Euripides, Dante and Shakespeare to Tyutchev,

11. Etkind, 'Bessmertie pamyati'; A. L. Crone, 'Antimetabole in *Rekviem*: The Structural Disposition of Themes and Motifs', in Rosslyn, *The Speech of Unknown Eyes*, vol. 1, pp. 27–41.

Nekrasov and Mayakovskii.[12] The most salient is highlighted by
Akhmatova herself when she places quotation marks around a phrase
from Pushkin which occurs in 'Dedication':

No krepki tyuremnye zatvory,
A za nimi 'katorzhnye nory'

But the prison bolts are firm,
And behind them lie the 'convicts' burrows'.

Pushkin's 1827 poem 'Vo glubine sibirskikh rud' ('In the depths of the
Siberian mines'), from which the quoted phrase is taken, is addressed
to the participants of the abortive Decembrist uprising.

Pushkin's poem was designed to encourage the convicted Decembrists and to reassure them that the ideals of freedom which they had
attempted unsuccessfully to uphold were still alive in the outside world
and would eventually prevail. The poem concludes:

Lyubov′ i druzhestvo do vas
Doidut skvoz′ mrachnye zatvory,
Kak v vashi katorzhnye nory
Dokhodit moi svobodnyi glas.
Okovy tyazhkie padut,
Temnitsy rukhnut − i svoboda
Vas primet radostno u vkhoda,
I brat′ya mech vam otdadut.[13]

Love and friendship will reach you
Past the sombre bolts,
As my free voice reaches you
In your convicts' burrows.
Your heavy fetters will fall,
Your dungeons will collapse,
And freedom will greet you at the entrance,
And your brothers will give you back your sword.

12. See M. Jovanović , 'K razboru "chuzhikh golosov" v *Rekvieme* Akhmatovoi',
Russian Literature, vol. 15, 1984, pp. 169–81; Etkind, 'Bessmertie pamyati'; M. M.
Kralin, 'Nekrasovskaya traditsiya u Anny Akhmatovoi', *Nekrasovskii sbornik*, no. 8,
1983, pp. 74–86.
13. Pushkin, *PSS*, vol. 3, p. 7.

The position in *Requiem*, however, is quite different. The prisons of the GULag are seen as impenetrable ('But the prison bolts are firm'); there is no hope of Akhmatova's voice reaching them, and it is to the survivors that the cycle is addressed. The contrast with Pushkin's poem, as Basker notes, throws 'into emphatic relief the utter bleakness of the modern period'.[14]

Similar effects are achieved by other references to external texts throughout *Requiem*. The pathos of the description of the woman crushed by the totalitarian state in poem No. 2 is increased by its overtly folkloric language, alluding to a pre-industrial world. The invocation of death in No. 8 achieves a particular intensification of emotion from its similarities to Pushkin's appeal to a dead lover in his poem 'Zaklinanie' ('Incantation') and from parallels in a poem by Chénier, 'Vienne, vienne la mort! – Que la mort me délivre' ('Let death come! – Let death deliver me'), with its appeals to the notions of justice and truth.[15] As Amert has noted, there are also ironic allusions to works of officially promoted Soviet literature which project a contented world grotesquely at variance with the one described by Akhmatova. In 'Dedication', for example, the lines 'Dlya kogo-to veet veter svezhii, / Dlya kogo-to nezhitsya zakat' ('For someone a fresh wind is blowing, For someone the sunset is luxurious') are a contemptuous echo of Vasilii Lebedev-Kumach's widely disseminated hymn to Stalinism, 'Pesnya o rodine' ('Song of the Motherland'), written in 1935, and in particular the lines:

Nad stranoi vesennii veter veet,
S kazhdym dnem vse radostnee zhit'.[16]

A spring wind is blowing across the country,
With every day life is more joyous.

Another function of literary allusion in *Requiem* is to indicate and memorialise poets known personally to Akhmatova who became victims of Soviet repression. There are, for example, several more or less direct allusions to the work of Mandelstam and Gumilev, who were by this stage completely unable to reach an audience directly.[17]

14. Basker, in Rosslyn, *The Speech of Unknown Eyes*, p. 14.
15. Ibid., pp. 17–18; Pushkin, *PSS*, vol. 3, p. 193; Etkind, 'Bessmertie pamyati', pp. 114–15.
16. See S. Amert, *In a Shattered Mirror: The Later Poetry of Anna Akhmatova*, Stanford, Calif. 1992, pp. 42–3.
17. See Basker, in Rosslyn, *The Speech of Unknown Eyes*.

Secret Writing

None of the poetry discussed so far in this chapter could be published in the Soviet Union, at least in its proper form, at the time of its writing. Indeed, most of it proved unpublishable until the advent of *glasnost'* in the late 1980s. In order to ensure that at least something of what she had to say got through to more than a circle of close friends, and appeared in print rather than rely on the hazardous processes of oral transmission for its survival, Akhmatova had recourse to several techniques designed to conceal meanings from the censorship. This is the case with perhaps the majority of the poems that she was to publish in 1940.

In the mid-1930s, of course, Akhmatova could not expect the early publication of any of her poetry, but she could nevertheless choose to write in a manner calculated to guarantee publication during the next period of relative thaw, even though this was not expected to grant full freedom of expression. Through Aesopian language texts could appear in print containing matter potentially disapproved of by the state, and these would ideally be decoded by the alert future reader.

Censors could be thrown off the scent, for example, by the deliberate inclusion of incorrect dates at the ends of poems. Already in *Anno Domini* Akhmatova had published a poem on the death of Gumilev in 1921 with the misleading date 1914 in order not to attract the attention of the authorities.[18] When she was able to publish again in 1940, the *Requiem* poem 'Sentence' appeared without its title and dated 1934. In this way it was dissociated from the worst phases of the Terror and could be interpreted not as a response to the passing of an arbitrary judicial sentence, but as a love poem in the tradition of Akhmatova's earlier work.

A more complex form of subterfuge was developed by exploiting the allusive extratextuality which was already a feature of Akhmatova's work in the 1910s, and which is clearly present under the surface in *Requiem*. The poetry of hints and allusions, where what was not stated directly was as important as the overt message of the text, became increasingly a political commentary on Stalinism, where Aesopian language was used to present a discourse superficially acceptable to the censorship. In this respect it is reference to the literary tradition that is Akhmatova's most important vehicle for the discussion of Russia's social predicament.

A key text is the 1936 poem 'Dante' (S1, 182), which Akhmatova later described as embracing 'all [her] thoughts on art' (S2, 184). On the surface this poem is an account of Dante's refusal to return from exile

---

18. Amert, *In a Shattered Mirror*, p. 9.

to his native Florence on the humiliating terms offered him by the government of the city in 1315:

> No bosoi, v rubakhe pokayannoi,
> So svechoi zazhzhennoi ne proshel
> Po svoei Florentsii zhelannoi,
> Verolomnoi, nizkoi, dolgozhdannoi. . .
> (S1, 182)

> But he did not walk barefoot,
> In a penitent's shirt, with a lighted candle,
> Through his beloved Florence,
> Treacherous, base and longed for. . .

However, as Pamela Davidson has noted, the poem is much more than this. In view of the keen interest of Akhmatova and her circle – especially Mandelstam and Lozinskii – in Dante's work and the particular significance of the city both for Dante and for the development of Italian literature, Florence provides 'an intensified image of the poet's city' and is clearly identified with St Petersburg.[19] The persecution of Dante by the Florentine authorities thus becomes an allegory for the attacks on Akhmatova and others, and more broadly on Russian culture as a whole, made by the Soviet state. The epigraph 'Il mio bel San Giovanni' ('my beautiful San Giovanni'), taken from *Inferno*, XIX, 18, refers, of course, to the principal cathedral of Florence, which stands as a symbol, as Davidson has suggested, for Dante's aesthetic sensibilities, for his 'exile and longing for his native city', and for his faith in his eventual return, not as a penitent in the way described in the poem, but in triumph.[20]

A further layer of meaning can be extracted by an examination of the passage in the *Inferno* from which the epigraph is taken. It appears in the description of the punishment of the Simonists, that is those guilty of buying or selling ecclesiastical preferment. Dante describes their crime in the following terms:

> O Simon mago, o miseri segnaci,
> che le cose di Dio, che di bontate
> devono essere spose, e voi rapaci
> per oro e per argento adulterate.

---

19. P. Davidson, 'Akhmatova's Dante', in Rosslyn, *The Speech of Unknown Eyes*, vol. 2, p. 206.
20. Ibid., pp. 216–17.

O Simon Magus! O wretched followers of his and robbers ye,
who prostitute the things of God, that should be wedded unto
righteousness, for gold and silver![21]

The significance of this passage for Akhmatova's poem is made clear
by an examination of its opening lines:

On i posle smerti ne vernulsya
V staruyu Florentsiyu svoyu.
Etot, ukhodya, ne oglyanulsya,
Etomu ya etu pesn' poyu.

Even after death he did not return
To his ancient Florence.
When he left, he did not look back,
It is to him that I sing this song.

The emphasis which Akhmatova places on negative actions here high-
lights the artistic integrity of Dante, and by implication of persecuted
writers of Akhmatova's own generation. In the fourth line she suggests
that it is this group alone who are deserving of being celebrated in her
own verse. There is, however, a definite implication that there exists
another group of writers which she will *not* celebrate, a group who
did 'look back' and did return to 'Florence', or, in other words, did
compromise their principles, and betray their duty as writers, just as the
Simonists betrayed their duty to God, for their own material advantage.
By evoking Dante's condemnation of the Simonists through her choice
of epigraph, Akhmatova is able to encode into a superficially innocuous
poem about fourteenth-century Italy her own attack on the self-serving
champions of Stalinist literature.

The device of invoking one thing by describing characteristics which
do *not* belong to another is one which Akhmatova learned primarily
from Pushkin. This so-called 'shadow portrait' is a frequent focus of
attention in her own essays on Pushkin and is a technique which Akhmatova uses not infrequently in her poetry.[22]

The theme of exile is taken up in several other poems of the mid-
1930s, notably 'Voronezh', which was written on the occasion of
Akhmatova's visit to Mandelstam there in 1936. This poem begins with

21. Dante, *Inferno*, London, 1970, pp. 202–3. Dent edition; translator not indicated.
22. See Wells, *Akhmatova and Pushkin*, pp. 28–9.

an idyllic and startlingly accurate picture of the town on a winter's day:

> I gorod ves' stoit oledenelyi.
> Kak pod steklom derev'ya, steny, sneg.
> (S1, 179)

> And the white town stands frozen.
> Trees and walls and snow seem under glass.

The description even strikes a note of triumph, evoking Peter the Great, who constructed a flotilla of ships there in the 1690s, the victory of the Russians over the Mongols in 1380 at the Battle of Kulikovo, not far from Voronezh, and concluding:

> I topolya, kak sdvinutye chashi,
> Nad nami srazu zazvenyat sil'nei,
> Kak budto p'yut za likovan'e nashe
> Na brachnom pire tysyachi gostei.

> And the poplars, like goblets brought together,
> Suddenly ring out more strongly above us,
> As if thousands of guests were drinking
> To our joy at a wedding feast.

This confident vision of Voronezh is thrown into stark relief by the concluding four lines of the poem, in which the metre is disrupted as well as the meaning:

> A v komnate opal'nogo poeta
> Dezhuryat strakh i Muza v svoi chered.
> I noch' idet,
> Kotoraya ne vedaet rassveta.

> But in the room of the disgraced poet
> Fear and the Muse keep watch in turns.
> And the night goes on,
> Which knows no dawn.

The superficial beauty and dignity of Voronezh is shown to conceal a state of moral corruption which is unable to tolerate the existence of a true poet.[23]

23. In its original published form this poem appeared without the last four lines. Emma Gershtein has suggested that they were not in fact written until the 1950s: *Novoe o Mandel'shtame*, Paris, 1986, pp. 93–5. N. Ya. Mandel'shtam, however, certainly implies that she was acquainted with them in 1936: *Vospominaniya*, pp. 234–5.

Analogous to the poem on Dante is the retelling of the story of Cleopatra which Akhmatova wrote a few months earlier. Her view of the
Egyptian queen is derived principally from Shakespeare's *Antony and
Cleopatra*, and her account of Cleopatra's downfall and suicide follows
the order of events in the play quite closely: Cleopatra kisses the dying
Antony; she kneels before Caesar; she is betrayed by her treasurer;
Dolabella tells Cleopatra that she and her children will be sent to Rome
in chains; Cleopatra reflects on the meaning of this for her; she jokes
with the Clown; and finally places the asp on her breast. What interests
Akhmatova above all is the dignity and courage with which Cleopatra
meets her fate, retaining her integrity in the face of political persecution
from Rome:

> A zavtra detei zakuyut. O, kak malo ostalos´
> Ei dela na svete – eshche s muzhikom poshutit´
> I chernuyu zmeiku, kak budto proshchal´nuyu zhalost´,
> Na smugluyu grud´ ravnodushnoi rukoi polozhit´.

> And tomorrow they'll put the children in chains.
> Oh, how little she still had to do on earth –
> Joke with the boy, and place the black snake,
> Like a final gesture of pity, on her dark breast
> With an indifferent hand.

In the form in which it was published in *From Six Books* 'Cleopatra'
was provided with two epigraphs, one from *Antony and Cleopatra* and
one from Pushkin. Each of these serves to highlight Cleopatra's dignity and tragic grandeur. Shakespeare's play, of course, begins with
a characterisation of Antony's love for Cleopatra as depraved, and of
Cleopatra herself as promiscuous and manipulative. However, when in
the fifth act she dresses in full regalia in preparation for her suicide,
much emphasis is placed on her fidelity to the dead Antony and to her
own sense of majesty. She proclaims:

> Husband, I come.
> Now to that name my courage prove my title!
> I am fire and air; my other elements
> I give to baser life.[24]

---

24. *Antony and Cleopatra*, V.ii.286–9.

Akhmatova's epigraph 'I am air and fire', presumably an accidental misquotation from this passage, evokes this triumphant moment before Cleopatra's death.

The other epigraph, 'Aleksandriiskie chertogi / Pokryla sladostnaya ten'' ('The halls of Alexandria were covered with delicious shade'), is taken from a poem customarily printed as the improvisation on the theme 'Cleopatra and her lovers' invented by the itinerant Italian poet in Pushkin's story *Egipetskie nochi* (*Egyptian Nights*). On one level it can be taken as a statement of finality and calm, reflecting Cleopatra's resignation in the face of her inevitable destruction. The idea of death is conveyed by the word 'shade', and qualified by 'delicious', 'sweet', suggesting relief. Associations of grandeur are expressed through the archaic word 'chertogi' used for 'halls'. At the same time, Pushkin's poem emphasises the opulence of Cleopatra's court and her self-assurance at the full height of her power, and thus stands in striking contrast to Akhmatova's account of her downfall. The epigraph thus leads to a deepening of the idea of majestic death.

A further layer of significance can be seen from an examination of the wider context of *Egyptian Nights*. An important theme in Pushkin's story is the nature of poetic inspiration. The aristocratic Charskii with his ideas of the independence and strong moral position of the author is contrasted with the Italian improviser, who gladly deals with any theme in order to make his living. The debate which takes place between them, of course, is never resolved, but the issue of artistic freedom is raised, and Cleopatra's behaviour is implicitly made to represent the ideal moral position of the poet. She becomes a double of Akhmatova herself and the persecution that she suffers at the hand of Augustus comes to stand for the condemnation of Akhmatova and her work under the Stalinist regime.[25]

The Theme of Dispossession

Closely related to the theme of exile in the poetry of the pre-war period is a strong theme of dispossession. From the late 1920s there are poems which convey the idea that the promise of Akhmatova's youth has somehow not been fulfilled. In 'Tot gorod, mnoi lyubimyi s detstva' ('That town, which I have loved since childhood', S1, 175), the city of St Petersburg is seen as a 'squandered inheritance'. Even though this poem ends on a positive note with the speaker's recognition of the

---

25. For a more detailed discussion of this poem see Wells, *Akhmatova and Pushkin*, pp. 74–9.

Russian language as a constant which has survived the passing of time,
her previous life has disappeared without trace:

> Vse uneslos' prozrachnym dymom,
> Istlelo v glubine zerkal. . .
> I vot uzh o nevozvratimom
> Skripach beznosyi zaigral.

> Everything swept off like transparent smoke,
> Smouldered to ashes in the depths of the mirrors. . .
> And then the noseless fiddler
> Began to play about the irretrievable.

In the mid-1930s Akhmatova returns to the imagery of her early poetry
to express a similar discontinuity:

> Ne prislal li lebedya za mnoyu,
> Ili lodku, ili chernyi plot? –
> On v shestnadtsatom godu vesnoyu
> Obeshchal, chto skoro sam pridet.
> (S1, 176)

> Hasn't he sent a swan for me,
> Or a boat, or a black raft?
> In the spring of 1916 he promised
> To come soon in person.

This resurrection of the theme of *By the Sea Shore* at a distance of
twenty years strikes a particularly incongruous note in the context of
Akhmatova's other poetry of the period, and serves to emphasise
the great gulf that exists between 1916 and 1936. But although the
speaker's memory of the Prince's promise is still bright, the ironic tone
of the final lines of the poem suggests that her faith in his keeping it is
no longer active:

> Chto mne delat'! Angel polunochi
> Do zari beseduyut so mnoi.

> What can I do? The midnight angel
> Talks to me till dawn.

These lines suggest too that the speaker is being forced to a re-
evaluation of the past, an idea which is taken up more explicitly in

another poem of 1936, 'Odni glyadyatsya v laskovye vzory' ('Some exchange fond glances', S1, 177), where the memory of pre-revolutionary Tsarskoe Selo, and of its cultural arbiter Nikolai Nedobrovo, to whom the poem is dedicated, becomes subject to the closest scrutiny:

> A ya vsyu noch' vedu peregovory
> S neukrotimoi sovest'yu svoei.

> But all night I negotiate
> With my indomitable conscience.

The notion that Akhmatova's contemporaries in literary St Petersburg and Tsarskoe Selo were somehow responsible for the destruction of Russian culture which took place under Soviet rule was to be enunciated with particular force in *Poem without a Hero*.

A similarly ambivalent attitude towards the memory of the past is found in the poems of 1940. In 'Moi molodye ruki' ('My young hands', S1, 184), it is clear that the speaker's youth forms an ineradicable part of her current view of the world:

> Ty neotstupen, kak sovest',
> Kak vozdukh, vsegda so mnoyu.

> You are as persistent as conscience,
> Always with me like the air.

Yet elsewhere she acknowledges a great distance between the present and a past which is gone forever and cannot be recreated. Thus in 'Podval pamyati' ('The Cellar of Memory', S1, 185), she uses a description of the basement which had previously housed the 'Stray Dog' cabaret as a metaphor for an account of a mental journey into the depths of memory. The speaker recognises that she cannot return there, for the past is now no longer what it was:

> Ya opozdala. Ekaya beda!
> Nel'zya mne pokazat'sya nikuda.

> I am too late. What a calamity!
> I cannot show myself anywhere.

At the same time, however, the present is characterised as profoundly insecure:

> Nu, idem domoi!
> No gde moi dom i gde rassudok moi?

> Well, let's go home!
> But where is my home, and where's my reason?

In 'The Cellar of Memory' the significance of the past is linked closely with the cultural environment of pre-revolutionary St Petersburg. In 'Iva' ('Willow', S1, 183), Akhmatova uses familiar allusive techniques to hint at a much broader sense of cultural loss. On the surface the heroine of 'Willow' begins by recalling her childhood in Tsarskoe Selo and goes on to lament that this is no longer accessible to her. The main focus of reminiscence, the heroine's favourite memory, is the willow tree itself, a traditional folkloric and literary symbol of grief. This memory, however, is seen as inaccessible, since the particular willow that the heroine remembers has been replaced by others which do not have the same emotive connotations. A return to the past is impossible and the recognition of this impossibility causes the heroine anguish, 'as if a brother had died':

> Tam pen´ torchit, chuzhimi golosami
> Drugie ivy chto-to govoryat
> Pod nashimi, pod temi nebesami.
> I ya molchu. . . kak budto umer brat.

> Its stump sticks up, and other willows
> Talk in other voices
> Under our, under those skies.
> And I am silent. . . as if a brother had died.

The epigraph to 'Willow', 'I dryakhlyi puk derev' ('And a decrepit bunch of trees'), is taken from Pushkin's poem 'Tsarskoe Selo', in which he addresses a deified 'Memory' and asks for those things which he associates with 'poetry, gaiety and peace' to be recalled to his mind.[26] 'Memory' is defined in the first line as 'preserver of pleasant feelings and past delights' and is clearly seen to be a powerful inspirational force in poetry. It is specifically the garden at Tsarskoe Selo, linked with the birth of Pushkin's talent and sensibility as a poet, which he asks to be restored to him, and his poem contains a eulogy of its charms, including the phrase Akhmatova has chosen for her epigraph.

26. Pushkin, *PSS*, vol. 1, pp. 371–2.

For Pushkin, a return is still possible through the agency of the god
Memory; for Akhmatova, as we have seen, it is not. As a result there is
a strong implication that the 'poetry, gaiety and peace' equated with the
garden in Pushkin's reminiscence are also lost for Akhmatova's heroine.
The poem comes to convey a sense of isolation from the poetic past as
well as the material and emotional past, and the willow tree or its stump
becomes a symbol for the poet attempting to continue writing in the
Pushkinian tradition, surrounded by hostile or foreign voices (the new
growth of trees) and reduced to silence.[27]

Another examination of the literary past is found in 'Predystoriya'
('Prehistory', S1, 253–4), begun in Leningrad in 1940, and later to become the first of a series of *Northern Elegies*. In it Akhmatova looks
back behind the changes that have been made to the architecture of the
city to the period immediately before her birth, to the environment of
the 1870s, which are seen, like the image of Tsarskoe Selo presented
elsewhere in her poetry, as a 'bridge to the experience of Akhmatova's
generation'.[28] The 'historical landscape' which is presented in 'Prehistory' has been acknowledged to be both accurate and highly
evocative.[29] It is rich in contemporary detail:

> Shurshanie yubok, kletchatye pledy,
> Orekhovye ramy u zerkal,
> Kareninskoi krasoyu izumlennykh,
> I v koridorakh uzkikh te oboi,
> Kotorymi my lyubovalis´ v detstve.

> The rustle of skirts, the checked plaids,
> The walnut frames around the mirrors,
> Which were amazed at Karenina's beauty.
> And in the narrow passages, the wallpaper
> We so admired as children.

There are numerous references to writers and literary works of
the period – to Tolstoi's *Anna Karenina* as in the above passage, to
Turgenev's novel *Fathers and Children* ('Ottsy i dedy neponyatny'
('Fathers and grandfathers are beyond comprehension')), to Nekrasov
and Saltykov-Shchedrin, whose homes on Liteinyi Prospect are
mentioned. Most particularly, Akhmatova's poem includes a condensed
account of the life and work of Dostoevskii. The opening lines of the

27. See Wells, *Akhmatova and Pushkin*, pp. 37–40.
28. S. Leiter, *Akhmatova's Petersburg*, Cambridge, 1983, p. 124.
29. K. Chukovskii, 'Chitaya Akhmatovu', *Moskva*, no. 5, 1964, p. 201.

elegy not only mention him by name, but offer a view of St Petersburg as if from Dostoevskii's writing desk:[30]

Rossiya Dostoevskogo. Luna
Pochti na chetvert' skryta kolokol'nei.
Torguyut kabaki, letyat proletki,
Pyatietazhnye rastut gromady
V Gorokhovoi, u Znamen'ya, pod Smol'nym.

Dostoevskii's Russia. The moon
Is almost a quarter hidden by the bell tower.
The pubs are open, cabs fly by,
Five-storey heaps are going up
On Gorokhovaya Street, at Znamen'e, near Smol'nyi.

Later the poem refers to many other places associated with Dostoevskii – Staraya Russa, Optina Pustyn', Baden – and to themes in his novels.[31] Dostoevskii is shown as the presiding genius of his age; having suffered both mock execution on Semenovskii Square and Siberian exile, he is able to penetrate to the essence of Russian society and to record it:

Stranu znobit, a omskii katorzhanin
Vse ponyal i na vsem postavil krest.
Vot on seichas peremeshaet vse
I sam nad pervozdannym besporyadkom,
Kak nekii dukh, vznesetsya. Polnoch' b'et.
Pero skripit, i mnogie stranitsy
Semenovskim pripakhivayut platsom.

The country shivers, but the Omsk convict
Has understood everything and given it up for lost.
And now he shuffles everything around,
And like some kind of spirit
Rises up over the primordial chaos.
Midnight strikes. His pen squeaks,
And many pages reek of Semenovskii Square.

At the same time there are many points that make it clear that the tradition represented by Dostoevskii is related to present actuality.

30. Verheul, *The Theme of Time*, pp. 172–3.
31. For a detailed discussion of this point see Amert, *In a Shattered Mirror*, pp. 73–88.

There are, for example, linking phrases which provide a distancing from the past and a return to the present. Thus Akhmatova writes: 'No vprochem, gorod malo izmenilsya' ('But still, the city has changed little'), 'Liteinyi, / Eshche ne opozorennyi modernom', ('Liteinyi Prospect, not yet disgraced by *style moderne*'), 'Tak vot kogda my vzdumali rodit'sya' 'So this is when we took it into our heads to be born'). It is through the memorial plaques erected after their deaths that the presence of the writers Nekrasov and Saltykov-Shchedrin is introduced into the poem. Moreover the stanza beginning 'I zhenshchina s prozrachnymi glazami' ('And a woman with transparent eyes'), which in context could be expected to comprise a description of a character from one of Dostoevskii's novels, is apparently based on Akhmatova's early memories of her mother, and thus creates an additional link between the worlds of Dostoevskii and Akhmatova herself. In 'Prehistory' Akhmatova uses Dostoevskii and the tradition he represents both as an artist and as a social commentator in the same way as she uses Pushkin elsewhere in her poetry, and it is quite appropriate that this poem should have been referred to as a 'myth of origins'.[32]

The epigraph to 'Prehistory', 'Ya teper' zhivu ne tam' ('I now live somewhere else'), suggests that for all the vividness of Akhmatova's portrayal of the past it is recognised as no longer accessible. The passage in Pushkin's *Domik v Kolomne* (*The House in Kolomna*) from which it is taken reads:

> Ya zhivu
> Teper' ne tam, no vernoyu mechtoyu
> Lyublyu letat', zasnuvshi nayavu [. . .][33]

> I know live somewhere else,
> But in faithful dreams
> I love to fly in my imagination [. . .]

This stresses that it is only in memory that the world of Dostoevskii can be reached. Moreover, although this is not stated explicitly, 'Prehistory' contains a series of ominous suggestions that, in spite of the transcending art of Dostoevskii, society of the 1870s contained the seeds of its own destruction: the coffins of the sixth line, for example; the irony of 'So this is when we took it into our heads to be born'; or the list of

32. Ibid., pp. 60–2.
33. Pushkin, *PSS*, vol. 4, p. 331.

social evils contained in the passage:

Vse raznochinno, naspekh, kak-nibud'. . .
Ottsy i dedy neponyatny. Zemli
Zalozheny. I v Badene – ruletka.

Everything is changing, hurried, anyhow. . .
Fathers and grandfathers are beyond comprehension.
Lands are mortgaged. And in Baden there is roulette.

As the effects of war in Europe began to be felt during the course of 1940 a further dimension was added to Akhmatova's fear of cultural dispossession: it was no longer merely *Russian* cultural values that were under threat. This is illustrated by two poems responding to events in Britain and France, which were later included in the cycle 'V sorokovom godu' ('In 1940'). The first of these characterises the fall of Paris as the ending of an era:

Kogda pogrebayut epokhu,
Nadgrobnyi psalom ne zvuchit
(S1, 195)

When an epoch is buried
No psalm is sung over the grave.

The only possible response to such enormity is silence. The second views Hitler's attempted invasion of Britain in terms of an unknown Shakespearean drama whose tragic consequences are potentially far worse than those of *Hamlet* or *King Lear* or *Macbeth*, so much so that the unfolding catastrophe is unbearable for the outside, Russian observer:

Tol'ko ne etu, ne etu, ne etu,
Etu uzhe my ne v silakh chitat'!
(S1, 196)

Only not this, not this, not this,
This we do not have the strength to read!

A more sustained discussion of the notion of cultural continuity is contained in the long poem *Putem vseya zemli* (*The Way of All the Earth*), also written in 1940. In a note on this poem Akhmatova linked it with the storm of Vyborg (Viipuri) during the Russo-Finnish War of 1939–40 and the subsequent peace treaty signed on 12 March 1940, in which Finland ceded a southern tract of land to the Soviet Union (SP,

511). It consists of a series of interconnected visions which link the current international crisis with ominous symbolic moments in the past. These, with the benefit of hindsight, appear to foreshadow the destruction threatening in the present. Temporal distinctions are blurred and events of different periods merge into 'a timeless co-presence of the past and the future'.[34] The military imagery of the first section certainly suggests the circumstances of 1940:

> 'Vot propusk, tovarishch,
> Pustite nazad. . .'
> I voin spokoino
> Otvodit shtyk.
>   (S1, 269)

> 'Here is my pass, comrade,
> Let me go back. . .'
> And the warrior calmly
> Turns his bayonet away.

Yet its applicability is not rendered explicit, and in subsequent sections reference is made to conflicts that are clearly in the past. Thus the First World War and its effects on European civilisation are evoked in the lines:

> Okopy, okopy, –
> Zabludish´sya tut!
> Ot staroi Evropy
> Ostalsya loskut.

> Trenches, trenches,
> You will lose your way!
> Only shreds of old Europe
> Still remain.

In the fifth section even earlier conflicts are recalled with the implication that the twentieth century was been shaped by their legacy: the Russo-Japanese War, which saw the ignominious defeat of the Russian army and navy and acted as one catalyst for the revolution of 1905; and behind this the Anglo-Boer War of 1899–1902, and perhaps the Dreyfus Affair of the 1890s. These events all took place within Akhmatova's

---

34. Verheul, *The Theme of Time*, p. 140.

lifetime, which is thus situated within a context of ever-increasing conflict.[35]

The central part of the poem also suggests discontinuities within Akhmatova's own artistic biography. In the second fragment she sees a vision of the Crimea, generally associated with the beginnings of creativity in her work. But now the Muse does not recognise her. Access to the world which she represents is cut off:

> Syuda ty vernesh´sya,
> Vernesh´sya ne raz,
> No snova spotknesh´sya
> O krepkii almaz.
> (S1, 270)

> You will return here,
> Return more than once,
> But again you will stumble
> On the hard diamond.

The third fragment presents a nightmarish vision of the heroine searching for something unspecified in an empty house, but finding instead a man with his throat cut. That this has been a recurrent dream and that it is in some way connected with the time of the First World War is suggested by the lines:

> Ved´ eto ne shutki,
> Chto dvadtsat´ pyat´ let
> Mne viditsya zhutkii
> Odin siluet.
> (S1, 271)

> For it is not a joke
> That for twenty-five years
> I have seen the same
> Eerie silhouette.

From the perspective of 1940 the time period mentioned here appears to point to 1915. It has been suggested that there is a specific connection between these lines and the complex of guilt which Akhmatova felt in connection with the death of Nedobrovo the following year.[36] It

---

35. Zhirmunskii, *Tvorchestvo Anny Akhmatovoi*, p. 137.
36. Verheul, *The Theme of Time*, pp. 147–8.

seems quite possible, however, that the fragment refers to some other figure entirely, or is a composite rendering of guilt towards the last pre-revolutionary generation.

As Verheul has noted, the visions which make up *The Way of All the Earth* are made coherent by two literary motifs whose imagery recurs throughout: the story of the lost city of Kitezh; and the testament of the Kievan prince Vladimir Monomakh, from which the epigraph purports to be taken. Kitezh, according to Russian legend, was miraculously saved from destruction by the Tatars in the thirteenth century and hidden at the bottom of a lake. Akhmatova follows rather the adaptation of the legend found in Rimskii-Korsakov's opera 'The Tale of the Invisible City of Kitezh and the Maiden Fevroniya', which focuses on the attempt of the last surviving inhabitant of the city, who was taken captive by the Tatars, to return to Kitezh. She succeeds in doing this, triumphantly, only in death. In *The Way of All the Earth*, the heroine's frustrated journey into the past parallels Fevroniya's wanderings, and the two are identified in the first fragment:

Menya, kitezhanku,
Pozvali domoi.
(S1, 269)

I, the woman of Kitezh,
Have been summoned home.

The final fragment of the poem returns explicitly to the legend, suggesting that escape from the nightmare visions of the past, and re-entry into the city of Kitezh, are only possible in death:

Teper´ s kitezhankoi
Nikto ne poidet
[. . .]
V poslednem zhilishche
Menya upokoi.
(S1, 272)

Now no-one will go
With the woman of Kitezh
[. . .]
Lay me to rest in my last
Dwelling place.

The woman of Kitezh announces her final journey using the traditional symbolic imagery of winter:

Velikuyu zimu
Ya dolgo zhdala,
Kak beluyu skhimu
Ee prinyala.
I v legkie sani
Spokoino sazhus´. . .
(S1, 272)

I have long awaited
Great winter,
And accepted it
Like a strict vow.
And I will sit calmly
In the light sledge. . .

The metaphor of sitting in a sledge is used in old Russian literature to indicate the approach of death.[37] In particular it is found in the introduction to the *Instruction of Vladimir Monomakh*, from which Akhmatova's epigraph is adapted. The epigraph reads 'V sanyakh sidya, otpravlyayas´ putem vseya zemli. . .' ('Sitting in a sledge, I set out on the way of all the earth. . .'), a conflation of Monomakh's 'Sedya na sanekh, pomyslikh v dushi svoei i pokhvalikh Boga' ('Sitting in a sledge, I thought in my heart and praised God') and the exhortation of the biblical King David: 'Vot, ya otkhozhu v put´ vsei zemli, ty zhe bud´ tverd i bud´ muzhestven' ('I go the way of all the earth: be thou strong therefore and shew thyself a man').[38] Both monarchs had a broadly similar purpose: to set out the proper paths of conduct for their successors. By implication, then, Akhmatova's poem contains a testament for future generations. A message is contained in the accumulation of portentous images from the past which threaten to be repeated in the accelerating conflict of the Second World War: if the lessons of the past are not learned they will be repeated in the present. At the same time there is a suggestion in the concluding fragment that the paradise of the heavenly Kitezh, finally attained by the heroine, also constitutes a home for artistic creation, which thus transcends the endemic dislocation of the

37. It perhaps derives from the custom of transporting a body for burial on sleigh. See J. Fennell and D. Obolenskii (eds), *A Historical Russian Reader: A Selection of Texts from the Eleventh to the Sixteenth Centuries*, Oxford, 1969, p. 166.
38. Ibid., p. 52; 1 Kings 2.2.

contingent world. On her final journey the heroine is thus accompanied by poetry and by its source:

Teper´ s kitezhankoi
Nikto ne poidet,
Ni brat, ni sosedka,
Ni pervyi zhenikh, –
Lish´ khvoinaya vetka
Da solnechnyi stikh,
Obronennyi nishchim
I podnyatyi mnoi. . .
(S1, 272)

Now no one will go
With the woman of Kitezh,
Neither brother, nor neighbour,
Nor first love, –
Only a pine branch
And a sunny verse,
Dropped by a beggar
And picked up by me. . .

In spite of its preoccupation with the themes of political repression, exile and cultural dispossession, Akhmatova's poetry of the 1930s and early 1940s nevertheless often succeeds, as here, in conveying a deep-rooted sense of hope. The poetry is itself very much an act of faith. Akhmatova's openly political verse depended for its precarious transmission on a small group of friends. The poetry she wrote for publication – whether she expected this to be immediate or at some unspecified point in the future – depends for the understanding of its political agenda on a highly sophisticated interpretative technique and on readers who understand that this needs to be applied. Not surprisingly, artistic creation is highly prominent as a theme in its own right and Akhmatova's writing is to be seen in terms of the creation of a poetic monument to her fellow citizens in Stalin's Russia and to the cultural values of humanism. In the relative thaw of 1940 Akhmatova's themes of the 1930s were to be combined in a literary monument on a much larger scale than anything she had attempted before, a work which would occupy her for the following two decades, the complex and often enigmatic *Poem Without a Hero*.

Poem Without a Hero

The themes which occupied Akhmatova through the 1930s receive their fullest treatment in *Poem Without a Hero*, begun in Leningrad in 1940, completed in its initial form in Tashkent in 1943 and finally declared finished in 1962. In this work Akhmatova aims at nothing less than an evaluation of half a century of Russian cultural and social history and an assessment of the role of the individual *vis-à-vis* the forces of destiny. The *Poem* is both a celebration of the cultural values of Akhmatova's youth and a condemnation of those political forces – Stalinism and war – which have sought to undermine them. At the same time it raises the question of who bears the responsibility for Russia's predicament, seeing this in the heedlessness of Akhmatova's own generation. The *Poem* too aims to remain within the pale of the Soviet censorship in order to achieve the widest possible dissemination of its message, but to reveal enough of its Aesopian compositional method to allow the sympathetic reader to interpret it correctly.

This is an extremely ambitious project, and one in which Akhmatova evidently did not altogether succeed. She herself frequently complained that readers of *Poem Without a Hero* seemed to find it difficult to understand, and she paid particular attention in the numerous rewritings of the work, with which she was almost obsessively occupied during the 1950s and 1960s, to clarifying its obscurities and to rendering it more accessible. Moreover, for all its virtuosity, and partly because of the lengthy time period over which it was written, *Poem Without a Hero* does not completely achieve the thematic unity at which it aims: the different perspectives which it offers are not quite brought into a single focus. Yet it remains a powerful and a compelling work, and, as the mounting body of criticism on it shows, one which is remarkably reluctant to give up all its secrets.

There is much about the text of the poem itself which remains enigmatic, often designedly so. The most complete critical edition, that of Elisabeth von Erdmann-Pandžić, lists over thirty different redactions, and there are doubtless more in Russian archives and personal collections.[1] The differences between them are often radical: the first 'completed' version of 1942 is, for example, half the length of the texts of the 1960s. The numerous variants are accompanied by a multiplicity of epigraphs, notes, dedications and introductory passages in prose. Then there are several bodies of writing, which while not *of* the text of *Poem Without a Hero*, are clearly closely associated *with* it: passages written in the same stanzaic structure but 'excluded' from the poem itself; prose passages in which Akhmatova cryptically discusses the composition and significance of the poem; separate works which according to Akhmatova 'accompanied' the writing of the poem, notably *Requiem* and the dramatic work *Enuma Elish*.

The principle of incoherence which can be detected in Akhmatova's refusal to define the exact boundaries of the poem can also be detected within it, as a brief account of its overt structure and narrative content will show.[2] The work has three main subdivisions: 'Devyat'sot trinadtsatyi god' ('Nineteen-Thirteen'), 'Reshka' ('Reverse') and 'Epilog' ('Epilogue'), each with its own compositional peculiarities. 'Nineteen-Thirteen', divided into four chapters and an intermezzo, comes the closest to having a linear plot. It begins with the figure of the Author alone in her flat in the Sheremetev Palace on the eve of the year 1941. The first lines evoke a traditional New Year's fortune-telling practice in which a young woman would seek a vision in two interreflecting mirrors between which two candles had been placed:

> Ya zazhgla zavetnye svechi,
>   Chtoby etot svetilsya vecher,
>   I s toboi, ko mne ne prishedshim,
>   Sorok pervyi vstrechayu god.
>
>   (S1, 277)

> I lit the magic candles
>   So that this evening should be bright,
>   And with you, who have not come to me,
>   I meet the New Year 1941.[3]

1. Elisabeth von Erdmann-Pandžić, *'Poema bez geroja' von Anna A. Achmatova: Varientenedition und Interpretation von Symbolstrukturen*, Cologne, 1987.

2. Here and below, unless otherwise indicated, I work from the text printed in S1, pp. 273–300.

3. On the fortune-telling theme in *Poem Without a Hero*, see D. N. Wells, 'Folk Ritual in Anna Akhmatova's *Poema bez geroya*', *Scottish Slavonic Review*, no. 7, 1986, pp. 75–8.

Instead of her absent lover, the author unexpectedly conjures up a masked ball from the year 1913.

Many of the characters present at this masquerade are based on Akhmatova's contemporaries in the artistic circles of St Petersburg during the 1910s. It is a mistake, however, to look for exact portraits in every case, for as Akhmatova herself noted, the characters of *Poem Without a Hero* developed according to a logic of their own: 'The Demon was always Blok. The Mile-Post – the Poet in General, the Poet with a capital P (something like Mayakovskii). The characters developed and changed, and life introduced new actors into the drama' (S2, 222). In line, moreover, with the traditional belief that New Year is the season when human beings are most closely in touch with the spirit world, it is also possible to detect the presence of supernatural figures alongside the earthly ones, including representatives of the devil.

In successive chapters the masked figures act out the central event – the suicide of a young dragoon cornet after discovering his actress-beloved with a rival. The episode is related more than once in varying amounts of detail and with disregard of strict chronological sequence. It is interrupted by numerous digressions describing the literary bohemia of 1913 and the city of St Petersburg, and projected simultaneously on to several different planes. The relationship between cornet, actress and the less sharply defined rival, for example, is also seen in terms of the Pierrot–Columbine–Harlequin triangle of the *commedia dell'arte* which features in so many literary works of the Russian Silver Age. The many links that exist between symbolic and historical personages, and the textual framework of the section, both strongly imply that the personal tragedy is emblematic of a broader historical one. The events of 1913 are to be seen as relevant to the present day of 1940.

'Reverse' comprises an authorial commentary on 'Nineteen-Thirteen'. This notes the bemusement of an editor on reading the work, and purports to explain it by commenting on its principles of composition, hinting at concealed depths within it and revealing, however enigmatically, the sources of its inspiration. 'Epilogue', which is dated 1942, is addressed to the city of Leningrad under siege and describes both the Author's attachment to her home and, in apocalyptic terms, her flight from it under the threat of war.

As this brief account suggests, *Poem Without a Hero* is essentially a modernist work. In terms of Bakhtinian discourse analysis, it is 'dialogic', proceeding from a constantly shifting point of perception and offering a series of fragments rather than a unified structure such as might be presented by a (characteristically monologic) realist novel: the linguistic construction of the text invites a plurality of readings.

Poem Without a Hero is in this respect not so much a narrative poem in the traditional sense as a lyric sequence after the manner of *Requiem* or the early poetic books, where the principle of organisation is reflection rather than progression.

Akhmatova herself suggested several parallels with other works which serve to elucidate her compositional method. In one comment on the poem she compares it with a work by the American writer Peter Viereck, whom she met when he visited Russia in the early 1960s: 'The following quotation explains everything: "This book may be read as a poem or verse play" – writes Peter Viereck (1961 "The Tree Witch") and then explains technically how a long poem is transformed into a play.'[4] Viereck's *The Tree Witch* is a lengthy dramatic poem dealing with questions of the subordination of spontaneity and creativity to the demands of method and order. What is important here, however, are Viereck's comments about the genre of his work. He insists that it can be read either as a lyrical work or as a drama, and provides notes on how typographical and other features should be interpreted in either case. For example, indentations 'suggest a mood change when read as a poem; a voice change when read as a play'. Viereck suggests several other oppositional characteristics which coexist in *The Tree Witch*. The work should be 'so staged and acted as to hover between material and magical explanations, never resolved'; two of the three voices of the poem, WE and THEY, are defined simultaneously as groups and as individual actors; the character and appearance of the WE group is defined 'as simultaneously middle-aged and schoolboy'; the tree-witch or dryad herself plays several different roles in the drama. Finally, Viereck insists that dramatic conflict can overcome the distinction between 'perused *verse*-play and performed verse-*play*': 'When involving us deep enough, songs are not merely about actions; songs *are* actions.'[5] In the blurring of categories, the breaking down of boundaries, the device of speaking simultaneously on different temporal and spatial levels, and the insistence that a new vision is thereby created, *Poem Without a Hero* is indeed, as Akhmatova suggests, close to Viereck's *The Tree Witch*.

Another parallel to Akhmatova's poetics can be found in Alain Robbe-Grillet's film *L'Année dernière à Marienbad* (*Last Year at Marienbad*), which received great critical acclaim after winning the Golden Lion at the Venice Film Festival in 1961. Akhmatova herself noted a

---

4. S2, 231. See I. A. Tlusty, 'Anna Akhmatova and the Composition of her Poema bez geroya 1940–1962', unpublished D.Phil. thesis, University of Oxford, 1984, p. 277.
5. Peter Viereck, *The Tree Witch: A Poem and Play (First of All a Poem)*, New York, 1961, pp. 11–13.

particular correspondence with *Prologue*, but comparison also with *Poem Without a Hero* is not out of place.[6] In *Last Year at Marienbad* Robbe-Grillet, in collaboration with Alain Resnais, applies the techniques of the *nouveau roman* to the medium of film. He wishes to replace conventional film narrative with a technique modelled more exactly on the working of the human mind:

> Its style is more varied, richer and less reassuring: it skips certain passages, it preserves an exact record of certain 'unimportant' details, it repeats and doubles back on itself. And this *mental time*, with its peculiarities, its gaps, its obsessions, its obscure areas, is the one that interests us since it is the tempo of our emotions, of our life.[7]

Robbe-Grillet's enigmatic account of a young man's seduction of a young woman on the strength of a promise she made to him the previous year at the resort of Marienbad is of course very different in overall conception and execution from Akhmatova's *Poem Without a Hero*, but in certain of its compositional features it is surprisingly similar. Both works, for example, include material from different periods of time without making the distinction between them explicit. In *Last Year in Marienbad* scenes from the past, present and future, the real and the imaginary are not clearly distinguished. In Akhmatova too, although the situation is considerably more complex and there is an additional moral level of interpretation, the lessons of 1913 are seen to hold good for 1940, and the figure of the heroine slides easily between the two. As in the film, so too in Akhmatova's poem the interchangeability of time frames is inscribed in the text through the pervasive imagery of mirrors and doubles.

Origins, Methods and Themes

In her prose about *Poem Without a Hero* Akhmatova comments several times on the impulses behind its writing. An examination of these passages will go some way to elucidating the various intermingled themes of the poem. Whether or not Akhmatova's statements on the matter can be held to be literally true, they are nevertheless important indicators of what she held to be significant in the work which dominated the last twenty-five years of her life.

6. K2, 312, 399. Amanda Haight notes that she sent Akhmatova a copy of the film script in 1966 after noting parallels with both *Prologue* and *Poem Without a Hero*: Haight, *Anna Akhmatova*, p. 192.
  7. A. Robbe-Grillet, *Last Year at Marienbad*, trans. R. Howard, New York, 1962, p. 9.

The immediate inspiration of *Poem Without a Hero* can be traced to the autumn of 1940, when Akhmatova claims that she discovered among her papers letters and poems which she had not previously read referring to 'the tragic event of 1913 which is related in *Poem Without a Hero*'. The 'tragic event' in question is evidently the suicide of the young soldier-poet Vsevolod Knyazev as a result of his unrequited love for Akhmatova's close friend the actor Ol´ga Sudeikina. Elsewhere Akhmatova notes that 'O[l´ga Sudeikina]'s things, in the midst of which I had lived for a long time, suddenly demanded their place in the poetic sun.'[8] It is thus Sudeikina rather than Knyazev or anyone else, who is the main initial focus of attention.

The first part of 'Nineteen-Thirteen' to be written was the section described in 'Instead of a Preface' as the 'Vestnik' ('Messenger'), beginning 'Ty v Rossiyu prishla niotkuda' ('You came to Russia from nowhere', S1, 285). In this short passage can already be seen several motifs which are of crucial importance to the poem as a whole. It came to lie at the heart of the second chapter of 'Nineteen-Thirteen', which is devoted to the heroine, where it links the actress figure of chapter one with Sudeikina. It also renders explicit her symbolic role as representative of her epoch, describing her as 'Kolombina desyatykh godov' ('Colombine of the 1910s'), and brings out the decorative function she was called on to fill in society by referring to her as 'belokuroe chudo' ('blond marvel') and 'Peterburgskaya kukla' ('Petersburg doll'). The passage, moreover, also emphasises her status as actor which allows her to embody numerous parts simultaneously, and, most importantly, associates her firmly with the narrator figure, the lyric 'I' of the poem. The figurative Akhmatova writes here that the actress is one of her doubles ('Ty odin iz moikh dvoinikov') and that she herself has inherited the actress' fame ('Ya – naslednitsa slavy tvoei'). The last line of the passage, 'Vizhu tanets pridvornykh kostei' ('I see the dance of court bones'), with its evocation of the neoromantic *danse macabre*, suggests the theme of death, destruction and guilt which is central to the story of the cornet and present in 'Nineteen-Thirteen' on other levels as well.

Akhmatova associated 'You came to Russia from nowhere' with another poem written at the same time, 'Ten'' ('Shade', S1, 196–7), originally called 'Sovremennitse' ('To a Contemporary'), and dedicated to another society beauty of the early twentieth century, Salomeya Andronikova. Andronikova becomes another double of the actress of 'Nineteen-Thirteen'. Her appearance to the poet's imagination after many years of absence is equally unexpected; she is associated with the

---

8. S2, 221, 223.

same abnegation of responsibility – her period of triumph is described as 'Tvoi bezoblachnyi i ravnodushnyi den'' ('Your cloudless and indifferent day'); both are associated with poets. The evocation of Andronikova, like that of Sudeikina, ends on an ominous note: 'A mne takogo roda / Vospominaniya ne k litsu. O ten'!' ('But this kind of memory does not suit me. O shade!').

In one note on her poem Akhmatova writes that the heroine is not meant as a portrait of Ol'ga Sudeikina. What is intended rather is a portrait of the epoch, of St Petersburg artistic circles of the 1910s.[9] This composite portrait indeed suggests many other models besides Sudeikina, Andronikova and Akhmatova herself. A convincing case has been made, for example, for a connection with Marina Tsvetaeva.[10] The text of the *Poem* incorporates, moreover, numerous figures from literature and art, who can be seen as Akhmatova's doubles: Donna Anna from Blok's treatment of the Don Juan legend, 'Shagi komandora' ('The Steps of the Commendatore'), Botticelli's Venus, the characters of Psyche and Confusion from contemporary plays by Yurii Belyaev. When composing the ballet libretto from *Poem Without a Hero*, Akhmatova thought additionally of the dancer Tamara Vecheslova.

'Shade' is the third poem of the cycle 'In 1940', devoted to the sufferings of western Europe at the beginning of the Second World War. The first two poems of the cycle are addressed to the cities of Paris and London, as they endure respectively German occupation and attack. These two cities were the homes of Sudeikina and Andronikova respectively and it is not surprising that Akhmatova's thoughts should have turned in 1940 to her friends who lived in them, nor that she should have been so struck by the difference between their lives in 1913 and in 1940. In the fourth and fifth poems of 'In 1940', Akhmatova draws a parallel between events of the present in western Europe and an unspecified past disaster in her own Russian experience, prophesying that this disaster is about to be repeated:

> I chto tam v tumane – Daniya,
> Normandiya, ili tut
> Sama ya byvala ranee,
> I eto – pereizdanie
> Navek zabytykh minut?
>
> (S1, 197)

---

9. V. Ya. Vilenkin, *V sto pervom zerkale*, 2nd edn, Moscow, 1990, p. 233.
10. I. Lisnyanskaya, *Muzyka 'Poemy bez geroya' Anny Akhmatovoi*, Moscow, 1991.

What is there in the mist –
Denmark, Normandy, or
Was I myself there earlier,
And is this a repeat of moments
Forgotten forever?

Akhmatova foresees the coming of war to Russia in 1941 and compares its arrival with that of the war of 1914, which brought revolution in its wake and mass destruction not only of human beings, but also of codes of behaviour and cultural traditions.

The figure of the cornet-Pierrot is identified as Knyazev in the same prose passages which make explicit the connection with Sudeikina, and, of course, the text of *Poem Without a Hero* contains numerous allusions both to Knyazev's life and to his poems – presumably the works referred to in Akhmatova's note about the events of the autumn of 1940.[11] But as Timenchik has pointed out, Knyazev's biography and the story of the cornet differ in many respects,[12] and as with the composite figure of Columbine, Akhmatova draws simultaneously on multiple sources to create her portrait of Pierrot. Indeed, in one of her prose notes, Akhmatova hints that Knyazev is not even the primary source for the cornet and that the true original impulse behind *Poem Without a Hero* lies not in the events of 1913, but in a similar episode which took place two years earlier:

> The first shoot (the first stimulus), which perhaps I concealed from myself for decades, was, of course, Pushkin's remark: 'Only the first lover produces an impression on a woman, like the first dead body in a war.' Vsevolod [Knyazev] was not the first dead body (and he was never my lover), but his suicide was so similar to another catastrophe – (24 Dec. 1911) – that for me they were forever fused.[13]

Timenchik asserts that the 'other catastrophe' alluded to here was the suicide of a certain Mikhail Lindberg in his military barracks in Vladikavkaz. What personal relationship may have existed between Lindberg and Akhmatova, however, remains unclear.[14] However, there appears to have been something of a vogue for suicide in artistic circles in the 1910s, and 1911 also saw the deaths, for example, of the poets Viktor

11. S2, 223.
12. R. D. Timenchik, 'Rizhskii epizod v "Poeme bez geroya" Anny Akhmatovoi', *Daugava*, no. 80, 1984, pp. 113–21.
13. Vilenkin, *V sto pervom zerkale*, pp. 233–4.
14. Timenchik, 'Rizhskii epizod', p. 121. A marginal note on one draft of the ballet libretto also points to Lindberg: see V. Ya. Vilenkin, 'Obraz "teni" v poetike Anny Akhmatovoi', *Voprosy literatury*, no. 1, 1994, pp. 68–9.

Gofman, whom Akhmatova had met in Paris, and Sergei Solov'ev, a cousin of Aleksandr Blok.[15]

The image of Knyazev-Pierrot in *Poem Without a Hero* can be associated much less ambiguously with Osip Mandelstam. The first dedication, for example, bears alongside the initials Vs. K. the official date of the anniversary of Mandelstam's death, and textual and biographical allusions have been found in it to both poets.[16] In the body of *Poem Without a Hero* the words spoken by the cornet before his suicide – 'Ya k smerti gotov' ('I am ready for death') – are a reflection of words spoken by Mandelstam to Akhmatova in February 1934, shortly before he was arrested for the first time.[17] The phrase is also to be linked with Gumilev through his play *Gondla*, which contains the lines: 'Ya vinom blagodati / Op'yanilsya i k smerti gotov' ('I am drunk on the wine of grace and am ready for death').[18] By virtue of the combination of the images of the three poets in the character of the cornet, their deaths are seen as on one level equivalent and the cornet's suicide in 1913 acquires a clear political meaning. The cornet represents not only the naivety and immaturity of a Knyazev, but also commemorates the destruction by the Soviet regime of a Mandelstam or a Gumilev. His death both prefigures the breakdown of civilisation that came with war and revolution after 1913, and foreshadows the deaths of individuals during the Terror of the 1930s.

That Akhmatova in writing *Poem Without a Hero* had an explicit political agenda is indicated by a note in which she links its genesis with the revolution of 1917:

> It is impossible to say when it [*Poem Without a Hero*] first began to sound in me. It either happened when I was standing with my companion on Nevskii Prospekt (after the dress rehearsal of 'Masquerade' on 25 February 1917), and the cavalry swept along the pavement like lava, or. . . when I was standing, no longer with my companion, on the Liteinyi Bridge at the time it was unexpectedly raised in broad daylight (an unprecedented event) in order to let the minesweepers through to the Smolnyi Institute to support the Bolsheviks (25 October 1917). How should I tell which?[19]

This passage is worth considering in some detail. February 25, 1917 marked a turning point in the Petrograd rising which heralded the over-

15. Zhirmunskii, *Tvorchestvo Anny Akhmatovoi*, pp. 145–6.
16. See R. Childers and A. L. Crone, 'The Mandel'štam Presence in the Dedications of *Poèma bez geroja*', *Russian Literature*, vol. 15, 1984, pp. 51–82.
17. II, 179.
18. N. S. Gumilev, *Sobranie sochinenii v chetyrekh tomakh*, ed. G. P. Struve and B. A. Filippov, Washington, 1962–8, vol. 3, p. 91.
19. S2, 221.

throw of the autocracy: a policeman was killed, apparently by Cossack troops sympathetic to the demonstrators who had massed on Znamenskaya Square.[20] October 25 is the date of the Bolshevik *coup d'état* which toppled Kerenskii's provisional government and proclaimed the transfer of power to the Soviets of Workers', Soldiers' and Peasants' Deputies. The event Akhmatova describes (somewhat inaccurately) in fact took place before the coup as the different political groups in Petrograd attempted to seize military control of key installations. The passage, then, associates *Poem Without a Hero* with revolution and with the assumption of power by the Bolsheviks; its textual insistence on the years 1913 and 1940 as marking significant transitions masks the more essential boundary formed by 1917. The mention of an unidentified companion gives Akhmatova's historical explanation of the origins of her poem an additional, personal component. At the beginning of the transitional period of 1917 Akhmatova is accompanied; at the end she is not. In the context of Akhmatova's love poetry it is difficult to interpret this 'companion' as anything other than a lover from whom she has been separated by historical circumstance.

The reference to 'Masquerade' also has implications for an understanding of *Poem Without a Hero*. February 25, 1917 was the date of the opening performance (not the dress rehearsal as Akhmatova states) of Meyerhold's celebrated production of Lermontov's *Maskarad* (*Masquerade*). Meyerhold is alluded to several times in *Poem Without a Hero*, and this play may well have been called particularly to Akhmatova's mind in 1940 when she began to write her poem, since a revival of *Masquerade* in Leningrad in December 1938 was the last work in the theatre that Meyerhold completed. Although they were not personally close, his arrest in June 1939 and death in a Moscow prison in February 1940 removed another important link between Akhmatova and the artistic world of 1913.

Meyerhold's production of *Masquerade* was very much in the avant-garde tradition of the day and has been regarded as the culmination of the Petersburg period of his work.[21] The potentialities of masks and masquerade for exploring the nature of illusion and for facilitating the passage of supernatural and demonic forces into the world of human beings had already been investigated in Meyerhold's earlier productions of such works as Blok's *Balaganchik* (*The Fairground Booth*), or *Sharf Kolombiny* (*Columbine's Scarf*), adapted from Schnitzler's *Der Schleier*

20. See G. Katkov, *Russia 1917: The February Revolution*, London, 1967, pp. 358ff.

21. E. Braun, *The Theatre of Meyerhold: Revolution on the Modern Stage*, London, 1979, p. 144. Details below on the production are taken from this work, pp. 135–44.

der Pierrette. Masquerade is a story of jealousy and revenge set in Petersburg society in the 1830s, combining a romantic melodrama with a satire on the hypocrisy and cynicism of aristocratic morals. In Meyerhold's production considerable emphasis was placed on the figure of the Stranger, who was interpreted as a demonic force impelling the hero, Arbenin, to poison his wife at a masked ball on suspicion of adultery. The Stranger then takes the leading role in revealing to Arbenin that his suspicions were groundless and driving him to madness. The character of the Stranger is one possible source for the mysterious figure 'bez litsa i nazvaniya' ('without a face or a name') who appears twice in Akhmatova's masquerade and is closely, if obscurely, linked with the demonic world and with the downfall of the cornet. Lermontov's Stranger has no name, but is referred to as a Mask (maska) and as Unknown (Neizvestnyi). He describes himself to Arbenin as having no single face of his own:

vezde ya byl s toboi,
Vsegda s drugim litsom, vsegda v drugom naryade.[22]

I have been with you everywhere,
Always with a different face, a different costume.

A further linguistic source for the expression 'without a face or a name' may be found in Lermontov's definition of a mask much earlier in *Masquerade*:

Pod maskoi vse chiny ravny,
U maski ni dushi, ni zvan'ya net – est' telo.[23]

Behind a mask all ranks are equal,
A mask has neither a soul nor a title – it has a body.

There is also a broader parallel between 'Nineteen-Thirteen' and *Masquerade* in that both works use a masquerade setting to show how an amoral and frivolous society can be the cause of unnecessary suffering and death. Further, the theme of Nero fiddling while Rome burns that asserts itself throughout 'Nineteen-Thirteen', where the artistic world is seen as engaging in role-playing while political forces are reshaping the world all around them, finds its reflection in the coincidence

22. M. Yu. Lermontov, *Polnoe sobranie stikhotvorenii v dvukh tomakh*, ed. E. E. Naidich, Leningrad, 1989, vol. 1, p. 507.
23. Ibid., pp. 413–14.

of Meyerhold's *Masquerade* opening on the same day that the February revolution began in earnest. There was much criticism of the production at the time for being irrelevant to the important issues of the day. But at the same time, some commentators at least have seen it as being, like *Poem Without a Hero*, a grim requiem for the passing of an era.

The Political Theme

Akhmatova's comments on the origins of *Poem Without a Hero* reveal that the story of the Petersburg masquerade is intended to point first of all to an examination of the history of Russia in the twentieth century and secondly to an investigation of the role of the poet in Russian society. Each of these themes provides a unifying thread through the various parts of the work.

The political theme is announced indirectly from the very beginning of *Poem Without a Hero* through the epigraph to the introductory prose passage headed 'Vmesto predsiloviya' ('Instead of a Preface'). This reads 'Inykh uzh net, a te daleche' ('Some are already dead, and the others are far away', S1, 273), and is a quotation from Pushkin's *Evgenii Onegin*. The line is taken from the last stanza of chapter eight of Pushkin's work, where he takes leave of his readers and notes that those to whom he read the first chapters are now either dead or far away. The immediate context reads:

> No te kotorym v druzhnoi vstreche
> Ya strofy pervye chital. . .
> Inykh uzh net, a te daleche,
> Kak Sadi nekogda skazal.[24]

> But those to whom in friendly meetings
> I read the first stanzas. . .
> Some are already dead, and the others are far away,
> As Sadi once said.

Although Pushkin carefully ascribes the phrase picked out by Akhmatova to the thirteenth-century Persian poet Sadi, by the time he came to use it in *Evgenii Onegin* it had acquired a definite contemporary meaning. The expression has, as Vladimir Nabokov has noted, a complex literary history in other authors as well as Pushkin.[25] What is important here is that by the time of *Evgenii Onegin* it had come

24. Pushkin, *PSS*, vol. 5, p. 191.
25. V. Nabokov (ed.), *Eugene Onegin*, rev. edn, London, 1975, vol. 3, pp. 245–7.

to constitute an unambiguous reference to Pushkin's friends in the Decembrist movement, who had suffered either execution or exile. Consequently, when Akhmatova used the phrase at the beginning of *Poem Without a Hero* it was clearly associated with both a literary and a political tradition. Akhmatova's poem both continues the literary tradition by incorporating and interpreting the texts of earlier writers and preserves the political awareness demonstrated by Pushkin.

In referring to the first readers of *Evgenii Onegin* in the passage which contains the words 'Some are already dead, and the others are far away', Pushkin also makes the point that his work is based on real experience and that the figures portrayed in it are drawn from life. He continues:

> Bez nikh Onegin dorisovan.
> A ta, s kotoroi obrazovan
> Tat´yany milyi ideal. . .
> O mnogo, mnogo rok ot´´yal![26]

> Onegin was painted without them.
> And she on whom the sweet ideal
> Of Tat´yana was based. . .
> Oh, fate has taken away so much. . .

Akhmatova uses the reference to Pushkin to make the same point about her own work. In this indirect way, she supplies a key for the informed reader to establish *Poem Without a Hero* as a statement about her own contemporaries in spite of the mystifying techniques with which it is permeated.

The implicit comparison between Akhmatova's contemporaries and the Decembrists is revealed on several different levels. In the prose introduction, which is the immediate context of her epigraph, Akhmatova dedicates her poem to the memory of its original audience: 'I dedicate this poem to the memory of its first listeners – my friends and fellow citizens who perished in Leningrad during the siege' (S1, 273). A note at the end of this passage reveals that at the time of writing the Author was in Tashkent. Thus a contrast between the dead and the distant, those in exile, is immediately established. This contrast in fact dominates the whole poem. Of the three dedications, the first two are written to dead addressees. They bear the dates of the deaths of Mandelstam and Sudeikina respectively, and both conclude with funereal images: the first with Chopin's funeral march, the second with the

26. Pushkin, *PSS*, vol. 5, p. 253.

words 'il' podsnezhnik v mogil'nom rvu' ('or a snowdrop in an open grave'). The third dedication is associated with the 'Guest from the Future', a figure who will be discussed later. For the present it is enough to note that although he is not dead, he is distant from the speaker in time and place.

The dichotomy continues into 'Nineteen-Thirteen'. In the 'Letter to N.', which forms an introduction to some early versions of *Poem Without a Hero*, Akhmatova, echoing the epigraph, notes some early reactions to her poem in Tashkent: 'he [a critic] said that I was settling some old accounts with the epoch (the 1910s) and with people who were either dead or who were unable to answer me' (S2, 223). Although Akhmatova's perhaps fictitious critic here appears to see the poem erroneously as a personal attack on her enemies from the 1910s, he has nonetheless noted correctly the categories of people to whom it is devoted. All or nearly all of Akhmatova's contemporaries from literary St Petersburg who are alluded to in 'Nineteen-Thirteen' were already dead or in exile.

On one level, of course, as has already been suggested, the poem commemorates the artistic achievement of the Silver Age.[27] Many of its representatives are referred to metonymically: Anna Pavlova, for example, is recognisable by allusion to her role in Fokine's *The Dying Swan*:

> No letit, ulybayas' mnimo,
> Nad Mariinskoi stsenoi prima –
> Ty – nash lebed' nepostizhimyi.
>
> (S1, 283)

> But with a false smile a ballerina
> Flies aver the Mariinskii stage –
> It is you, our inscrutable swan.

Chaliapin is identified by his voice:

> I opyat' tot golos znakomyi,
> Budto ekho gornogo groma,–
> Nasha slava i torzhestvo!
>
> (S1, 284)

---

27. See V. V. Ivanov, '"Poema bez geroya", poetika pozdnei Akhmatovoi i fantasticheskii realizm', in S. Dedyulin and G. Superfin (eds), *Akhmatovskii sbornik*, vol. 1, Paris, 1989, pp. 132–3.

And again that familiar voice
Like the thundering of a mountain echo,
Our glory and our triumph![28]

Writers are frequently alluded to by direct or indirect quotation from
their work. For example:

Poem Without a Hero	*Source*

Na ch´em serdtse 'palevyi
            lokon'
        (S1, 288)

On whose heart lies a 'pale-
    blond' curl

            Skol´ko raz videl palevyi
                    lokon. . .

            How many times have I seen a
                    pale-blond curl
                    (Knyazev)

No mne strashno: voidu sama
                ya,
Kruzhevnuyu shal´ ne snimaya,
Ulybnus´ vsem i zamolchu.
        (S1, 279)

But I am afraid: I myself will
        come in,

Without taking off my lace shawl.
I will smile to everyone and fall silent.

            'Krasota strashna' — vam
                    skazhut —
            Vy nakinete lenivo
            Shal´ ispanskuyu na plechi.

            'Beauty is terrible,' they will tell
                    you,

28. See B. Kats and R. D. Timenchik, *Anna Akhmatova i muzyka: issledovatel´skie
ocherki*, Leningrad, 1989, pp. 167–8, 194–5.

You will throw your Spanish
shawl
Lazily on to your shoulders
(Blok: 'Anne Akhmatovoi'
('To Anna Akhmatova'))

Kruzhevnoi ronyaet platochek
[. . .]
I bryullovskim manit plechom.
(S1, 294)

She drops her lace handker-
chief . . .
And beckons with a Bryullovesque
shoulder.

Krasavitsa, kak polotno
Bryullova. . .
Ne popravlyala alogo platochka,
Chto spolz u nei s zhemchuzh-
nogo plecha.

A beauty, like a canvas by
Bryullov. . .
Not adjusting her scarlet shawl,
Which has fallen from her
shoulders
(Kuzmin)[29]

The allusions, frequently covert, to Knyazev, Kuzmin, Gumilev, Mandelstam and others which abound in *Poem Without a Hero* were for a long time the only way in which these poets, in many respects typical of Akhmatova's generation and of the poetry of the 1910s and 1920s, could be represented in print in the Soviet Union, even in periods of relative thaw. Many of the people she refers to in this way were not in sympathy with the Soviet government, and had been destroyed or exiled by it. Akhmatova's work is thus a tribute to her fellow poets, who would otherwise be forced into permanent silence.

The story of the downfall of the cornet in 'Nineteen-Thirteen' is

---

29. See R. D. Timenchik, V. N. Toporov and T. V. Tsiv'yan, 'Akhmatova i Kuzmin', *Russian Literature*, vol. 6, 1978, pp. 224, 240; V. N. Toporov, *Akhmatova i Blok (k probleme postroeniya poeticheskogo dialoga: 'blokovskii' tekst Akhmatovoi)*, Berkeley, 1981, p. 46.

accompanied by a complex symbolic structure of premonitions of disaster. Not only does the masquerade of chapter one, for example, refer to the devil and his works, but the subtitle to the section as a whole, 'A Petersburg Tale', brings to mind Pushkin's 'Petersburg tale', *Mednyi vsadnik* (*The Bronze Horseman*), which recounts the unenviable fate of an ordinary man caught up by the natural and man-made forces behind the great flood of 1824. Chapter three of 'Nineteen-Thirteen' is particularly rich in ominous events: it describes carriages sliding from the bridges across the Neva, drums beating for an execution and the city succumbing to the curse placed on it by the Empress Evdokiya. All this leads up to the onset of the terrible 'Nastoyashchii dvadtsatyi vek' ('True Twentieth Century') (S1, 286–7). The sense of foreboding here is enhanced by a reference to the feverish world of Dostoevskii's Petersburg novels: 'Dostoevskii i besnovatyi / Gorod v svoi ukhodil tuman' ('The bedevilled town of Dostoevskii disappeared into its fog'). There is also a series of indirect references to scenes of ill omen in *The Bronze Horseman* and in Pushkin's tale of pride before a fall, *Skazka o zolotom petushke* (*The Tale of the Golden Cockerel*). For example, the account of the flood in *The Bronze Horseman* can be compared with Akhmatova's description of the river Neva. In both cases the Neva is uncontrollable. Akhmatova's lines 'Po Neve i protiv techen'ya, – / Tol'ko proch' ot svoikh mogil' ('Along the Neva and against its current, only away from its graves') echo a similar mention of graves in Pushkin: 'Groba s razmytogo kladbishcha / Plyvut po ulitsam' ('Coffins from a flooded cemetery float along the streets'). Similarly, Akhmatova's line 'V Letnem tonko pela flyugarka' ('The weather-vane sang thinly in the Summer Garden') recalls the fateful crowing of Pushkin's golden cockerel.[30]

The nature of the 'True Twentieth Century' which the death of the cornet foreshadows is alluded to several times during the course of 'Nineteen-Thirteen'. The framing passages, of course, connect it unambiguously with the horrors of the Second World War. Chapter four, in addition, sketches an alternative death for the cornet in the fighting against the Central Powers in 1914–15:

> Glyadi:
> Ne v proklyatykh Mazurskikh bolotakh,
> Ne na sinikh Karpatskikh vysotakh. . .
> On – na tvoi porog!
>
> (S1, 289)

30. Pushkin, *PSS*, vol. 4, pp. 387, 486; see T. V. Tsiv'yan, 'Zametki k deshirovke "Poemy bez geroya"', *Trudy po znakovym sistemam*, no. 5, 1971, p. 272.

Look:
Not in the cursed Masurian marshes,
Not on the blue Carpathian heights. . .
He is on your doorstep!

'Nineteen-Thirteen' also contains oblique links with the domestic situation in the Soviet Union between the wars. It has already been noted that the premature death of the cornet is linked with that of Mandelstam and Gumilev, but there are also passages which on one level repeat the common experience of the Terror. For example,

I ya slyshu zvonok protyazhnyi,
I ya chuvstvuyu kholod vlazhnyi,
Kameneyu, stynu, goryu. . .
(S1, 278)

And I hear a prolonged ringing,
And I feel a damp chill,
I turn to stone, freeze, burn. . .

connects the heroine's fortune-telling experiment in chapter one with a midnight visit from the secret police. The line 'Ty kak budto ne znachish´sya v spiskakh' ('It's as if you are not on the list'), which is found in the description of the masquerade, echoes an official expression used by prison authorities to inform relatives whether or not they were holding a particular individual.

These passages may seem of little significance in themselves, but in the light of the prose introduction to 'Reverse' they fall into clearer perspective. Here Akhmatova writes: 'The wind is howling in the stovepipe and in this howl can be detected the very deeply hidden and very cleverly concealed fragments of a Requiem' (S1, 290), implying that the themes of her own *Requiem* sequence are also present in *Poem Without a Hero*. The Requiem theme is most directly seen in 'Reverse' through a series of 'missing stanzas' indicated by dots. Akhmatova appends a note which suggests that the lines are left blank in imitation of Pushkin in *Evgenii Onegin*, leaving the reader to recall that at least some of Pushkin's stanzas were omitted for reasons of political censorship.[31] Akhmatova's missing stanzas, which circulated in *samizdat* separately from the main text of *Poem Without a Hero*, contain a strong

31. Or at least that Pushkin liked to hint that this was the case. See Amert, *In a Shattered Mirror*, pp. 117–20.

statement of the Requiem theme, which again combines the motifs of death and exile:

> Ty sprosi u moikh sovremennits,
> Katorzhanok, stopyatnits, plennits,
> I tebe porasskazhem my,
> Kak v bespamyatnom zhili strakhe,
> Kak rastili detei dlya plakhi,
> Dlya zastenki i dlya tyur'my.
>
> (III, 116)

> Ask my contemporaries –
> Convicts, exiles, prisoners –
> And we will tell you
> How we lived in delirious fear,
> How we brought up our children for execution,
> For torture and for prison.

Death and distance become much more central themes in 'Epilogue'. Set explicitly in 1942, the section is addressed to the city of Leningrad under siege and to its inhabitants who are either dead or facing death in its defence or scattered 'kto v Tashkente, kto v N´yu-Iorke' ('Some in Tashkent, some in New York', S1, 297). The Author describes her own escape from the city 'ne stavshii moei mogiloi' ('which has not become my grave') into the exile of an evacuee in Central Asia. The parallel between the eastward route of refugees from the fighting in European Russia and that of the earlier victims of Stalinist oppression is unavoidable. Akhmatova writes:

> I otkrylas´ mne ta doroga,
> Po kotoroi ushlo tak mnogo,
> Po kotoroi syna vezli.
>
> (S1, 298)

> And that path opened out before me
> Which so many have travelled,
> On which my son was taken.

And in a still more overt reference to the camps, omitted from most redactions of 'Epilogue' and replaced by a line of dots, Akhmatova describes a prisoner being taken to and returned from interrogation, a figure whom she identifies as her own double (II, 130).

The Metapoetic Theme

'Nineteen-Thirteen' contains among its numerous references to other texts many reminiscences of different treatments of the legend of Don Juan. Depending on the version, for example, either 'Nineteen-Thirteen' or *Poem Without a Hero* as a whole bears the epigraph 'Di rider finirai / pria dell'aurora' ('You will stop laughing before dawn') from Da Ponte's libretto to Mozart's *Don Giovanni*. There are many allusions too to Blok's poem 'The Footsteps of the Commendatore'.[32] 'Nineteen-Thirteen' can easily be read in the light of the story of Don Juan as an account of punishment following inexorably from wrongdoing. The cornet's death and the collapse of pre-revolutionary society can thus be seen as the consequence perhaps of the sexual licence displayed in the Intermezzo between chapters one and two, or of the irresponsible addiction to masks and role-playing revealed in the masquerade.[33] The figure of Don Juan has often been identified as Blok,[34] yet it is perhaps a mistake in the mirror-world of *Poem Without a Hero* to lay too much stress on any single identification. More important is the theme of guilt which the Don Juan 'line' in the poem brings to the fore and the connection between the guilt of 1913 and the poem's present in 1940.

The only character who spans both periods of the poem's action is the Author. She is deeply implicated in the events of 1913 – she is after all the double of the actress – but at the same time she has outgrown the superficiality of that world by the benefit of her subsequent experience. Her ambiguous relationship to the past is summarised by the lines that follow her encounter with her younger self in the course of the masquerade:

> Ya zabyla vashi uroki,
> Krasnobai i lzheproroki! –
> No menya ne zabyli vy.
> (S1, 279)

> I have forgotten your lessons,
> Phrase-mongers and false prophets!
> But you haven't forgotten me.

32. See Toporov, *Akhmatova i Blok*, pp. 36–40. W. Rosslyn, 'Don Juan Feminised', in A. McMillin, (ed.), *Symbolism and After: Essays on Russian Poetry in Honour of Georgette Donchin*, London, 1992, pp. 102–3, contains a succinct summary of Akhmatova's allusions to the Don Juan legend.
33. See ibid., pp. 104–6.
34. E.g. A. L. Crone, 'Blok as Don Juan in Akhmatova's "Poema bez geroia"', *Russian Language Journal*, nos. 121–2, 1981, pp. 147–55.

Guilt and responsibility attach themselves to the Author from the beginning of the masquerade as the only actor in the drama still alive. At one point she deliberately takes on the role of tragic chorus (S1, 285), and at the end of 'Nineteen-Thirteen' its writing is seen as an act inspired by conscience:

> Eto ya – tvoya staraya sovest´ –
> Razyskala sozhzhennuyu povest´
> I na krai podokonnika
> V dome pokoinika
> Polozhila – i na tsypochkakh ushla. . .
>
> (S1, 289)

> It was I – your old conscience –
> Who hunted out the burned story
> And placed it on the edge of the windowsill
> In the house of the deceased – and tiptoed away. . .

Since, as has already been noted, the tragedy of 1913 also embraces the destruction caused by Terror and war, this passage may be read as an assertion of the poet's reluctant duty both to preserve the past and to chronicle the present for the benefit of future generations. The techniques which are available for doing this, and which are applied in the writing of 'Nineteen-Thirteen', form the main subject of 'Reverse'. One meaning of this title is 'the other side of the coin', and indeed 'Nineteen-Thirteen' and 'Reverse' do form inseparable parts of a single whole.[35]

Akhmatova's analysis of 'Nineteen-Thirteen' in 'Reverse' can be divided into several sections, each of which illuminates a particular aspect of her work. The Author's discussion with her editor leads her into a reflection on her inability to escape from the poem. Akhmatova employs a succession of metaphors to describe its tenacity. It is a musical box mechanically pouring out its sound, a poison whose action cannot be stopped, an irresistible ballet libretto. The Author wishes that the poem would in fact leave her alone, but it will not because it is closely linked with matters of conscience. In describing one of the dia-

---

35. See J. Faryno, 'Akhmatova's *Poem Without a Hero* as a *Moneta* and as a Revelation', *Essays in Poetics*, vol. 16, no. 2, 1991, pp. 80–1.

bolic characters of the masquerade:

> Sam izyashchneishii satana,
> Kto nad mertvym so mnoi ne plachet,
> Kto ne znaet, chto sovest´ znachit
> I zachem sushchestvuet ona.
> (S1, 292)

> Most elegant Satan himself,
> Who will not weep with me over the dead,
> Who does not know what conscience means
> Or why it exists.

she is painting a shadow portrait of herself, announcing her own intention to mourn the dead and insisting that she does understand the meaning of conscience. The notion of moral dilemma is reinforced by references to Keats' sonnet 'To Sleep', in which he enjoins sleep to 'Save me from curious conscience, that still lords / Its strength, for darkness burrowing like a mole', to Maeterlinck's *L'Oiseau bleu* (*The Blue Bird*), where Night is accompanied both by Sleep and by his sister whom 'it is better not to name', and to the moral choice facing Hamlet at Elsinore (S1, 291).

The second section (stanzas VIII–XII) returns to the scene at the beginning of 'Nineteen-Thirteen', that is, to the Author waiting in her flat, but before the idea of the poem has come to her:

> V dver´ moyu nikto ne stuchitsya,
> Tol´ko zerkalo zerkalu snitsya,
> Tishina tishinu storozhit.
> (S1, 292)

> No one knocks at my door,
> The mirror dreams only of the mirror,
> Silence watches over silence.

In this bleak environment, the Author is accompanied by her 'Sed´-maya' ('Seventh'). This appears to be a reference to Akhmatova's 'seventh book' of verse, that is, her poetry of the late 1930s and early 1940s, which could not be published at the time.[36] This poetry is described as 'polumertvaya i nemaya' ('half-dead and mute') and the explanation for this is to be found in the description of the Terror found in the omitted stanzas which have already been described.

---

36. But see Amert, *In a Shattered Mirror*, pp. 111–12.

The stanza which follows (XIII) notes and dismisses one possible alternative for continuing to speak under these conditions, the 'official hymn', the dominant genre of Stalinist adulatory verse. Yet the need for a voice of Sophoclean intensity to bridge the gap between memory and remembrance ('pomnit'' and 'vspomnit'') is insistent, partly because of the onus of responsibility which has fallen on to the Author's shoulders. This insistence is expressed in stanza XV, in which Akhmatova ingenuously contrasts her present task with the supposed simplicity and apoliticality of her early work:

> Bes poputal v ukladke ryt´sya. . .
> Nu, a kak zhe moglo sluchit´sya,
> Chto vo vsem vinovata ya?
> Ya – tishaishaya, ya – prostaya,
> 'Podorozhnik', 'Belaya staya'. . .
> Opravdat´sya. . . no kak, druz´ya?
> (S1, 293)

> The devil drove me to rummage in this chest. . .
> But how did it come about
> That it is I who am guilty of everything?
> I who am so quiet, so simple. . .
> 'Plantain', 'White Flock'. . .
> I must defend myself. . . but how, my friends?

The following stanzas list the instruments of Akhmatova's defence. Foremost among them is 'plagiarism', the use of quotation and allusion to put forward indirectly themes that could not be broached outright. The metaphor of the triple-bottomed casket ('U shkatulki zh troinoe dno') is used to describe the poetry of secret meanings created in this way. 'Invisible ink' and 'mirror writing' serve a similar purpose.

The last section of 'Reverse' (stanzas XX–XXIV) examines the broader structural question for *Poem Without a Hero* of its relationship to the genre of the romantic narrative poem. This is an issue that will be discussed in more detail on pp. 125–8; for the present it may simply be noted that Akhmatova's Muse here insists that she is not a product of nineteenth-century romanticism, but an independent and vital being in her own right. She declares:

> Vovse net u menya rodoslovnoi,
> Krome solnechnoi i basnoslovnoi,
> I privel menya sam Iyul´.
> (S1, 295)

I have no pedigree at all
Except from the sun and from legend,
And July himself brought me here.

As a result her collaborative achievement with the Author will be an artistically valid and original one, as is expressed by the metaphor with which 'Reverse' ends: 'I ya tsarskim moim potseluem / zluyu polnoch' tvoyu nagrazhu' ('And with my royal kiss I will reward your malevolent midnight', S1, 295).

It is in 'Epilogue' that the parallel implied between 1913 and 1940 is made most explicit. The portents of 'Nineteen-Thirteen' have come to pass: 'Epilogue' is set and dated at the height of the Leningrad blockade and tells of destruction, separation and diaspora. Both the material fabric of the city and its cultural values are lost as the Author escapes to Asia. The theme of destruction is reinforced by three epigraphs which refer to the theme of the accursed city and thus look back to similar allusions in 'Nineteen-Thirteen'. Superficially the Pushkin epigraph 'Lyublyu tebya, Petra tvoren'e' ('I love you, creation of Peter') stands in opposition to the other two: an allusion to the Empress Evdokiya's curse on the city and a quotation from Annenskii's poem 'Peterburg' ('Petersburg') describing a political execution. The broader context of *The Bronze Horseman*, however, is also evoked and the Author's view of the city seen to be a mixture of love and horror.

Yet in spite of the overall apocalyptic tenor of 'Epilogue', there are muted indications that not everything is lost. Most significantly, the person of the Author, although sent into uncertain exile, is nevertheless spared death, and has therefore been vouchsafed the opportunity to present to the world the encoded message that is *Poem Without a Hero*. This theme of survival is reflected in several metaphors in the course of 'Epilogue'. Most importantly, the elegy to the city of Leningrad which it contains suggests that even if the city is destroyed physically something of its spirit will nevertheless be retained in the mind of the Author. She suffers with her city certainly, but by surviving she also implicitly preserves it:

Razluchenie nashe mnimo:
Ya s toboyu nerazluchima,
Ten' moya na stenakh tvoikh,
Otrazhen'e moe v kanalakh.
(S1, 297)

Our separation is imaginary:
You and I cannot be separated,
My shadow is on your walls,
My reflection in your canals.

Some versions of 'Epilogue' end with an allusion to Shostakovich and his Seventh 'Leningrad' Symphony, the first part of which Akhmatova took with her when she flew out of the city in 1941.[37] Shostakovich's symphony, like *Poem Without a Hero* itself, is an artistic monument to the act of survival in Russia in the 1930s and 1940s. By mentioning it here Akhmatova suggests the possibility of an eventual cultural revival. This is indeed foreshadowed by an image of renewal in the midst of destruction which is found in the prose introduction to 'Epilogue': 'In the Sheremetev garden the lime trees are flowering and a nightingale is singing' (S1, 296).

The Lyrical Theme

A further dimension is added to *Poem Without a Hero* by the lyrical theme associated in the first instance with the guest the Author was originally expecting on the eve of 1941 at the beginning of 'Nineteen-Thirteen'. This does not provide such a strong unifying force as either the political or metapoetical strands of the poem, but nevertheless creates a further link between at least 'Nineteen-Thirteen' and 'Epilogue'.

The traditional purpose of Russian New Year's fortune-telling was for young women to learn who their husbands would be. The figure who does not appear at the beginning of 'Nineteen-Thirteen' is thus to be seen in terms of the lyric hero or 'beloved' of Akhmatova's love poetry. He is evoked at various stages in *Poem Without a Hero*, where he holds out the promise of spiritual support for the Author-heroine even if his presence can at the same time prove inimical to her. Like other characters in *Poem Without a Hero*, the 'beloved' has several prototypes in real life which are merged poetically into a composite whole.

There are three principal manifestations of the 'lyrical theme'. The first is associated with the 'Guest from the Future' who is the subject of an italicised passage which occurs in the middle of the description of the masquerade (S1, 279). This figure, who is defined as alive while the other participants in the masquerade are dead, appears to be the same as the Author's expected visitor. He is referred to as: 'Chelovek, chto ne poyavilsya / I proniknut´ v tot zal ne mog' ('A person who did not appear, and was unable to enter that hall'). His presence is deeply des-

37. SP, 378.

ired by the Author, who declares:

> Gost' iz Budushchego! – Neuzheli
> On pridet ko mne v samom dele,
> Povernuv nalevo s mosta?

> Guest from the Future – Will he
> Really come to me,
> Turning left from the bridge?

This italicised passage is linked closely to the third dedication of *Poem Without a Hero* (S1, 275–6). This is connected to the masquerade through its reference to Epiphany, part of the Christmas–New Year carnival period, and to fortune-telling through its epigraph from Zhukovskii's ballad 'Svetlana', which describes in some detail the type of divinatory practice in which the Author engages at the beginning of 'Nineteen-Thirteen'. Moreover, the description of the hero of the third dedication, that of a beloved whose love is fatal for the heroine, mirrors exactly that of the 'Guest from the Future' as he appears in other works of Akhmatova, including notably *Prologue*. The hero's love token is death itself:

> No ne pervuyu vetv' sireni,
> Ne kol'tso, ne sladost' molenii –
> On pogibel' mne prineset.

> But it's not the first bunch of lilac,
> Not a ring, not the sweetness of prayers –
> It is death that he will bring me.

In writing the third dedication, Akhmatova had in mind Isaiah Berlin, whose last visit to her in 1946 had been at Epiphany,[38] and whom she saw as a cause of the calamitous Zhdanov decree of later that year, but at the same time as uniquely able to understand the import of her poetry. It is perhaps also of him that she is thinking in 'Reverse' when she outlines the response of a reader of the future and again uses the image of lilac:

> I togda iz gryadushchego veka
> Neznakomogo cheloveka
> Pust' posmotryat derzko glaza,
> I on mne, otletivshei teni,

---

38. Haight, *Anna Akhmatova*, p. 149.

Dast okhapku mokroi sireni
V chas, kak eta minet groza.
(S1, 294)

And then let the eyes of a stranger
Look at me boldly
From a future century,
And he will give me, a fleeing shade,
An armful of wet lilac
As this storm passes.

These passages relating to the 'Guest from the Future' were added at a relatively late stage in the history of the composition of *Poem Without a Hero*. The 'lyrical theme' as such, however, existed from a much earlier point: in the 'lyric digression' of chapter three of 'Nineteen-Thirteen'. Here too the redeeming presence of the beloved is associated with disaster and with inaccessibility. In chapter three, the succession of ominous images which has already been discussed is followed by a short paean to Tsarskoe Selo which recalls several expressions from Pushkin's elegies to the town, referring to waterfalls, gardens and the Muses. The passage concludes by confirming the importance of Tsarskoe Selo for the Author and stressing the association between it and a specific proponent of the lost ideal:

Razve ty mne ne skazhesh´ snova
Pobedivshee smert´ slovo
I razgadku zhizni moei?
(S1, 287)

Won't you say to me again
The word which overcomes death
And explain to me the purpose of my life?

In her prose notes on the poem Akhmatova linked this passage with Nedobrovo, emphasising the importance his friendship continued to have for her throughout her life: 'I only allowed you into the lyric digression, you to whom ¾ of the poem belongs, just as I am ¾ made up of you'.[39] The peculiar concentration of Pushkin references associated with chapter three of 'Nineteen-Thirteen' also serves to connect this passage with Nedobrovo, who was well known for his absorption with the Russian poetry of the early nineteenth century and for the 'aura of

39. Zhirmunskii, *Tvorchestvo Anny Akhmatovoi*, p. 43.

Pushkin interests which surrounded him'.[40] One of the most prominent allusions to Pushkin is found in the prose introduction to the chapter. This describes what follows as 'poslednee vospominanie o Tsarskom Sele' ('final memory of Tsarskoe Selo'), evoking Pushkin's two poems entitled 'Vospominaniya v Tsarskom Sele' ('Memories in Tsarskoe Selo'), both of which put forth an idyllic view of the past contrasted sharply with the present.[41] The effect of these allusions to Pushkin's elegies is to associate Nedobrovo and the vitality which he represents firmly in the past, superseded in the present by the advent of the 'True Twentieth Century'.

Early versions of 'Epilogue' bear the dedication 'Gorodu i drugu' ('To my city and my friend'), the friend here being Vladimir Garshin, whose name also preceded 'Reverse'. In redactions of the early 1940s the elegy to Leningrad in 'Epilogue' was accompanied by an unambiguous evocation of a male figure capable of giving meaning to the Author's life:

> Ty moi groznyi i moi poslednii,
> Svetlyi slushatel´ temnykh brednei,
> Upovan´e, proshchen´e, chest´.
> Predo mnoi ty gorish´, kak plamya,
> Nado mnoi ty stoish´, kak znamya,
> I tseluesh´ menya, kak lest´.
> (SP, 441)

> You my stern one and my last,
> Bright listener to my dark fantasies,
> My hope, my absolution and my honour.
> You burn before me like a flame,
> You stand over me like a banner,
> And you kiss me like flattery itself.

Yet as with the previous manifestations of the theme, the Author's friendship with the hero is doomed, in the same way that her association with Leningrad-St Petersburg is doomed. In a striking metaphor Akh-

---

40. R. D. Timenchik, 'Akhmatova i Pushkin: zametki k teme', *Pushkinskii sbornik*, no. 2, Riga, 1974, p. 44. Akhmatova is known to have re-read Nedobrovo's 1914 article on her work in 1940 at about the time *Poem Without a Hero* was begun: see Chukovskaya, *Zapiski*, vol. 1, p. 108.

41. Pushkin, *PSS*, vol. 1, pp. 83–8; vol. 3, pp. 155–6. For a more detailed discussion of the theme of Pushkin and Nedobrovo, see Wells, *Akhmatova and Pushkin*, pp. 56–9.

matova links the misfortunes of hero and heroine with the fate of the country at large:

> Nas neschastie ne minuet,
> I kukushka ne zakukuet
> V opalennykh nashikh lesakh. . .
> (S1, 297)

> Misfortune will not pass us by,
> And the cuckoo will not cry
> In our singed forests. . .

When Akhmatova fell out with Garshin in 1944 she removed the overt references to him in *Poem Without a Hero* and amended the lines reflecting her relationship with him to read:

> Ty ne pervyi i ne poslednii
> Temnyi slushatel' svetlykh brednei,
> Mne kakuyu gotovish' mest'?
> Ty ne vyp'esh', tol'ko prigubish'
> Etu gorech' iz samoi glubi –
> Eto nashei razluki vest'.
> (S1, 297)

> You are not the first and not the last
> Dark listener to my bright fantasies,
> What revenge are you planning for me?
> You will not drink up, only sip at
> This bitterness from the very depths –
> This is the news of our parting.

In the context of the 'lyrical theme' the alteration of this passage has the effect first of all of obscuring the fact that the addressee of these lines is a 'beloved' and not, for example, the tree in the Sheremetev garden that was the subject of earlier lines. Secondly, the emphasis is now placed on revenge, separation and loss rather than on the revitalising power of love, even when it is doomed, which is the central theme of the earlier version. As a result, for *Poem Without a Hero* as a whole the notion that the Author's poetry is sustained not only by a moral and political imperative in the face of the destruction of the cultural values of St Petersburg, but also by deep emotional commitment at a personal level is undermined. Part of the connection between 'Epilogue' and 'Nineteen-Thirteen' is broken and the pathos of the Author's flight in

'Epilogue' and the implicit potential for renewal correspondingly underplayed.

Pushkin, Genre and Style

Akhmatova spent much time studying Pushkin's narrative poems and comparing them with their Byronic models,[42] and when she came to write *Poem Without a Hero*, she was acutely aware of the narrative poem tradition. For Akhmatova, Pushkin's *Evgenii Onegin* was without question the culminating point of the genre, and a work whose influence subsequent writers of narrative poetry were obliged to overcome. Discussing *Poem Without a Hero* with the critic D. Khrenkov, Akhmatova commented: 'Let us recall the first Russian *poema*, *Evgenii Onegin*. Let us not be confused by the fact that its author called it a novel. . . But *Evgenii Onegin* appeared and brought down a boom-gate after it. Anyone who tried to make use of Pushkin's "discovery" met with failure.'[43] Elsewhere, Akhmatova defines *Poem Without a Hero*'s position within the narrative poem tradition: 'It is an anti-Onegin piece, and herein lies its advantage. For *Onegin* "spoiled" . . . both Lermontov's long poems and Blok's *Retribution*.'[44] '*Evgenii Onegin* killed the Russian narrative poem by its perfection, both Baratynskii's and those of other poets; it was no longer possible to write in this way.'[45] The importance of *Evgenii Onegin* as a model for Akhmatova is again suggested by a short poem of the 1960s, which compares *Onegin* to a cloud dominating the speaker of the poem and being all-sufficient to her:

> I bylo serdtsu nichego ne nado,
> Kogda pila ya etot zhguchii znoi. . .
> 'Onegina' vozdushnaya gromada,
> Kak oblako, stoyala nado mnoi.
> (S1, 212)

> And my heart needed nothing
> When I drank this burning heat. . .
> The airy mass of *Onegin*
> Stood over me like a cloud.

---

42. See III, 312–17.
43. D. Khrenkov, '"Tainy remesla" Beseda s A.A. Akhmatovoi', *Literaturnaya gazeta*, 23 November 1965, p. 3 (reprinted in II, 294–5).
44. D. E. Maksimov, 'Akhmatova o Bloke', *Zvezda*, no. 12, 1967, p. 190.
45. N. Struve, 'Vosem´ chasov s Annoi Akhmatovoi', in II, 341.

Evgenii Onegin is, of course, reflected in a wide variety of ways in *Poem Without a Hero*. Some contextual correspondences have already been mentioned alongside those with other narrative poems by Pushkin, but there are also parallels in form. Both works make use of a complex compositional framework of literary allusion, multiple layering and encoding.[46] Both are saturated with literary reference to their authors' contemporaries and predecessors. Both authors make use of autobiographical material, mythologised and encoded in their texts. Both works contain numerous thematic layers, combining a love story with a discussion of artistic method and a wide variety of other themes. Both works make extensive use of digression, missing stanzas and misleading authorial notes.[47]

In order to get away from the 'Onegin intonations' that Akhmatova saw dominating the narrative poem genre, she had recourse to several techniques. Not the least of these was in the area of verse structure. The technical accomplishment of the 'Onegin stanza' could not be challenged on its own ground. An early attempt by Akhmatova to write a narrative poem in the Pushkin tradition, 'Russkii Trianon' (S1, 171–2), was abandoned precisely because it did not succeed in escaping the tradition.[48] Blok's attempt to capture the spirit of his age in *Vozmezdie (Retribution)* is hampered by a reliance on Pushkinian iambic tetrameter, incorporating, as in Pushkin, ironic and punning rhymes. Together with a significant amount of direct reference to Pushkin, and a degree of stylistic imitation of *The Bronze Horseman* and *Evgenii Onegin*, this feature tends to root the work in the nineteenth-century past, rather than in the present.[49] Akhmatova avoids this, in the same way that she considered Nekrasov, Mayakovskii and Blok in *Dvenadtsat' (The Twelve)* to have avoided the same issue,[50] and in spite of her own frequent allusion to Pushkin, through innovation in form.

In general, the strophic structure of Akhmatova's verse is conservative, being based on the quatrain. In *Poem Without a Hero*, however,

46. Tsiv'yan, 'Zametki k deshirovke "Poemy bez geroya"', pp. 273–4.
47. See L. L. Saulenko, 'Pushkinskaya traditsiya v "Poeme bez geroya" Anny Akhmatovoi', *Voprosy russkoi literatury* (L'vov), vol. 36, no. 2, 1980, pp. 42–50; Yu. N. Chumakov, 'Ob avtorskikh primechaniyakh k "Evgeniyu Oneginu"', *Boldinskie chteniya*, Gor'kii, 1976, pp. 58–72.
48. Zhirmunskii, *Tvorchestvo Anny Akhmatovoi*, p. 132; Akhmatova, 'Avtobiograficheskaya proza', p. 8.
49. F. D. Reeve, *Aleksandr Blok: Between Image and Idea*, New York, 1962, pp. 193–4. For a discussion of the moral polemic with *Vozmezdie* in *Poema bez geroya* as well as formal differences between the two works, see S. Driver, 'Axmatova's *Poèma bez geroja* and Blok's *Vozmezdie*', in W. N. Vickery (ed.), *Aleksandr Blok Centenary Conference*, Columbus, Ohio, 1984, pp. 89–99.
50. Khrenkov in II, 295.

she moulds the three-stress dol´nik into a new type of strophe. This has much in common with the 'step' format used by Mayakovskii and other Futurists. In Akhmatova this device is not used so much as a mark of punctuation, as it is in Mayakovskii's declamatory verse, as to produce a form midway between stanzaic narrative and continuous verse.[51] This 'Akhmatova stanza' is an open form, capable of indefinite extension. Because of the simple rhyme scheme – each strophe has two or more rhymed lines, and the strophes are linked by rhyming end lines – each forms a unit in which an idea can be treated at whatever length it requires, and new ideas added at any point without disturbing the verse structure. The technique of rhyming the last lines of the strophes gives the verse a forward movement which is increased by the step format. The system brings with it considerable flexibility, being used with some strictness in 'Reverse', where the stanzas are uniform and numbered, as Akhmatova puts forward a supposedly reasoned analysis of the first part of *Poem Without a Hero*. In 'Nineteen-Thirteen', on the other hand, the strophic structure is frequently interrupted or broken and the strophe length varies from three to six lines in conformity with the prevailing spirit of Carnival.[52]

Another important way in which Akhmatova distances *Poem Without a Hero* from *Evgenii Onegin* is, paradoxically, the manner in which she refers to it. Blok's *Retribution* suffers from taking Pushkin's narrative poem style too deliberately and exclusively as a model. Akhmatova avoids this pitfall of exclusivity, as has been suggested, by drawing on several traditions at once. Alongside the Pushkinian narrative poem 'line' in *Poem Without a Hero*, there is much reference to Symbolist and Acmeist authors, to the traditions of the theatre and folk ritual, and to the works of Akhmatova herself. The presence of numerous 'lines' allows Akhmatova to treat each of them with some irony, and to stand back from each of them in turn. An example of this can be seen in one function of the epigraph 'S Tat´yanoi nam ne vorozhit´. . .' ('We shall not tell fortunes with Tat´yana'). As well as evoking Tat´yana's fear at the thought of the fortune-telling ritual, Akhmatova offers a mild parody of Pushkin's method in *Evgenii Onegin*. Just as Pushkin denies that he intends to describe a fortune-telling vision, and then immediately relates Tat´yana's dream, which is in effect precisely such a vision, Akhmatova,

51. On one level *Poem Without a Hero* conducts a dialogue with Mayakovskii. See A. Subbotin, *Gorizonty poezii*, Sverdlovsk, 1984, pp. 238–54, and 'Mayakovskii i Akhmatova', *Ural*, no. 6, 1983, pp. 177–84.

52. As T. V. Tsiv´yan has noted, the existence of numerous variant forms of *Poem Without a Hero* serves a similar function. See T. V. Tsiv´yan, '"Poema bez geroya": Eshche raz o mnogovariantnosti', in Dedyulin and Superfin, *Akhmatovskii sbornik*, p. 125.

through the epigraph, denies that she is going to describe the fortune-telling process, and then begins by doing precisely that, giving an account of the narrator sitting up alone on New Year's Eve between two candles in a mirror-filled room. Similarly, although the mystifying authorial notes to *Poem Without a Hero* are clearly modelled on Pushkin's notes to *Evgenii Onegin*, they also serve to parody it. When Akhmatova cites Pushkin's example as a justification for leaving blank stanzas in 'Reverse', and produces a similar statement by Pushkin appealing to the authority of Byron for the same practice (S1, 300), the overstatement of the case has a distinctly ironic effect.

Perhaps the most far-reaching challenge presented by *Poem Without a Hero* to the tradition of the narrative poem and of *Evgenii Onegin* lies in its attitude to time and narrative. Notwithstanding the complexities of its structure and the numerous digressions that it contains, *Evgenii Onegin* is dominated by a single linear plot, following the fortunes of a single hero. *Poem Without a Hero* cannot be reduced in any sense to such a simplistic formula. Its three sections do not contribute to a common plot on a narrative level. 'Reverse', indeed, in terms of the temporal progression of a story, consists entirely of authorial digression. Even 'Nineteen-Thirteen', the most obviously narrative section of *Poem Without a Hero*, does not make use of a linear plot construction. Furthermore, the time scales of the three sections of *Poem Without a Hero* are all distinct. In terms of narrative structure, Akhmatova's poem is in many ways closer to a lyric sequence than a narrative poem.

The title of *Poem Without a Hero*, of course, states that there is no hero. This in itself represents a challenge to the narrative poem—*Onegin* tradition. The only figure that remains constant throughout *Poem Without a Hero* is the authorial 'I' of the narrator, although even this divides into two at one point where the author comes face to face with her former self. This feature too relates *Poem Without a Hero* more nearly to a lyric tradition than a narrative one. It has been suggested that the role of 'hero' is taken over by a sort of collective human consciousness.[53] Certainly, ideas are split between several figures, which are each other's doubles. In 'Epilogue' Akhmatova's perspective gradually widens as she addresses first a tree outside the Sheremetev Palace, then the city of Leningrad, then her fellow exiles at home and abroad, concluding with a conventional symbol: the personification of Russia leading the path into Siberia, and at the same time thirsting for revenge. This conception of the hero, however, is equally novel in terms of the traditional narrative poem.

---

53. Pavlovskii, for example, suggests this in his discussion of *Poem Without a Hero* as a 'Poema sovesti': Pavlovskii, *Anna Akhmatova*, pp. 156, 161ff.

Yet for all its looseness of structure and its conscious rejection of the usual conventions of narrative verse, *Poem Without a Hero* remains more than simply a collection of lyric fragments. The underlying thematic unity provided by its insistent development of the political, metapoetic and lyrical themes together with the consistency attained by the use of its distinctive strophic form give it a forward momentum which approaches quite closely to narrative. The work may not exactly be a narrative poem, but it is certainly a lyric narrative.

The narrative element, however, while undeniably present, is often obscured by the very proliferation of material which is intended to support it and by the necessary and deliberate obliqueness of Akhmatova's approach. Unity is not promoted either by the length of time over which *Poem Without a Hero* was written or by the changes in Akhmatova's conception of it which took place in the course of its composition. This would matter little if the individual parts of the poem were self-sufficient like the poems of the early books or even of *Requiem*. But with *Poem Without a Hero* this is not the case. The individual sections and subsections are bound together by a structure of titles, epigraphs and introductions which demand that the work be considered as a whole. It is, as I have shown, possible to do this, but it seems there will always be elements that do not fit easily into any interpretative schema. If this is a weakness, however, it is also a strength, for alongside its eloquent indictment of Stalinism and its memorialisation of Stalin's victims, alongside its examination of the processes of writing and its assertion of the redemptive power of both cultural and emotional commitment, *Poem Without a Hero* is permeated by a deep sense of mystery. The intriguing complexity of its construction and the challenge of its intertextuality thus ensure that its messages will continue to be explored profitably by future generations of readers.

–6–

1946 and *Prologue*

During the war years, Akhmatova wrote a number of broadly program-matic pieces on patriotic themes, and also a group of poems relating to her sojourn in Central Asia. On the whole these are not among her best or most significant works, and, compared with much of her other poetry, seem one dimensional, lacking its pervasive intertextuality. Yet they are not without merits of their own and their unembellished expression of both hope and anxiety captured a major note of wartime thinking. Poems such as 'Muzhestvo' ('Courage'), published in *Pravda* in 1942, both caught the public eye and allowed the government to claim Akh-matova as a Soviet poet:

> My znaem, chto nyne lezhit na vesakh
> I chto sovershaetsya nyne.
> Chas muzhestva probil na nashikh chasakh.
> I muzhestvo nas ne pokinet.
>
> (S1, 199)

> We know what is hanging in the balance
> And what is now taking place.
> The hour of courage has struck on our clocks.
> And courage will not desert us.[1]

The confidence of Akhmatova's wartime writing was to some extent carried forward into her poems composed in the years immediately fol-lowing the war, notably for example in the love cycle 'Cinque' (S1, 219–20), which will be discussed in the next chapter. But whatever new directions Akhmatova's verse may have been heading in by the begin-ning of 1946, its development was dealt a serious blow by the Central Committee resolution against her of August that year. Any place she

---

1. A. Naiman, 'Uroki poeta', *Literaturnaya gazeta*, 14 June 1989, p. 8, suggests that alongside the patriotic theme this poem points to the courage required of the poet in Stalin's Russia.

might have won in Soviet literature was lost and her official status returned to what it had been in the 1930s.

Not only was her material position once more precarious as a result of the anathemas pronounced against her, but Akhmatova also adopted similar stratagems in her writing. Relatively little appears to have survived the destruction of Akhmatova's papers which she resorted to in 1949 in the hope that the NKVD would thereby be deprived of material it could use against her recently re-arrested son. There is, however, a small number of short poems which constitute a direct response to the Zhdanov resolution and the isolation which it produced. In 'Vse ushli i nikto ne vernulsya' ('Everyone left and no one has returned', III, 72–3), for example, Akhmatova catalogues the misfortunes which have befallen her over twenty years and reflects that for reasons she finds difficult to explain her life has nevertheless been spared. She has been allowed a licence to speak similar to that of the 'holy fools' of the Russian middle ages:

> I do samogo kraya dovedshi,
> Pochemu-to ostavili tam –
> Budu ya gorodskoi sumasshedshei
> Po pritikhshim brodit´ ploshchadyam.

> And after taking me to the very edge,
> They for some reason left me there –
> I shall wander the silent squares
> Like the town madwoman.

The short and apparently unfinished cycle 'Cherepki' ('Potsherds', III, 73–4) repeats in miniature the central theme of *Requiem*: the grief of a mother for her son separated from her by political imprisonment. The image of the son to his mother is contrasted boldly with the role of 'vagabond, rebel, conspirator' which has been forced on him by the authorities. The voice of his mother is shown as able to reach him across the thousands of miles of separation:

> Sem´ tysyach i tri kilometra. . .
> Ne uslyshish´ kak mat´ zovet
> V groznom voe polyarnogo vetra,
> V tesnote obstupivshikh nevzgod.

Seven thousand and three kilometres. . .
Can you not hear your mother calling
In the dread howling of the polar wind,
Hemmed in by adversity.

There is, in addition, a note of guilt, a feeling that she is herself
responsible in some way for the misfortune that has befallen both herself and her son, that she has somehow mismanaged the political
situation:

Komu i kogda govorila,
Zachem ot lyudei ne tayu,
Chto katorga syna sgnoila,
Chto Muzu zasekli moyu.
Ya vsekh na zemle vinovatei
Kto byl i kto budet, kto est',
I mne v sumasshedshei palate
Valyat'sya – velikaya chest'.

To whom and when have I said
Why I do not hide from people,
That hard labour has left my son to rot,
That my Muse has been flogged to death.
I am more guilty than anyone on earth
In past or present or future,
And to lie about in a madhouse
Would be a great honour for me.

As in the 1930s, the scope for direct artistic reflections of the political situation was limited, and Akhmatova again had recourse to the
strategies of Aesopian writing. An important vehicle for the expression
of Akhmatova's ideas at this time was her writing on Pushkin. Although
Akhmatova worked on several projects in the immediate post-war
period, the only one which both survived the burning of her papers in
1949 and saw publication in her lifetime was her essay on *Kamennyi
gost'* (*The Stone Guest*), Pushkin's reworking of the story of Don Juan.
This essay was completed in the spring of 1947 and read privately to
groups of Pushkin scholars in both Leningrad and Moscow. It was sub-
mitted to the journal *Zvezda* the same year, though it was not in fact
published for over a decade.[2] Although Akhmatova made numerous
revisions when preparing her essay for the press in 1958 (S2, 382), it is

2. A. Akhmatova, '"Kamennyi gost'" Pushkina', *Pushkin: Issledovaniya i mat-
erialy*, vol. 2, Moscow, 1958, pp. 171–86.

safe to assume that these did not substantially affect its arguments, and that the printed version is in all essential respects equivalent to the manuscript of 1947.

Akhmatova's essay on *The Stone Guest* is, of course, a valid and useful contribution to Pushkin studies. It examines what she calls the 'lyric basis' ('liricheskoe nachalo') of Pushkin's play and focuses particularly on the way Pushkin has made changes to the traditional treatment of the Don Juan theme in accordance with the concerns which dominated his own life in 1830, the time the play was written. The figure of Don Juan thus comes closely to resemble Pushkin himself: he is a poet, an aristocrat of ancient lineage; he has been banished from the capital city, to which he has returned illegally. The action has been transferred from Seville to Madrid in order to make this last point clearer, and the situation reflects Pushkin's own exile from St Petersburg to his country estate at Boldino and his desire to return to the capital. The character and function of the Commendatore have also been changed. He is now Juan's equal, socially and in age, and is the husband, not the father, of Donna Anna. At the end of the play he does not call upon Juan to repent, for in Akhmatova's reading Juan has already done so and found genuine happiness in a newly inspired love for Donna Anna.

A large part of the Commendatore's motive in bringing about Juan's downfall is jealousy from beyond the grave, and the latter's situation is tragic because it is precisely because of his redemption that he is afraid at the moment of his destruction. Akhmatova links this fear of the loss of happiness – a fear which Juan had not experienced in his duels with the Commendatore or with Don Carlos, or at the time the statue accepted his invitation in the graveyard – with Pushkin's thoughts immediately preceding his marriage: would Natal´ya Nikolaevna, the society beauty, so many years his junior, return his affections unreservedly and remain true to him even after his death? Akhmatova concludes that the themes of revenge and of faithfulness beyond the grave sound equally loudly in *The Stone Guest* (S2, 84), and, as she puts it in her notes for a revised version of her article in the late 1950s, 'Pushkin as it were divides himself between the Commendatore and Juan' (S2, 133).

Akhmatova supports her arguments meticulously by detailed reference to the text of *The Stone Guest*, by comparisons with other works written by Pushkin at around the same time and by quotation from Pushkin's letters. Yet her essay can easily be read in terms not of Pushkin's biography, but her own. Stephanie Sandler has written of Akhmatova's article as a lyrical reassessment of her life and work prompted by the Zhdanov resolution.[3] In the light of the techniques used in Akhmatova's poems of the 1930s, however, it is possible to go further and to see Akhmatova's essay as also containing a number of deliberately encoded statements relating to her predicament.

At the very beginning of her essay, Akhmatova notes the change which had taken place in Pushkin's relationship with his readers between the romantic works of his youth and the more reflective, problematic writing of his maturity. 'All Pushkin's contemporaries', she writes, 'ecstatically recognised themselves in *The Prisoner of the Caucasus*, but who would agree to recognise themselves in Evgenii from *The Bronze Horseman*?' (S2, 72). Akhmatova suggests that the process of a poet outgrowing his or her readers is a common one, and refers to the draft of Pushkin's unfinished article on Baratynskii, where he notes the same process taking place with regard to the latter. It is difficult to believe that Akhmatova did not intend here an ironic allusion to the change in her own relationship to her readers that was brought about in 1946, and to Zhdanov's comments that the Soviet reader had no more use for her writing, which had, he claimed, remained firmly entrenched in the past: 'What is there in common between this poetry and the interests of our people, our government? Absolutely nothing.'[4]

If, in writing *The Stone Guest*, Pushkin 'punishes himself – himself as young, careless and sinning' (S2, 84), Akhmatova's essay is deeply aware of the parallel with developments in her own poetry and poetic image. As has already been noted, Akhmatova's poetry from the late 1920s onwards and particularly *Poem Without a Hero* shows a strong theme of guilt about the past and the responsibility of Akhmatova's generation for the excesses of revolutionary terror and Stalinism. Linking the Author in *Poem Without a Hero* with Don Juan, Rosslyn concludes: 'The traditional characters of the Don Juan myth are internalised and, within one single character, play out a drama in which the unthinking immorality of youth is severely condemned by maturity, which consciously accepts the retribution meted out to it, as a means of purgation and atonement.'[5] By 1946, however, Akhmatova's poetry had already begun to radiate a new self-confidence as a result of the public recognition of her work during the war years, and it is perhaps not fanciful to suggest that she saw Zhdanov's condemnation of her on the basis of a partial reading of her early work, his characterisation of her poetic persona as a 'harlot-nun whose sin is mixed with prayer',[6] as the

3. S. Sandler, 'The Stone Guest: Akhmatova, Pushkin and Don Juan', *Stanford Slavic Studies*, vol. 4, no. 2, 1992, pp. 40–1.

4. Quoted in Haight, *Anna Akhmatova*, p. 145.

5. Rosslyn, 'Don Juan Feminised', p. 118.

6. Quoted in Haight, *Anna Akhmatova*, p. 144.

tragic legacy of a past which had already been redeemed just as in her reading Don Juan had been redeemed by his love for Donna Anna at the moment of his end in *The Stone Guest*.

Yet if Akhmatova casts herself as Don Juan in her essay on *The Stone Guest*, she also projects on to him the image of Gumilev. As Sandler has noted, Gumilev fits the role of Don Juan in terms of both his biography and his self-image in his poetry.[7] Akhmatova also confirms this identification by means of a 'shadow portrait'. Before Pushkin, she writes, 'So far as I know, it had not occurred to anyone to make Don Juan a poet.' However, Gumilev in fact had done precisely this. Within the terms of his aesthetics the lyric speaker of the sonnet 'Don Zhaun' ('Don Juan') and the protagonist of 'Pyatistopnye yamby' ('Five-Foot Iambics'), who compares one side of his nature with Don Juan, may both be identified with the hero-poet who is the principal figure in the majority of Gumilev's poems.[8] Gumilev's longest interpretation of the Don Juan legend, *Don Zhuan v Egipte* (*Don Juan in Egypt*), has often attracted comments on the highly poetical nature of Juan's speech, particularly when contrasted with that of the more prosaic Leporello.[9] The punishment of Don Juan-Akhmatova is thus made, as elsewhere in Akhmatova's writing, to apply to her generation as a whole.[10]

Gumilev is an important presence behind another of Akhmatova's essays, 'Pushkin i nevskoe vzmor´e' ('Pushkin and the Neva Coastline'), which although the surviving typescripts bear the date 1963, appears also to have its origins around 1946 or 1947. In 1965, Akhmatova claimed that she had been working on the topic for nearly twenty years (S2, 238), and an early date is also suggested by parallels in imagery with the 1945 poem, 'Est´ tri epokhi u vospominanii' ('Memories have three epochs'), which covers related thematic ground.[11] In her article Akhmatova links the descriptions of desolate St Petersburg coastlines which are found in several of Pushkin's works with the remote island of Golodai, believed to be the burial site of those Decembrists who were executed in the wake of the failed coup of 1825. She suggests

7. Sandler, 'The Stone Guest', pp. 38–40.
8. Gumilev, *Stikhotvoreniya i poemy*, pp. 143, 220–2.
9. See R. Karpiak, 'The Sequels to Pushkin's *Kamennyi gost´*: Russian Don Juan Versions by Nikolai Gumilev and Vladimir Korvin-Piotrovskii', in S. D. Cioran, W. Smyrniw and G. Thomas (eds), *Studies in Honour of Louis Shein*, Hamilton, Ont., 1983, p. 84; V. Setchkarev, 'Gumilev – dramaturg', in Gumilev, *Sobranie sochinenii*, vol. 3, pp. viii–ix.
10. On another level, as Sandler points out, in regard to the theme of jealousy beyond the grave, Gumilev is given the role of the avenging Commendatore while Akhmatova takes that of Donna Anna. See Sandler, 'The Stone Guest', pp. 38, 41.
11. See S. Amert, 'Akhmatova's "Pushkin i nevskoe vzmor´e"', *Transactions of the Association of Russian-American Scholars in the U.S.A.*, vol. 23, 1990, pp. 200–2.

that like others at the time Pushkin was concerned to preserve their memory, and that his detailed knowledge of the landscape was due to extensive explorations which he made there in the late 1820s and early 1830s (S2, 125). She goes on to discuss the theme of burial in Pushkin more generally and to liken his concern for the dead Decembrists with Antigone attempting to honour her dead brother in spite of King Creon's orders that no funeral should be held. As we have seen, reference to the Decembrists in Akhmatova's writing often points to a hidden bio-political theme, and behind the overt level of discourse she is referring here to her own fruitless search over the island of Golodai for the grave of Gumilev in order to accord it the obsequies which had similarly been denied him by the Soviet authorities.[12]

Another vehicle for the expression of politically sensitive views was, ironically, the superficially loyal Soviet verse which Akhmatova published in 1950 in an attempt to appease the authorities with regard to the fate of her son. The poems in question comprise the cycle 'Slava miru' ('In Praise of Peace'), which was published over three issues of *Ogonek* in 1950, and two other poems, 'Govoryat deti' ('The Children Speak') and 'Primorskii Park Pobedy' ('Coastal Victory Park'), which were not published until 1954, but which were included in the manuscript of a small collection of verse with the title *Slava miru! (In Praise of Peace!)*. This collection was offered to the publishing house of the Writers' Union in 1950, but the project came to nothing.[13] In later years Akhmatova did not admit these poems as belonging properly to the corpus of her poetry, and even attempted to erase those of them that were printed in her 1958 collection from copies which she presented to her friends.[14] Criticism too has until recently also ignored them beyond briefly noting the circumstances under which they were written and commenting on their low technical standard.[15] However, it is now becoming clear that the poems are not quite so straightforward as they appear. The eulogy of Stalin, particularly in the book version of the poems, reaches the point of the grotesque in lines such as:

Legenda govorit o mudrom cheloveke,
Kto kazhdogo iz nas ot strashnoi smerti spas.[16]

---

12. See N. Ya. Mandel´shtam, *Vtoraya kniga*, 4th edn, Paris, 1987, p. 164. Gumilev's grave was later located elsewhere.

13. For a discussion of the background and fate of this volume see K2, 326–31. *In Praise of Peace!* also included some poems of the war years and a small number of translations.

14. K2, 332.

15. E.g. II, 393–4.

16. II, 50; cf. K2, 52, 328.

Legend speaks of a wise man,
Who saved each of us from a terrible death.

As Amert has suggested, the technical shortcomings of the verse structure, so different from Akhmatova's usual accomplishment, undermine
the optimism of the words, and thus constitute a form of resistance.[17]

In his discussion of the editorial history of Akhmatova's 1950 book
manuscript, Kralin has put forward the view that fear of Akhmatova's
Aesopian language contributed substantially to the editors' unwilling-
ness to publish. Thus the concluding lines of 'Gde aromatom veyali
mussony' ('Where monsoons wafted their aroma'):

Eshche vopyat o pravote svoei, –
Ubiitsy i muchiteli detei.

(II, 154)

The murderers and torturers of children
Still sing of their innocence

which are (rather ambiguously) directed at the side opposing the Soviet
Union in the Korean War, suggest rather, for the reader of *Requiem* and
Akhmatova's other poems of the 1930s, the figures of Stalin and his
accomplices. Moreover, the Mayakovskii epigraph with which Akhmatova prefaced this poem, although at first sight seeming to appeal to the
impeccable authority of the prototypical Soviet poet, in fact has quite
unexpected connotations. As Amert has noted, the line 'Akh, zakroite,
zakroite glaza gazet!..' ('Oh, cover, cover the eyes of the newspapers!..') is taken from a 1914 anti-war poem by Mayakovskii in
which the patriotic optimism of the newspapers is contrasted with the
private grief of a woman whose son is killed in the fighting. The implication is that in Akhmatova's poem too the public rhetoric conceals an
inner suffering.[18]

Another poem, 'Coastal Victory Park' (K2, 60–1), returns to the
thematics of Akhmatova's essay on 'Pushkin and the Neva Coastline'.
In describing the construction of the park on one of the islands in the
Neva delta as a memorial to the victory of the Second World War,

---

17. S. Amert, '"*Bol'shim Maiakovskim putem*": Akhmatova and the *Kazennyi
gimn*', in Rosslyn, *The Speech of Unknown Eyes*, vol. 2, pp. 260–1.
18. Ibid., pp. 261–3.

Akhmatova recalls also the landscape of Golodai:

Eshche nedavno ploskaya kosa,
chernevshaya unylo v nevskoi del´te,
kak pri Petre, byla pokryta mkhom
i ledyanoyu penoyu omyta.

Only recently this low headland,
Extending, dark and cheerless, into the Neva delta,
Was covered in moss as in the days of Peter,
And washed with icy foam.

As Shigeki Kaji has suggested, the allusion here to those works of Pushkin which Akhmatova notes in her essay as containing a memorial of the Decembrists implies a statement of her own concern for the proper burial of Gumilev.[19] The theme of triumph over nature, manifested in the planting of trees by the population in order to establish the park, thus becomes a symbolic expression of hope in the future of Russia, not so much in terms of Stalinist 'progress', as in the context of a popular will to recognise the injustices of the past and to build a more humane society in the future.

A similar faith can be seen in 'V pionerlagere' ('In a Pioneer Camp', S1, 332), also written in 1950. On the surface this is a propagandistic hymn of praise to the promise of the new generation represented by a group of Pioneers at Pavlovsk. However, the epigraph which was added for republication of the poem in Akhmatova's 1961 collection adds a further dimension. It is taken from Pushkin's elegy '. . .vnov´ ya posetil' ('. . .again I have visited'), which describes the speaker's visit to a former place of exile, stresses the changes wrought by time and concludes with a confident expression of trust that the younger generation will remember the past, and specifically not forget the author of the poem.[20] The lines chosen by Akhmatova – 'Zdravstvui, plemya / Mladoe, neznakomoe!' ('Greetings, young, unknown breed') – refer to a group of trees which has grown up since the speaker's youth in Pushkin's poem. Akhmatova maintains this association between the new generation and young trees in her own poem: 'plyasali deti / Pod legkoi setkoi molodykh vetvei' ('the children danced under the light network of the young branches'). The parallel suggests a concern not mentioned explicitly in Akhmatova's poem with the *past* of Akhmatova and her contemporaries, which she hopes will not be forgotten. The particular

19. S. Kaji, 'O slavoslovii Anny Akhmatovoi', *Japanese Slavic and East European Studies*, vol. 12, 1991, 45–60.
20. Pushkin, *PSS*, vol. 3, pp. 345–6.

setting that Akhmatova chooses for her poem, Pavlovsk, like Tsarskoe Selo long associated with poetic achievement, hints that she is perhaps also prophesying a regeneration of genuine poetic sensibility.

Prologue

Once Akhmatova had declared her *Poem Without a Hero* complete in 1962 she felt the need for another major project to replace it, and returned to the theme of the persecution of the writer by the state which had been the subject of the play *Enuma Elish* written in the 1940s in Tashkent. The original version of this work had been destroyed after Akhmatova's return to Leningrad, but now she sought to reconstruct it, and in doing so inevitably incorporated into it her experience of the 1946 Central Committee resolution against her. Analysis of the play is hindered by the fact that it remained unfinished and indeed fragmentary at Akhmatova's death. The recent reconstruction by Mikhail Kralin nevertheless allows at least a tentative reading of the work which consumed most of her energies in her final years.[21]

Akhmatova left a very brief note on the structure and composition of the first, Tashkent, version of her play: 'The play *Enuma Elish*, consisting of three parts: 1) On the staircase, 2) Prologue, 3) Under the staircase. Written in Tashkent after the typhus (1942), finished at Easter 1943' (K2, 385). Akhmatova read the work to a number of people in Tashkent, but the only surviving account of it appears to be that of Nadezhda Mandelstam, who states that the play was also staged informally with Akhmatova herself playing the part of the heroine.[22] Mandelstam summarises the theme of the play as the trial before a writers' tribunal of the heroine, who is then sent straight to prison.[23] The heroine is summoned before a body of literary bureaucrats in the middle of the night and appears in her nightgown. Before the trial, writers are seen agitating to attend in order to add their own voice of condemnation to that of the judges. At the trial itself, the heroine is quite ignorant of the nature of the charges against her and is seen to represent a totally different world from that of her accusers. She goes off calmly to prison where she recites poetry prophesying the preservation of humane values while the chorus of writers continues to utter strings of propagandistic clichés.

Two important themes stand out in Mandelstam's account. First the evocation in the character of the heroine of the sense of hallucination which she sees as the experience of many in Stalin's Russia, and sec-

---

21. See K2, 259–312.
22. Mandel'shtam, *Vtoraya kniga*, pp. 395–401.
23. Ibid., p. 397.

ondly the sharpness of the satirical edge. Mandelstam compares the work with the attacks on government bureaucracy contained in the plays of the nineteenth-century dramatist Aleksandr Sukhovo-Kobylin, and notes particularly Akhmatova's fine ear for the empty phrases of official speech.

Mandelstam felt, however, that the 1960s version of *Prologue* (as *Enuma Elish* came increasingly to be called) was a betrayal of the work as it had existed in Tashkent. It seems unlikely, though, that she can have been fully acquainted with the drafts of the new play, and by her own admission she did not make the attempt to come to terms with Akhmatova's new conception of it.[24] Moreover, the Tashkent version as she describes it appears to correspond only to the third and final part of Akhmatova's later conception.

The surviving fragments of the 1960s version of the play indicate that it had become much broader in scope than its Tashkent antecedent. As Kralin suggests, it was perhaps this very expansion of thematic material which was the major factor hindering completion of the work. Whereas the relatively free structure of *Poem Without a Hero* had been able to accommodate new characters and new themes almost seamlessly, it was a different matter with the stricter form of the drama, and with the greater need for explicit referentiality implied by the medium of prose.[25] It is not surprising that Akhmatova seems to have given more and more attention to the section of the drama that was written in verse, that is the scenes from the play *Prologue, or Dream Within a Dream* purportedly written by the unknown heroine. It is significant too that she came increasingly to refer to the work as a whole by this name.

The only fully coherent extant section of the new drama is the third part, the trial of the heroine, and it is instructive to compare it with Mandelstam's account of the earlier version. The basic situation is the same. The heroine, X ('Iks'), appears in her night-clothes and in a state of somnambulistic trance before a bench of implacable judges. She responds to the list of preposterous charges with incomprehension, and is subject to the same hallucinatory abusive logic of the show trials:

— I heard her praising James Joyce. . .
— Some say she was sent here by the enemy and came down by parachute. . .
— I myself saw something falling from the sky. . .
— She crossed over the border. . . Swam over the river Pyandzh . . .

24. Ibid., pp. 407–14.
25. K2, 386–7.

— She was selling passports at the Alaisk market. . .
— She stole a submarine [to make her escape] . . .
[— Old poet: She made light signals to the Germans. X (finally unable to restrain herself): Where from?
Rival: What does it matter where from? The important thing is where to.] (K2, 268)

There are, however, two main differences between the published version of the trial scene and Mandelstam's account of the Tashkent play. In the later draft, although many of the heroine's accusers are writers, the impetus for her prosecution is shown to come from the state. The chairman of the tribunal is identified as Comrade Zh., clearly alluding to Zhdanov. This figure is called away at the beginning of the trial by a telephone call from Moscow, from where he is presumably receiving his instructions. Other judges also represent key state institutions of social control. 'Someone in a light blue cap', who reads out the criminal charges against X, is wearing the uniform of the NKVD. A key role in the prosecution is played by the duplicitous 'Best friend in a public prosecutor's uniform'. Moreover, the explicit image of Stalin is present in the form of his portrait and as 'Someone with a Georgian accent' who is heard threatening the editor who had earlier allowed the performance of X's play. The fact that it is no longer simply a writers' group which leads the attack on X and her work makes the satirical attack on Soviet society more generally explicit.

The second major difference lies in the conclusion to the scene. Instead of continuing to assert the authority of her poetry from prison, in the printed version of the play the heroine collapses under the pressure of the allegations against her and dies. Immediately, the mob of her persecutors move on to their next project and X is forgotten. The only character who grieves over her death is a blind beggar whom she had helped earlier in the play, and even he is unable to remember her name.

The third part of *Enuma Elish*, the scene of the trial, deals with the consequences of literary creativity in a totalitarian society. The first part, although very little of it has survived, appears to have been concerned with the processes by which literature was written and accepted for publication. The lengthy stage direction which begins Kralin's reconstruction mentions some of the literary bureaucrats who reappear in part three, the Secretary of Unhuman Beauty, for example. The act concludes with the arrival of a telegram from Moscow announcing that the heroine's play, *Prologue*, has been accepted for production. The only dialogue extant from the first act consists of the heroine asking the blind beggar Vasya to tell her fortune. His answer is gnomic and full of

Anna Akhmatova

foreboding:

> Ne beri sama sebya za ruku,
> Ne vedi sama sebya za reku,
> Na sebya pal´tsem ne pokazyvai,
> Pro sebya skazku ne rasskazyvai. . .
> Idesh´, idesh´ i spotknesh´sya.
>
> (K2, 260)

> Do not take yourself by the hand,
> Do not lead yourself across the river,
> Do not point to yourself with a finger,
> Do not tell about yourself. . .
> You keep on going and you'll stumble. . .

The first act is followed by an interlude (or interludes) set in the wings of the theatre as *Prologue* is being played. This contains a satire on the need for constant rewriting to comply with the changing requirements of censorship. X runs in from the stage complaining that the ending is not complete, and a mysterious figure in a yashmak, who is her double, undertakes to finish it. At the same time the interlude introduces the theme of the Guest from the Future, in love with X, but separated from her by time and space, which is the principal theme of the second act and of *Prologue* itself.

Other scenes (which Kralin includes in the drafts of Act Two) are also set in the wings of the theatre as *Prologue* is under way. In one of them the assistant producer complains to the director that X is departing from the text. The director is at first alarmed, fearing that political comment is involved; when he is told that X is talking about love, and moreover in verse, he is mollified and, evidently ignorant of the possibilities of Aesopian language, allows the play to continue (K2, 276–7). Another scene satirises the wartime paranoia about the behaviour of foreigners:

Younger:	[. . .] And the foreigner. . .
Older (interrupting):	. . .the one with sticking plaster over his eye?
Younger:	Yes. He's in the director's office. The authorities have been notified.
Older:	I should think so. It could be a signal. There is a war on. (K2, 277)

The remains of the second act are extensive, but do not form an easily intelligible whole. It is not, for example, easy to determine how far the second act was intended to consist of X's play and how far it comprised X's commentary on it. The matter is not rendered any more

–142–

straightforward by the fact that X plays the central character in her own drama. Nevertheless, several thematic strands present themselves as important.

First, the political theme of Act Three is unambiguously fore-shadowed in X's conversations with the Guest from the Future, who is destined to bring about her downfall. Thus in one fragment the agent of her destruction is spelled out by name:

On. Ty znaesh', chto zhdet tebya?
Ona. Zhdet, zhdet. . . Zhdanov. (K2, 279)

He: Do you know what is awaiting you?
She: What awaits me . . . is . . . Zhdanov.

The majority of the fragments consist of dialogue between X and two related characters from the future, who appear to her in a dream: the Guest from the Future and the Voice. Although the main topic of their discussion is the tragic denouement of Act Three, this is expanded on to a far broader metaphysical level.

It is this blurring of the political satire to which Mandelstam objects so strongly in her comments on the 1960s version of *Prologue*. According-ing to her the tragedy of the earlier version lay 'in such ordinary day-to-day matters as the persecution of people for what they thought and said, their use of two different languages, the mutual estrangement and lack of understanding between them'.[26] Mandelstam complains that the focus of the new version of the play has shifted, and that the main con-cern has become the separation of two lovers in time. The question revolves around the precise roles played by the Guest from the Future and the Voice. Although these appear to be different names for the same character their parts in the remaining fragments of the play do not wholly coincide.

The Guest from the Future who appears in *Prologue* is the same fig-ure who is the addressee of the third dedication to *Poem Without a Hero*, and who is the subject of the italicised passage in the description of the masquerade in chapter one of 'Nineteen-Thirteen'. He appears also in the two related cycles of poems 'Cinque' and 'Shipovnik tsvetet' ('The Wild Rose Blooms'). The textual and conceptual interrelations between all these works are unmistakable. For example, the Bach Chaconne which heralds the arrival of the Guest from the Future in *Prologue* (K2, 263) is also connected with him in *Poem Without a Hero* ('Polno mne ledenet' ot strakha, / Luchshe kliknu Chakonu Bakha, / A za nei voidet

26. Mandel'shtam, *Vtoraya kniga*, p. 407 (trans. Max Hayward in N. Mandelstam, *Hope Abandoned*, London, 1974, p. 409).

chelovek' ('Enough of freezing with terror, better I should call up Bach's Chaconne, and behind it someone will enter', S1, 275)), and in 'The Wild Rose Blooms' ('On byl vo vsem. . . I v bakhovskom Chakone' ('[Your arrival] was in everything. . . In the Bach Chaconne', S1, 223)). The description of the Guest's arrival in *Poem Without a Hero* and one fragment of *Prologue* are almost identical.

Poem Without a Hero:

> Gost´ iz Budushchego! – Neuzheli
> On pridet ko mne v samom dele,
> Povernuv nalevo s mosta?
>   (S1, 279)

> The Guest from the Future! – Will
> He really come to me,
> Turning left from the bridge?

Prologue:

> You will speak that word when the war is over, on Twelfth Night, seven thousand kilometres from here in the old palace – after turning left from the bridge. (K2, 280)

Another fragment prefaces the arrival of the Guest with an entire poem from the 'Cinque' cycle, 'Znaesh´ sam, chto ne stanu slavit'' ('You know yourself that I will not praise', K2, 278).

The role that the Guest from the Future plays in *Prologue* is also substantially that of the figure described in the third dedication to *Poem Without a Hero*. He is on the one hand someone with whom the heroine will enter into a deep spiritual union, who will come to her as a lover, but whose coming will have tragic and inevitable consequences. The following passage summarises the situation:

She: Shall I tell you what we shall fear when we meet?
He: Tell me.
She: Dying of tenderness for each other.
He: Yes, we feared dying of tenderness for each other. . .
She: But that is not the worst.
He: The horror that will rise up from our meeting will destroy us both.
She: No, only me. (K2, 279)

The Voice perhaps represents the Guest from the Future in more generalised, abstracted terms. He and the heroine are cast in the roles of inseparable lovers, even though their love is seen as destructive, because they share a primeval knowledge which is denied to others:

> Ottogo, chto ya delil s toboyu
> Pervozdannyi mrak. . .
> Ch'ei by ty ni delalas' zhenoyu,
> Prodolzhalas' (ya teper' ne skroyu)
> Nash prestupnyi brak.
>
> (K2, 284)

> Because I shared with you
> The primordial darkness. . .
> Whoever's wife you became
> (I will not conceal it now)
> Our criminal marriage still continued.

They are destined never to meet except in dreams, and in a sense are fatally separated from one another in time:

> No mayachit istina prostaya:
> Umer ya, a ty ne rodilas'. . .
>
> (K2, 294)

> But the simple truth looms up:
> I have died, and you are not yet born. . .

But on the other hand the couple are always together as they are continually reincarnated in different literary and historical images. The Voice notes: 'I have been with you so often. When you prayed as Margarita and danced as Salome, and deceived your husband as Emma Bovary [. . .]' (K2, 265), and elsewhere:

> Rimlyaninom, skifom, vizantiitsem
> Byl svidetel' srama tvoego.
>
> (K2, 285)

> As a Roman, as a Scythian, as a Byzantine,
> I was a witness to your shame.

On one level the Voice represents poetic inspiration which will always inevitably lead the poet into trouble. As X notes in one fragment: 'You were, are and will be the thing I most of all feared in life and without which I could not live. You were – inspiration.' The poet is unable to resist the impulse to creativity, even when she can see this creativity leading to her own destruction. The Voice also recognises this in one of the most haunting of Akhmatova's later lyrics:

> Bud´ ty trizhdy angelov prelestnei,
> Bud´ rodnoi sestroi zarechnykh iv,
> Ya ub´yu tebya svoeyu pesnei,
> Krov´ tvoyu na zemlyu ne proliv.
>
> (K2, 265)

> Even if you were three times as beautiful as angels,
> Even if you were the sister of the river willows,
> I would kill you with my singing,
> Without spilling your blood on the ground.

Whatever form *Prologue* might eventually have taken, it is difficult to see the political satire it contains as being diminished by the exchanges between X and the Guest from the Future and the Voice. On the contrary, the framework provided by Acts One and Three, and the link with *Poem Without a Hero*, have the effect of politicising the personal relationships which are explored. The fate which separates the lovers becomes a function of the historical circumstances of the Stalinist state. At the same time the political persecution of X as a writer is projected on to a broader philosophical plane by its juxtaposition with the lyric matter of Act Two. As in *Poem Without a Hero*, the political theme is strengthened by its continuation at other parallel thematic levels.

It is, of course, true that the 'lyrical theme' of *Poem Without a Hero* acquires in *Prologue* a much more forceful enunciation. The relationship between heroine and hero, so central to Akhmatova's early poetry, had been to a very large extent neglected in her political verse of the 1930s and 1940s. The fragments of *Prologue* provide a striking and clear example of how political and love themes can be combined to the enhancement of each. Akhmatova may not have succeeded in completing in *Prologue* a large-scale work of synthesis along these lines, but, as the following chapter will show, smaller-scale successes can be seen in many of her poems of the post-war and especially post-thaw period.

-7-

The Flight of Time

The particular combination of themes – political, metapoetical and lyrical – which characterises *Poem Without a Hero* and can also be seen to underlie *Prologue* is found more generally in Akhmatova's poetry of the 1950s and 1960s. As the spectre of Stalinism and war gradually recede, the political component of her writing becomes less urgent, allowing her to focus as well on questions of memory and time, of cultural continuity and the function of poetry. At the same time, the late period sees the renewal of Akhmatova's love poetry, enriched and expanded by a wealth of historical and philosophical experience.

From the point of view of form, one striking characteristic of Akhmatova's late poetry is her extensive use of the poetic cycle as a compositional device. By the 1950s this had for practical purposes taken over from the poetic book as Akhmatova's preferred means of expression. Approximately two-thirds of the poems Akhmatova published after the war are contained in cycles, varying in length from two to fourteen poems, and many of those which did not appear during her lifetime were also arranged in sequences in manuscript. It is notable that these cycles were not always stable. Akhmatova would frequently alter their composition, moving individual poems from one to another, excluding some poems and incorporating others. Thus the version of 'Secrets of the Craft' published in *Poems* (1961) contains only six poems; by *The Flight of Time* the cycle had been expanded to ten. The sequence 'Shestnadtsatyi god' ('Nineteen-Sixteen'), which appeared in *From Six Books*, was broken up into separate poems and its central portion included in *The Way of All the Earth*. There were projects to unite a series of elegiac poems to Akhmatova's contemporaries under the title 'Venok mertvym' ('A Wreath for the Dead') and to bring together poems of the 1930s as a cycle called 'Iz zavetnoi tetradi' ('From a Secret Notebook').[1]

The title that Akhmatova chose for the collection of her verse which she issued in 1965 was *The Flight of Time*. This was the only book that she published after the 1920s over which she had any real degree of

1. S1, 243–8; K1, 241–8.

editorial control, and its 471 pages present, within the constraints of the Soviet censorship, a reasonably full view of her poetry from the lyrics of the 1910s through to her work of the mid-1960s. It is reasonable to suppose therefore that the title *The Flight of Time* was chosen with some care, and to examine its significance for Akhmatova's late poetic thought in some detail.

Verheul has argued at length that the theme of time is central to Akhmatova's poetry from a very early stage.[2] If anything it achieves an even greater significance in the poetry of the late period, often being considered abstractly and with a philosophical detachment that is absent from Akhmatova's early work. The title *The Flight of Time* also has certain intertextual implications. The main reference is, of course, to Horace's ode 'Exegi monumentum' ('I have erected a monument') and to the series of Russian imitations of it, notaby those by Derzhavin and Pushkin. In Horace's poem, 'the flight of time' ('fuga temporum') is cited among a list of phenomena which will be unable to destroy the literary monument which he has created in his writing. By alluding to Horace's assertion of the durability of art Akhmatova thus also emphasises the significance of her own poetic achievement. In one short poem not published in her lifetime Akhmatova asks:

> No kto nas zashchitit ot uzhasa, kotoryi
> Byl begom vremeni kogda-to narechen?
> (S1, 211)

> But who will protect us from the horror that
> Was once called the flight of time?

Akhmatova's answer to this question is clear: the poet.

Examination of Pushkin's adaptation of Horace in his 'Ya pamyatnik vozdvig nerukotvornyi' ('I have erected a monument not made by hands') suggests some aspects of the poet's role which seem particularly apt in the context of Akhmatova's writing of the 1930s and 1940s.[3] Pushkin, for example, proclaims the poet as leader and as defender of the weak:

> v moi zhestokii vek vosslavil ya svobodu
> I milost´ k padshim prizyval.

---

2. Verheul, *The Theme of Time*.
3. Pushkin, *PSS*, vol. 3, p. 373.

in my cruel age I have praised freedom
And called for mercy to the fallen.

He emphasises the poet's independence, and stresses not only that his own poetry will survive, but that other poets will continue to write in the same tradition and that the poetry of one writer can survive in the work of another:

I slaven budu ya, dokol´ v podlunnom mire
Zhiv budet khot´ odin piit.

And I shall be praised so long as in this sublunary world
There remains alive a single poet.[4]

The Pushkin context of 'I have erected a monument', arrived at through Horace's ode, establishes Akhmatova's title *The Flight of Time* as a summary of the central content of her work and points out those themes which she particularly wished to highlight for the benefit of future generations of readers. As will become clear, the regenerative movement implied here, the confidence which Akhmatova expresses in her future readers, is an important factor in her late poetry. Even while suggesting that the past tradition is cut off, Akhmatova asserts the power of poetry to transcend the linearity of time.

Time and memory are, from one point of view, already the central themes of the cycle of *Northern Elegies*, written mostly in the 1940s. We have already seen that the first of these, 'Prehistory', looks to the age of Dostoevskii and defers to the great novelist's perspicacity as an artist and as a social commentator. The subsequent elegies show a gradual movement away from this ideal, which recedes ever further into the inaccessible past.[5]

In 'Tak vot on — tot osennii peizazh' ('There it is, that autumn landscape', S1, 256), written in Tashkent in 1942, the joy which greeted the formation of a relationship fifteen years ago is ironically contrasted with the guilt and emotional stress of the subsequent separation:

ty nebesa,
I khory zvezd, i khory vod molila
Privetsvovat´ torzhestvennuyu vstrechu
S tem, ot kogo segodnya ty ushla. . .

4. See L. L. Saulenko, 'Imya knigi (o traditsii v poetike A. Akhmatovoi)', *Voprosy russkoi literatury* (L´vov), vol. 40, no. 1, 1984, pp. 89–94; M. Sukhanova, 'Fuga temporum', *Russian Literature*, vol. 30, 1991, pp. 337–42.
5. See Verheul, *The Theme of Time*, p. 153.

You begged the heavens
And the choirs of the stars and the choirs of the waters
To greet this triumphant meeting
With the person you left today.

Two elegies of 1945 restate the same basic theme. In one of these the speaker compares herself to a river whose course has been altered:

Menya, kak reku,
Surovaya epokha povernula.
Mne podmenili zhizn'. V drugoe ruslo,
Mimo drugogo potekla ona,
I ya svoikh ne znayu beregov.
(S1, 256)

The stern era
Has changed my course as if I were a river.
My life has been replaced. It has begun to flow
In another channel, past the other,
And I no longer know my own banks.

Like the river the heroine feels no continuity with her former self, or rather with the self she would have become if fate had not intervened. Yet although the heroine is privy only to tantalising glimpses of this potential other life, the poem ends with a note of ironic acceptance as she remarks that her potential 'double' would no doubt look on her own 'real' life with envy. Acceptance is also the dominant motif of 'Memories have three epochs' (S1, 257–8), which traces the gradual process by which memories of the past lose their clarity and their relevance to the present. In the third age of memory the past has become quite foreign:

Bezhim tuda, no (kak vo sne byvaet)
Tam vse drugoe: lyudi, veshchi, steny,
I nas nikto ne znaet – my chuzhie.
My ne tuda popali. . . Bozhe moi!

We flee there, but (as happens in dreams)
Everything is different: people, things, walls,
And no one knows us – we are strangers.
We have gone to the wrong place. . . My God!

Once the shock of realising this disjunction between past and present has been faced, Akhmatova suggests, we come to a realisation that contact with the past is not only not possible, but also not especially desirable.

'Cinque'

The fatalism of the *Northern Elegies*, however, yields to an emphasis on the transcendence of time and place in Akhmatova's post-war love poetry, particularly in the three major cycles of poems 'Cinque', 'The Wild Rose Blooms' and 'Polnochnye stikhi' ('Midnight Verses'). On one level these continue the modality of Akhmatova's early love lyrics in that they are dominated by the physical absence of the figure of the beloved. At the same time, however, they preserve the memory of the beloved on a much broader and more permanent plane than in the early verse, and commemorate the lasting emotional transformation which the heroine has undergone through the experience of love.

The five poems which comprise 'Cinque' are dated between November 1945 and January 1946, and were first published not long after their composition in the journal *Leningrad* under the title 'Pyat´ stikhotvorenii iz tsikla "Lyubov´"' ('Five Poems from the "Love" cycle').[6] There are several other poems written at roughly this time on a similar theme which may originally have been intended to form part of this cycle, but it had crystallised in its final form under the title 'Cinque' as early as the 1946 *Selected Poems*. The significance of this Italian title remains unclear, though it must be assumed that it conceals some personal or literary association with the addressee of the cycle – whether, as has often been claimed, this is Isaiah Berlin, whose visits to Akhmatova occurred at around the time the poems were written,[7] or perhaps Vladimir Garshin, or perhaps even more probably a conflation of several different figures.

However this may be, the first three poems of 'Cinque' put forward what is, for Akhmatova, an unexpectedly positive vision of the experience of love. The relationship between two people has placed them outside the world of ordinary human activity, as is conveyed in strikingly simple terms at the beginning of the first poem:

Kak u oblaka na krayu,
Vspominayu ya rech´ tvoyu.

---

6. *Leningrad*, nos. 3–4, 1946.
7. Haight, *Anna Akhmatova*, pp. 140–3.

A tebe ot rechi moei
Stali nochi svetlee dnei.
(S1, 219)

As if on the edge of a cloud,
I remember your speech.

And for you, my words
Made the nights brighter than day.

The imagery of light which is seen here repeats itself in later comparisons between love and dawn. But it is the power of speech, emphasised
here at the beginning of the cycle, which is the most powerful point of
contact between the lovers, and which marks a significant movement of
renewal. Thus in the second poem it is their voices alone which are still
capable of speech:

V navsegda onemevshem mire
Dva lish´ golosa: tvoi i moi.
(S1, 219)

In a world which has forever fallen silent
There are only two voices, yours and mine.

In the third, a single word from her beloved gives the heroine renewed
sources of strength.

The final two poems of the cycle, on the other hand, emphasise separation. The night-time conversations of the second poem may have
been turned to rainbows as a token of their transcendental significance,
but by the fourth it is clear that it is only tokens that remain. We are
again in the familiar territory of memory and loss. The heroine is seen
searching for a suitable memorial for 'nashei vstrechi gorchaishii den''
('the most bitter day of our meeting'). The fifth and final poem raises
the question of guilt and queries the mechanisms of fate.

This last poem ends, however, on a note which suggests that the costs
of the relationship, the pain of separation and of greater evils which are
only hinted at (but which appear in retrospect to be foreshadowing the
catastrophic events for Akhmatova of August 1946), were, after all, a
price worth paying. In spite of everything, the meeting was marked by

the light of a dawn:

> I kakoe nezrimoe zarevo
> Nas do sveta svodilo s uma?
>   (S1, 220)

> And what invisible glow
> Drove us to madness before dawn?

Because of the overwhelming nature of the experience, it cannot be totally lost. The various epigraphs which were attached to the different publications of the cycle serve to emphasise the totality of the emotional response, to underline the unity of gratification and suffering which the poems describe. The line from Annenskii which accompanies the earliest publications of 'Cinque', 'Pyat´ roz, obruchennykh steblem' ('Five roses, joined by a single stem'), makes clear that the different moods expressed in the five poems of the cycle are all parts of a single whole just as the five fingers of the woman of Annenskii's poem are inseparable from the hand to which they belong.[8] Annenskii's actually rather inept poem also considers an amatory paradox, concluding a catalogue of the addressee's charms with the contrasting jealous note:

> I mne budut snit´sya, almeya,
> Slova, chtob tebya oskorbit´.

> And in my dreams, dancing-girl,
> I will hear words to insult you with.

The quotation from Baudelaire's 'Une Martyre' ('A Martyr'), which has most consistently been attached to 'Cinque' in one form or another from the 1946 *Selected Poems* to *The Flight of Time*, documents another case in which passion is linked with destruction. The French poem, of course, describes a much more extreme situation than Akhmatova's: a sado-masochistic experiment which has led to the death of its female participant. Following a detailed description of the decapitated body and its surroundings and a speculative account of the circumstances accompanying its death, Baudelaire concludes his poem with the thought that although the woman's murderer is still alive in the world the two are, on a deeper level, permanently united because of their joint

---

8. Annenskii, *Stikhotvoreniya i tragedii*, p. 138.

complicity in the crime:

> Ton époux court le monde, et ta forme immortelle
>   Veille près de lui quand il dort;
> Autant que toi sans doute il te sera fidèle,
>   Et constant jusques à la mort.[9]

> Your husband roams the world, and your immortal form
>   Watches near him when he sleeps;
> Probably just as you are he will be faithful to you
>   And constant unto death.

Moreover, the craftsmanship of Baudelaire's writing and the fiction that he is describing in painterly terms the canvas of an old master both attest to a permanent transformation of the gruesome events into art. In choosing the last two lines quoted above for her epigraph Akhmatova reinforces the notion of the inseparability of the heroine and her beloved notwithstanding the obstacles – even to the point of death – which may be placed between them. She also asserts the power of her poetry to create a permanent record of this inseparability.

'The Wild Rose Blooms'

'Cinque' is linked in several ways to the later cycle 'The Wild Rose Blooms' (S1, 221–6). This is particularly evident from the early version of the cycle which was published in Akhmatova's 1961 *Poems* (S61, 266–72).[10] Here the cycle begins with two poems which are thematically very close to 'Cinque', and which are associated with it in some of the surviving manuscripts.[11] In the final version of 'The Wild Rose Blooms' they bear the date 1946. Entitled respectively 'Nayavu' ('Awake') and 'Vo sne' ('Asleep'), they confirm the ability of memory to overcome separation both in the waking world, where for the heroine material objects are transcendentally imbued with the presence of the beloved, and in sleep, which allows the couple to communicate through the medium of dreams. At the same time, they echo the element of foreboding with which 'Cinque' concluded, and the realisation that physical

9. C. Baudelaire, *Les Fleurs du mal*, ed. Antoine Adam, Paris, 1961, p. 131.

10. References will be given to *Stikhotvoreniya (1909–1960)*, Moscow, 1961 (S61), and to S1 as appropriate. On the textual history of the cycle see M. R. Satin, 'Akhmatova's "Shipovnik Tsvetet": A Study of Creative Method', unpublished Ph.D. thesis, University of Pennsylvania, 1977, pp. 17–22.

11. SP, 488.

separation is inevitable and irremediable is brought to the fore:

> I vremya proch´, i prostranstvo proch´. . .
> No i ty mne ne mozhesh´ pomoch´.
> (S61, 267, S1, 221)

> And time is gone, and space is gone. . .
> But even you cannot help me.

The remainder of 'The Wild Rose Blooms' contains a further elaboration and expansion of these ideas. Thus the immanent presence of the figure of the hero, notwithstanding his physical absence, is asserted in 'Son' ('Dream'):

> On byl vo vsem. . . I v bakhovskoi chakone,
> I v rozakh, chto naprasno rastsveli,
> I v derevenskom kolokol´nom zvone
> Nad chernotoi raspakhannoi zemli.
> (S61, 268, S1, 223)

> It was in everything. . . In Bach's Chaconne,
> And in the roses, which had bloomed in vain,
> And in the ringing of the village bells
> Over the blackness of the ploughed earth.

The transformation which he has effected on the life of the heroine is commemorated in 'Vospominanie' ('Memory') (i.e. 'Ty vydumal menya. Takoi na svete net' ('You invented me. There is no one like that on earth', S61, 270–1, S1, 224)): 'I ty prishel ko mne, kak by zvezdoi vedom' ('And you came to me as if brought by a star'). And the unspecified costs of the relationship are highlighted particularly in the sixth poem of the original cycle entitled, 'Liricheskoe otstuplenie' ('Lyric Digression', S61, 270), which concludes:

> I ne pervuyu vetv´ sireni,
> Ne kol´tso, ne trepet molenii –
> On pogibel´ mne prineset.

> And he will bring me
> Not the first branch of lilac,
> Not a ring, not the trembling of entreaty,
> But destruction.

This poem, in modified form, was later to become the third dedication to *Poem Without a Hero* (S1, 275–6), illustrating once more the strong thematic link which exists between all Akhmatova's late poetry and the principle of recyclisation which is central to it.

There are several ways in which 'The Wild Rose Blooms' extends the themes of 'Cinque'. Central to the later cycle is the idea of the non-meeting ('nevstrecha'). This is on one level a reflection of Akhmatova's decision not to see Isaiah Berlin when he returned to Russia briefly in 1956, the year most of the poems of the cycle were written, for fear that to do so might lead to the rearrest of her son. For all the pain which it brings with it, Akhmatova turns the 'non-meeting' into a triumph reflecting the irrelevance of actual separation. This is to give a name to the phenomenon which has already been seen in 'Cinque', and in spite of the doubts about the process that are expressed in what was the fifth poem of the original cycle – 'Tainstvennoi nevstrechi / Pustynny torzhestva' ('The celebrations over our secret non-meeting are hollow', S61, 269, S1, 222) – the act of naming gives Akhmatova's experience a tangibility that it would otherwise lack.

The power of the creative act is a theme of major importance in 'The Wild Rose Blooms'. Already in 'Cinque' Akhmatova had spoken of the 'Posvyashchenie sozhzhennoi dramy / Ot kotoroi i pepla net' ('Dedication of a burnt drama, of which not even the ashes remain') as a possible gift to her addressee. In the early version of 'The Wild Rose Blooms' this motif is repeated twice. The first occasion follows a triumphant description of the arrival of the hero in 'Dream' and suggests, paradoxically, that his coming will lead to new poetic inspiration allowing the reconstruction of the poetry Akhmatova was forced to destroy during the years of Stalinism:

> I vot pishu, kak prezhde bez pomarok,
> Moi stikhi v sozhzhennuyu tetrad´.
> (S61, 268, S1, 223)

> And now, as before, with no corrections,
> I write my poems in a burnt notebook.

This is a version of Bulgakov's famous dictum 'manuscripts do not burn', and the sentiment is confirmed in the poem 'Memory', where the hero's presence appears to contradict the fear which led to the burning of poems:

> I ty prishel ko mne, kak by zvezdoi vedom,
> Po oseni tragicheskoi stupaya,
> V tot navsegda opustoshennyi dom,
> Otkuda uneslas´ stikhov sozhzhennykh staya.
> (S61, 271, S1, 224)

And you came to me as if led by a star
Across the tragic autumn,
To that forever empty house
From which a flock of burnt verses had flown off.

The image of the 'wild rose' is used to confirm this access of creative strength. Its memorialising function is stressed in the epigraph to the cycle: 'No v pamyat' toi nevstrechi / Shipovnik posazhu' ('In memory of that non-meeting I will plant a wild rose').[12] Its significance can also be seen from the conclusion of the fourth poem of the original cycle:

Shipovnik tak blagoukhal,
Chto dazhe prevratilsya v slovo,
I vstretit' ya byla gotova
Moei sud'by devyatyi val.
            (S61, 269, S1, 223)

The fragrance of the wild rose was so strong
That it even turned into a word,
And I was ready to meet
The ninth wave of my fate.

The poetic word, as symbolised by the wild rose, is able both to replace in a sense the figure of the cycle's addressee and to serve as a source of protection against the blows dealt by historical and emotional fate.

This reading is supported by the intertextual implications of the image of the wild rose. The most immediate of these is the passage in Pushkin's *Evgenii Onegin* from which the title of Akhmatova's cycle is apparently taken. In describing the overgrown grave of the poet Vladimir Lenskii, Pushkin writes:

Tam solovei, vesny lyubovnik,
Vsyu noch' poet; tsvetet shipovnik.[13]

There the nightingale, lover of the spring,
Sings all night. The wild rose blooms.

In, for example, the Scottish ballad tradition, the dog-rose is a common symbol of regeneration, associated particularly with the graves of star-

12. This epigraph was transferred in the later redaction to one of the poems which appeared there for the first time: 'Drugaya pesenka' (S1, 222–3).
13. Pushkin, *PSS*, vol. 5, p. 142.

crossed lovers. In the context of *Evgenii Onegin*, Lenskii's grave is now forgotten by anyone except Pushkin in his role as narrator. By using the phrase 'The Wild Rose Blooms' as the title for a sequence of poems to the secret figure from whom she is separated, Akhmatova thus asserts the importance of remembering and stresses the regenerative force that memory may contain.

The later version of 'The Wild Rose Blooms', as published in *The Flight of Time* and adopted as definitive in subsequent editions of Akhmatova's poetry, is marked by a clearer statement of these themes and by a broader set of intertextual references which serve to confirm them and set them in a wider cultural context. One effect of the various additions and changes which Akhmatova made is to shift the emphasis of the cycle away from the personal emotional experience of the heroine and the way in which her life has been transformed by contact – or indeed non-meeting – with the addressee. The expanded cycle focuses much more on the role played by poetry in the preservation of personal and collective memory.

Most prominently, the revised cycle insists on the motif of the burnt notebook from the very beginning by incorporating it into a subtitle. The work is now 'Shipovnik tsvetet: iz sozhzhennoi tetradi' ('The Wild Rose Blooms: From a Burnt Notebook'). The importance of this theme is reinforced in the new five-line introductory poem to the cycle which, like the opening of 'Nineteen-Thirteen', evokes a contrast between an expected festive meeting and a disconcerting and ominous reality:

> Vmesto prazdnichnogo pozdravlen´ya
> Etot veter, zhestkii i sukhoi,
> Prineset vam tol´ko zapakh tlen´ya,
> Privkus dyma i stikhotvoren´ya,
> Chto moei napisany rukoi.
>
> (S1, 221)

> Instead of a festive greeting
> This wind, cruel and dry,
> Will bring you only the smell of burning,
> An aftertaste of smoke,
> And poems written by my hand.

Poetry is clearly linked with burning here, but at the same time there is an implication that it is not to be entirely destroyed by fire: the poems are nevertheless brought to the addressee on the wind.

The poem which opens the cycle proper and is given the number 1 is entitled 'Sozhzhennaya tetrad´' ('A Burnt Notebook') and is uncompromisingly literary in its content. It refers to the burning of the notebook of poems, contrasting it with another collection, containing less sensitive material no doubt, which has succeeded in achieving publication:

> Uzhe krasuetsya na knizhnoi polke
> Tvoya blagopoluchnaya sestra,
> A nad toboyu zvezdnykh stai oskolki
> I pod toboyu ugol´ki kostra.
>
> (S1, 221)

> Your successful sister is already
> Standing prettily on the bookshelf,
> But above you are the splinters of flocks of stars,
> Below you the coals of a fire.

'A Burnt Notebook' was written in 1961 and Akhmatova presumably had in mind the slim and highly selective volume of her poems and translations which appeared in 1958.

In the lines that follow, the personification of the burnt book is expanded and rendered more concrete, as the manuscript pleads for its life and finally gives up the ghost, cursing the author who created it:

> Kak ty molila, kak ty zhit´ khotela,
> Kak ty boyalas´ edkogo ognya!
> No vdrug tvoe zatrepetalo telo,
> A golos uletaya, klyal menya.

> How you pleaded, how you wanted to live,
> How you feared the pungent fire!
> But suddenly your body trembled
> And your voice, as it flew off, cursed me.

It is, of course, a literary commonplace to address a book as a human being. The context of burning in Akhmatova's poem finds a striking parallel in an epigram by the eighteenth-century French writer Jean-Baptiste Rousseau which contains the lines:

> Vous me dites qu'il faut brûler mon livre.
> Hélas! le pauvre enfant ne demandait qu'à vivre.[14]

14. J.-B. Rousseau, *Œuvres*, Paris, 1869, p. 417 (spelling modernised) (*Epigrammes*, III, xviii).

You tell me that I should burn my book.
Alas, the poor child only asked to live.

The correspondence here draws attention to the traditional conception
of poetry as a child to be adopted, and gives added poignancy to Akhmatova's account of the enforced burning of her own poems.

Yet Akhmatova's book of verse rises from the ashes immediately
after its immolation, transformed by the forces of nature into an artistic
phenomenon of another genre:

I srazu vse zashelesteli sosny
I otrazilis' v nedrakh lunnykh vod.
A vkrug kostry svyashchenneishie vesny
Uzhe veli nadgrobnyi khorovod.

And straight away the pines began to rustle
And were reflected in the depths of the moonlit waters,
And around the fire the most holy spirits of springtime
Were already leading the funeral dance.

In spite of all attempts to suppress it, the book is refusing to die. The
choice of the term 'nadgrobnyi khorovod' ('funeral dance'), with its
evocation of Slavonic folk practice, to describe this phenomena is particularly apposite in view of the considerable energy which Akhmatova
devoted, as we have seen, to preserving the memory of her fellow
citizens and writers which would otherwise have been obliterated by the
cultural logic of Stalinism. Akhmatova's encoded poetry of the 1930s
and 1940s is itself a form of 'funeral dance'.

Akhmatova's title 'A Burnt Notebook' inevitably invites comparison
with Pushkin's poem 'Sozhzhennoe pis'mo' ('A Burnt Letter'). Amert
has suggested formal correspondences (in metre, lexicon and rhetoric)
between the two poems.[15] Most important, however, is the parallel
in theme. Pushkin's poem describes the burning of a love letter at the
beloved's request. Although the process of burning the letter is painful
for the speaker, he nevertheless manages to find some solace in the
contemplation of the ashes. The poem concludes:

Grud' moya stesnilas'. Pepel milyi,
Otrada bednaya v sud'be moei unyloi,
Ostan'sya vek so mnoi na gorestnoi grudi. . .

15. Amert, *In a Shattered Mirror*, p. 146.

My breast contracted. Dear ash,
My one poor joy in my desolate fate,
Stay forever with me on my sorrowful breast. . .

Amert finds the situation here opposite to that found in Akhmatova's poem, where by implication no ashes are left and 'the material *telo* (body) of the notebook is destroyed, and the *golos* (voice) flees from the fire, cursing the persona, not consoling her.'[16] However, as we have seen, the notebook's *soul* has clearly survived in the form of the dance, and by extension as the wild rose and as Akhmatova's new cycle of verse. Consequently, Pushkin's insistence on the power of memory to console can be read as a supporting context to Akhmatova's poem and not as an ironic commentary.

The words 'burnt notebook' also have a second Pushkinian reference: to the notebooks Pushkin burned following the Decembrist débâcle. This allusion points to the existence of hidden meanings in Akhmatova's cycle, preserved in the same way that Pushkin incorporated parts of his memoirs into other works. Akhmatova's ideal reader is thus encouraged, for example, to read the cycle as an evocation of her meetings with Isaiah Berlin and their consequences, and the subtitle once again insists that prohibited information can nevertheless be stated if it is presented in encoded form.

Another significant addition to the revised version of 'The Wild Rose Blooms' is the English epigraph 'And thou art distant in humanity'. The phrase is taken from Keats' long poem *Isabella, or the Pot of Basil*, which, like Akhmatova's cycle, addresses the themes of love, separation and memory. In brief, Isabella's lover, Lorenzo, is murdered by her brothers, who are intent on making a more advantageous match for her. Lorenzo appears to Isabella in a dream, revealing the circumstances of his death and the location of his grave. Isabella finds his body and conceals Lorenzo's head in a pot of basil, which flourishes, watered by her tears. Puzzled by Isabella's devotion to the basil plant, her brothers eventually steal it and, overcome by the evidence that their crime has been found out, flee into exile. Separated from Lorenzo for the second time, Isabella falls into a decline and shortly dies of grief.

The flourishing basil plant which preserves the memory of an absent lover is a clear parallel to Akhmatova's wild rose and provides a further expansion of the motif of regeneration in 'The Wild Rose Blooms'. The Keats epigraph, however, focuses more directly on another aspect of the separation theme. The line chosen by Akhmatova is taken from

16. Ibid., p. 147.

Lorenzo's speech to Isabella when he appears to her to announce that he is dead:

> I am a shadow now, alas! alas!
>   Upon the skirts of human-nature dwelling
> Alone. I chant alone the holy mass,
>   While little sounds of life are round me knelling,
> And glossy bees at noon do fieldward pass,
>   And many a chapel bell the hour is telling,
> Paining me through. Those sounds grow strange to me,
>   And thou art distant in Humanity.[17]

Lorenzo dwells on the impossibility of a meeting with Isabella which results from the gulf between the world of the dead where he resides and that of humanity in which Isabella still lives.

For Akhmatova's cycle this context has two implications. First it suggests that 'The Wild Rose Blooms' is to be read on one level as elegy and that the memorialisation of the obscure figure of the addressee can be taken as standing as an epitaph for a whole group of people who may have been the subjects of the burned poems of the 1930s. The quatrain which concludes the later redaction of the cycle would appear to confirm that its subject was a historical period:

> I eto stanet dlya lyudei
> Kak vremena Vespasiana,
> A bylo eto – tol´ko rana
> I muki oblachko nad nei.
> (S1, 226)

> And this will come to seem
> Like the age of Vespasian,
> But this was only a wound
> With a small cloud of suffering over it.

Secondly, the Keats epigraph serves to confuse the issue of who is alive and who is dead – is it the speaker or the addressee? – and to draw attention to the space between the human and the spirit worlds in which communication from one to the other is possible. If the speaker of the epigraph text and of the poems is held to be the same, then, paradoxically, she must be dead and the addressee alive. If, moreover, the

17. *The Poems of John Keats*, ed. M. Allott, London, 1970, p. 343.

addressee is taken to be based on Isaiah Berlin, who came to Akhmatova from England, the country also of Keats, a contrast may be implied between the spiritually 'dead' world of Stalinist Russia and the 'living' world of western Europe which he represents. The same consideration applies to the earlier cycle 'Cinque', which in the form in which it was published in the 1946 *Selected Poems* bore the same quotation from Keats as one of its epigraphs. Significantly, in the opening poem of 'Cinque', the addressee is specifically referred to as being alive, in implicit contrast to the speaker: 'No zhivogo i nayavu, / Slyshish´ ty kak tebya zovu' ('But alive and awake, do you hear me calling you?', S1, 219).

Still further intertextual references are introduced into 'The Wild Rose Blooms' through other poems which belong to the later redaction. A layer of allusion to Dante and to his separation from his beloved Beatrice has been identified in several of the poems.[18] The most prominent additional external text, however, is the story of Dido and Aeneas which lies at the heart of the eleventh poem of the revised cycle, 'Ne pugaisya,– ya eshche pokhozhei' ('Don't be afraid, I can even more closely'). This takes as its epigraph a quotation from Virgil's *Aeneid*, 'Protiv voli ya tvoi, tsaritsa, bereg pokinul' ('Against my will, Empress, I left your shores'). These words are spoken by Aeneas to Dido when they meet in the underworld after her suicide. They form part of his justification for leaving her notwithstanding her love for him and his promises to remain with her in Carthage: he has been divinely ordained to proceed to Italy where he will found Rome and thereby restore the lost honour and glory of Troy.

As with her treatment of other mythological and semi-mythological subjects Akhmatova adopts the generally neglected point of view of the woman in the story. As Amert has noted, 'Don't be afraid. . .' enters into a polemic with Virgil insofar as it draws attention to Aeneas' lack of faith towards Dido, but at the same time 'testifies to Dido's supreme faithfulness to him, as well as to the workings of a memory powerful enough to transcend the Lethean oblivion of death'.[19] It might be added that the concluding lines of Akhmatova's poem dwell on the glories of Rome and that the emergence of the new city from the ruins of Dido's

18. See M. B. Meilakh and V. N. Toporov, 'Akhmatova i Dante', *International Journal of Slavic Linguistics and Poetics*, vol. 15, 1972, pp. 44–6; Amert, *In a Shattered Mirror*, pp. 138–40.
19. Amert, *In a Shattered Mirror*, p. 137.

love for Aeneas constitutes a further reflex of the motif of the wild rose:

> Ty ne znaesh', chto tebe prostili. . .
> Sozdan Rim, plyvut stada flotilii,
> I pobedu slavoslovit lest'.
>
> (S1, 226)

> You do not know what you were forgiven. . .
> Rome was founded, flocks of vessels sail,
> And flattery extols victory.

The image of the wild rose is found again in another late cycle, 'Gorodu Pushkina' ('To Pushkin's Town', S1, 236–7), where it is contrasted with the rose proper: 'Odichalye rozy purpurnym shipovnikom stali' ('The roses have gone wild and become a purple sweetbriar'). Although the focus is slightly different here, the two poems that make up 'Gorodu Pushkina', like 'Shipovnik tsvetet', insist on the validity of the regenerative process and the power of memory to transform. The first poem of the cycle, written in 1945, is a lament at the destruction of Tsarskoe Selo. The physical damage caused by the Second World War threatens the poet's contact with the past, and with the literary tradition which the town represents:

> O, gore mne! oni tebya sozhgli. . .
> O, vstrecha, chto razluki tyazhelee!..

> Oh, sorrow! They have burnt you. . .
> Oh, meeting, heavier to bear than separation!..

The vision of loss expressed here is, however, balanced by the second poem (written in 1957, by which time Tsarskoe Selo was to some extent rebuilt). The narrator is reconciled to the physical loss of Tsarskoe Selo, since the past is now indelibly preserved in her memory: 'I tuda ne vernus'! No voz'mu i za Letu s soboyu / Ochertan'ya zhivye moikh tsarskosel'skikh sadov' ('I shall not go back there! But I shall take with me across the Lethe the living outlines of my gardens at Tsarskoe Selo'). The poem shows strong faith in the cyclical regeneration of poetry. Just as the poetic Golden Age of Pushkin was reflected in the Silver Age of Akhmatova's youth, so fifty years later it reappears in the present represented by the mature Akhmatova and the poets of the new Khrushchev generation. It is in this context that the wild rose motif reappears:

> Etoi ivy listy v devyatnadtsatom veke uvyali,
> Chtoby v strochke stikha serebrit´sya svezhee stokrat.
> Odichalye rozy purpurnym shipovnikom stali,
> A litseiskie gimny vse tak zhe zazdravno zvuchat.
> > (S1, 237)

> The leaves of this willow faded in the nineteenth century
> To stand out silver and a hundred times fresher in a line of verse.
> The roses have gone wild and become a purple sweet briar,
> But the hymns from the Lyceum raise toasts as before.

'To Pushkin's Town' is dominated by the presence of Pushkin, as I have shown elsewhere,[20] and the last line quoted above, referring to the youthful and exuberant creativity of Pushkin and his contemporaries at the famous Tsarskoe Selo Lyceum, confirms the persistence of the Golden Age as a model for future generations.

Pushkin is associated directly with the regenerative moment in many of Akhmatova's other works of the late 1950s. In one unfinished poem she notes Pushkin's posthumous domination of the city of St Petersburg and of the historical period which, ironically, precipitated his death:

> . . . poeta ubili,
> Nikolai pravei, chem Likurg.
> Chrez stoletie poluchili
> Imya – Pushkinskii Peterburg.
> > (III, 89)

> . . . the poet was killed,
> Nicholas was more just than Lycurgus.
> A century later it was called
> Pushkin's Petersburg.

The triumph of Pushkin after his death is also the main subject of Akhmatova's shorter prose sketches about the poet. In 'A Word about Pushkin' ('Slovo o Pushkine', II, 275–6), she demonstrates how Pushkin's image outgrew the slander which surrounded him in the 1830s: 'The whole epoch [. . .] slowly began to be called after Pushkin.' In 'Pushkin and the Children' ('Pushkin i Deti', III, 311), Akhmatova relates an anecdote explaining how the influence of a group of children

---

20. Wells, *Akhmatova and Pushkin*, pp. 97–101.

overturned a bureaucratic decision to remove a statue of Pushkin from a Leningrad square.

Like 'To Pushkin's Town', the fragmentary 'Bol'shaya ispoved'' ('Great Confession') contains, alongside a lament for the loss of the poetic tradition, a suggestion that, by following the example of Pushkin, the speaker may be able to recreate it:

> Eshche ya slyshu svezhii klich svobody,
> Mne kazhetsya, chto vol'nost' moi udel,
> I slyshatsya 'Sii zhivye vody'
> Tam, gde kogda-to yunyi Pushkin pel.
> (S1, 378)

> I can still hear the pure cry of freedom,
> I think that liberty is my fate,
> And 'these living waters' can still be heard,
> Where once the young Pushkin sang.

Akhmatova again associates Pushkin with images of renewal – 'the pure cry of freedom', 'liberty', 'these living waters' are all allusions to his work – and implies that the cultural values of Pushkin and his contemporaries are capable after all of resurrection in the present.[21]

'Midnight Verses'

The third major lyric cycle of Akhmatova's late poetry is 'Polnochnye stikhi' ('Midnight Verses', S1, 230–4). In many respects this constitutes a further development and expansion of the themes of 'Cinque' and particularly 'The Wild Rose Blooms'. It is, if anything, however, even more difficult of interpretation. The same principle of fragmentation applies as in the earlier sequences, so that the connections between the constituent parts are not always clear. The cycle is subject too to Akhmatova's delight in mystification and cryptographic expression.

One path into the mysteries of 'Midnight Verses' is through close consideration of the first numbered poem of the cycle, 'Predvesennyaya elegiya' ('Elegy on the Approach of Spring'). This picks up the image of fir trees from 'A Burnt Notebook', and shows another paradoxical moment of triumph resulting from a separation. The poem is worth quoting in full:

Predvesennyaya elegiya

. . . toi qui m'as consolé.
Gérard de Nerval

Mezh sosen metel' prismirela,
No, p'yanaya i bez vina,
Tam, slovno Ofeliya, pela
Vsyu noch' nam sama tishina.
A tot, kto mne tol'ko kazalsya,
Byl s toi obruchen tishinoi,
Prostivshis', on shchedro ostalsya,
On nasmert' ostalsya so mnoi.
(S1, 231)

Elegy on the Approach of Spring

. . . you who consoled me
Gérard de Nerval

The snowstorm fell quiet among the pines,
But, drunk with no wine,
There, like Ophelia,
Silence itself sang to us all night.
And he who only showed himself to me
Was wedded with that silence,
After saying goodbye he lavishly remained,
He remained with me until death.

Just as the book of poems is reborn from the fire in 'The Burnt Note-book', so the enigmatic third person of 'Elegy on the Approach of Spring' remains with the heroine even after his departure. The idea of the friend who consoles is encapsulated at the beginning of the poem in the epigraph, which is taken from Nerval's famous sonnet 'El Des-dichado'.[22] As has been shown by Vladimir Toporov and Tat'yana Tsiv'yan, the context of this quotation is closely related to that of 'Elegy on the Approach of Spring' and to 'Midnight Verses' as a whole.[23] The

22. G. de Nerval, *Œuvres*, ed. H. Lemaitre, Paris, 1966, p. 693. Although S1 cites Nerval exactly, other texts substitute the feminine for the original masculine form: 'toi qui m'as consolée'. See SP, 247; I, 301.
23. V. N. Toporov and T. V. Tsiv'yan, 'O nervalianskom podtekste v russkom akmeizme (Akhmatova i Mandel'shtam)', *Russian Literature*, vol. 15, 1984, pp. 34–7.

punctuation with which it begins inevitably draws attention to the first half of Nerval's line, which reads in full, 'Dans la nuit du tombeau, toi qui m'as consolé' ('In the night of the tomb, you who consoled me'). The idea of night and tomb functions in the cycle as a theme equal in importance to that of consolation. It is stressed by the title 'Midnight Verses' and by the general epigraph taken from 'Reverse' with its evocation of sterility and spiritual death:

> Tol'ko zerkalo zerkalu snitsya,
> Tishina tishinu storozhit. . .
>
> (S1, 230; cf. S1, 292)

> The mirror dreams only of the mirror,
> Silence watches over silence.

The isolation of the heroine is underlined in different poems by a series of expressions taken from related semantic fields conveying the idea of negativity or threat. We find, for example, expressions like, 'Nad skol'kimi bezdnami pela' ('Over how many abysses have I sung', No. 2), 'Kak vyshedshie iz tyurmy / My chto-to znaem drug o druge / Uzhasnoe' ('Like people who have come out of prison, we know something terrible about each other', No. 3). 'V zazerkal'e' ('Through the Looking-Glass', No. 3) conjures up a mirror world in which the heroine and her past are endlessly reflected in a series of stereotyped actions from which she is unable to escape.

The two themes of isolation and consolation converge in the motif of the non-meeting, which is restated forcefully in the introductory lines to 'Midnight Verses':

> Razluku naverno, neplokho snesu,
> No vstrechu s toboyu – edva li.
>
> (S1, 230)

> Separation, probably, I can bear fairly well,
> But a meeting with you – scarcely.

As in 'The Wild Rose Blooms', while the heroine's friend or lover is physically absent, memory reunites the couple and consoles the heroine in her present solitude. Death or distance is overcome and the creative act of memory is equivalent to an actual resurrection. It is often music that serves as a catalyst in this process:

> V kotoruyu-to iz sonat
> Tebya ya spryachu ostorozhno.
> (No. 5, S1, 232)[24]

> In one of the sonatas
> I will hide you carefully.

> My s toboi v Adazhio Vival´di
> Vstretimsya opyat´.
> (No. 6, S1, 233)

> We shall meet again
> In Vivaldi's Adagio.

Regeneration and reunion can also occur through dreams, as in the concluding verse of the cycle, 'Vmesto poslesloviya':

> A tam, gde sochinyayut sny,
> Oboim – raznykh ne khvatilo,
> My videli odin, no sila
> Byla v nem, kak prikhod vesny.
> (S1, 234)

> But where dreams are made
> There were not enough for both of us.
> We saw the same one, but it contained
> A force like the arrival of spring.

The regeneration myth, in its various forms in ancient tradition, is, of course, central to Nerval's cycle *Les Chimères*, in which 'El Desdichado' is found. The line in Nerval immediately following the one chosen by Akhmatova contains an adaptation of the myth in a cry for the return of the past: 'Rends-moi le Pausilippe et la mer d'Italie' ('Give me back Posilippo and the Italian sea'). One of the clearest statements of this theme in the poem is found in the line, 'Et j'ai deux fois, vainqueur, traversé l'Achéron' ('And twice, victorious, I have crossed the Acheron'), with its insistence that death can be overcome. In the lines before and after this Nerval too associates this triumph with dreams and

24. In the first published version of the cycle, and in a manuscript of *Beg vremeni*, this piece of music was identified as Beethoven's piano sonata op. 110. See A. A. Akhmatova, 'Polnochnye stikhi', *Den' poezii* (Moscow), 1964, p. 61; S1, 431.

with music (cf. 'J'ai rêvé dans la grotte où nage la sirène' ('I have dreamed in the cave where the siren bathes') and 'Modulant tour à tour sur la lyre d'Orphée' ('Modulating in turn on Orpheus' lyre')). By evoking 'El Desdichado', Akhmatova not only generalises her experience by comparing it with that of Nerval, but also places it on a mythological plane by indirectly recalling the legends of Orpheus, Osiris and Cybele, all of whom are assimilated by the French poet.

As N. A. Struve has observed, 'Midnight Verses' is also a very much a work which takes poetry itself as a central theme.[25] However, the status given to the poetic word in the later cycle is different from that accorded it in 'The Wild Rose Blooms'. Certainly poetry is to some extent associated with the regenerative process in 'Elegy on the Approach of Spring'. It is *singing* here which precedes the statement of the hero's continued metaphorical presence. The redemptive power of singing is indicated still more clearly in the third poem of the cycle, 'Trinadtsat' strochek' ('Thirteen Lines', S1, 232), where its momentum is reinforced by the anaphoric repetition of 'I' ('And'):

I vkrug tebya zapela tishina,
I chistym solntsem sumrak ozarilsya,
I mir na mig odin preobrazilsya,
I stranno izmenilsya vkus vina.

And around you the silence began to sing,
And the twilight was lit up by a pure sun,
And the world was transformed for a moment,
And the taste of wine was strangely changed.

Moreover, the last poem of the cycle proper ends with the word 'stikhi' ('verses') in stressed position, suggesting that it is to be taken as a key term. Reference to poetry here is, however, ambivalent. The emphasis produced by the rhetoric is undermined by the epithet 'okayannye' ('cursed'), by the uncertainty of the verb 'bormochet' ('mumbles') and by an obscure association with earlier sins:

I nikakim ne vnemlya slavoslov'yam,
Perezabyv vse prezhnie grekhi,
K bessonneishim pripavshi izgolov'yam,
Bormochet okayannye stikhi.

(S1, 233)

25. N. A. Struve, 'O "Polnochnykh stikhakh"', in Ketchian, *Anna Akhmatova 1889–1989*, pp. 186–93.

And ignoring all eulogies,
Forgetting all earlier sins,
Pressing herself to the most sleepless of pillows,
She mumbles cursed lines of verse.

The second poem of the cycle, 'Pervoe preduprezhdenie' ('First Warning') likewise contains associations between poetry and negative imagery: 'Nad skol'kimi bezdnami pela' ('Over how many abysses did I sing'), 'i gul zatikhayushchikh strochek' ('And the hum of lines as they fade away').

The source of poetry in 'Midnight Verses' is, paradoxically, silence, and this is made clear in lines such as 'silence itself sang to us all night' and 'And around you the silence began to sing'. Yet the role of silence in the cycle is not confined to the production of poetry; it is on the contrary a highly complex category embracing a range of contradictory impulses. An explanation can be found by examining the general epigraph from 'Reverse' which has already been quoted.[26] In *Poem Without a Hero* the lines of the epigraph immediately precede the following stanza, to which attention is drawn in 'Midnight Verses' by three intruded dots of suspension:

I so mnoyu moya 'Sed'maya',
Polumertvaya i nemaya,
Rot ee sveden i otkryt,
Slovno rot tragicheskoi maski,
No on chernoi zamazen kraskoi
I sukhoyu zemlei nabit.
(S1, 292)

And with me is my 'Seventh',
Half-dead and dumb,
Her mouth is twisted and open,
Like the mouth of a tragic mask,
But it is daubed with black paint
And packed with dry earth.

As has been noted above, 'Seventh' here refers to a suppressed collection of Akhmatova's poetry, and this stanza contains a statement

26. The role of silence was emphasised to an even greater extent in the earlier version of the cycle where the epigraph consisted only of the second line: 'Tishina tishinu storozhit. . .'. The connection with *Poem Without a Hero* is further indicated in this version by the fact that the seven poems of the cycle were followed by another stanza which later appeared in 'Reverse'. See *Den' poezii*, p. 62; S1, 294.

relating to the personal costs associated with writing poetry – of preserving the integrity of the poetic word – during a period of political and cultural repression.

Read in the light of 'Reverse', 'Midnight Verses' becomes neither simply a cycle of love poems nor only a discussion of 'mere poetry' as Struve would have it, but also a further example of Akhmatova's poetic indictment of Stalinism. Silence is not just a source of poetry, not simply a vehicle for the resurgence of memory, but a metaphor for the Terror, for the anxiety of the midnight anticipation of a visit from the NKVD. The sense of entrapment which has already been identified in the context of the heroine's isolation applies not only to her relationship to the past, but also to her freedom of action in the present.

The sixth poem of 'Midnight Verses', 'Nochnoe poseshchenie' ('Visit at Night'), connects a night-time visitation with fear and paralysis in the lines 'Protekut v nemom smertel'nom stone / Eti polchasa' ('This half-hour will pass in a silent deathly moan'), and in its final quatrain:

> I togda tebya tvoya trevoga,
>   Stavshaya sud'boi,
> Uvedet ot moego poroga
>   V ledyanoi priboi.
>   (S1, 233)

> And then the fear
>   Which has become your fate
> Will take you away from my door
>   Into the icy waves.

That this poem in particular is intended to be read in the context of the Terror is further suggested by its epigraph: 'Vse ushli i nikto ne vernulsya' ('Everyone left and no one has returned', III, 72–3). These words represent a further reflex of the expression 'Some are already dead and the others are far away' which has already been discussed (pp. 107–9) in terms of its political connotations in the context of *Poem Without a Hero*. They are also the first line of a poem of the late 1940s which deals explicitly with the effects of the purge years and the forced separation from friends. 'Everyone left and no one has returned' also refers to the cultural threat of Stalinism, and particularly its attempts to stifle an independent literature:

> Oskvernili prechistoe Slovo,
> Rastoptali svyashchennyi glagol.

> They have defiled the immaculate Word,
> Trampled the holy speech.

It ends, however, as has already been noted, with a statement relating to Akhmatova's own activity as a poet, comparing the compulsion to speak out against the destruction of social and cultural values with the prophetic utterances of the traditional Russian 'holy fool'.

The question of the role of the poet is taken up directly in two places in 'Midnight Verses'. The first passage notes the temptation of silence as a means of self-preservation:

> I dazhe ya, komu ubiitsei byt´
> Bozhestvennogo slova predstoyalo,
> Pochti blagogoveino zamolchala,
> Chtob zhizn´ blagoslovennuyu prodlit´.
> (S1, 232)

> And even I, who had the prospect
> Of murdering the divine word,
> Almost reverentially fell silent,
> In order to prolong this blessed life.

The seventh poem of the cycle, on the other hand, suggests that in fact the true poet is not ultimately in a position to choose silence. Rather this silence, together with the midnight silence of the politics of Terror, is an inevitable source of poetry irrespective of the wishes of the poet herself. The grammatical subject of the verbs in this poem is nowhere stated, but it can be assumed to be silence itself ('tishina'), in its role as producer of poetry:

> Byla nad nami, kak zvezda nad morem,
> Ishcha luchom devyatyi smertnyi val,
> Ty nazyval ee bedoi i gorem,
> A radost´yu ni razu ne nazval.
> (S1, 233)

It was above us like a star over the sea,
Searching with its beam for the fatal ninth wave,
You called it misfortune and grief,
But not once did you call it joy.

It is this silence too which is seen 'muttering accursed verses' in the poem's final line.

'Midnight Verses' thus combines inextricably the three themes which dominate Akhmatova's later work as a whole: love, poetry and political oppression. The relative prominence of these components varies to some extent in the three late cycles which have been examined. In 'Cinque' it is the love theme which is to the fore while the metapoetic and political assume a subsidiary role. In 'The Wild Rose Blooms', particularly in its revised form, it is the function of poetry in linking past, present and future which is predominant. 'Midnight Verses', however, presents a synthesis in which the three elements are in more or less equal balance. The power of both love and poetry to overcome the 'flight of time' is put fully to the service of the preservation of political and historical memory. Each of the major themes supports the others by providing them with an additional metaphorical context, and the three strands meet in their appropriation of the dialectics of time and space. Yet the cycle is constructed in such a way that it can be read primarily as a love cycle: its metapoetic and political layers can only be reached by careful and contextual reading. With all its haunting obscurity 'Midnight Verses' is thus perhaps the culmination of Akhmatova's late cryptographic style.

Conclusion

The many layers of 'Midnight Verses', written at the end of Akhmatova's career, make it in design and execution a very different type of work from the early lyrics of *Evening*. And, of course, a distinct pattern of evolution can be traced in Akhmatova's poetry from its beginnings in the 1910s to the mid-1960s. In general this is a progression towards greater and greater complexity, towards an ever greater density of meaning. As we have seen, the superficial clarity and simplicity of Akhmatova's early poetry already belies the considerable multiplicity of readings which is revealed on closer examination of her texts. Her earliest work is, nevertheless, very closely focused on the relationship between hero and heroine, and although there is frequently a strong literary or metapoetic element, this is normally subordinated to the theme of love. A great deal of care is taken with the arrangement of poems in books, and indeed the book itself is a major vehicle of artistic expression, allowing an interplay of themes and images not possible within the bounds of a single poem. By *White Flock* this concept reaches its most elaborate form as the public themes of poetic transformation and war provide a counterpoint to the private emotions of the heroine.

In *Anno Domini*, written in the aftermath of the Revolution and at a time when the new Soviet government was still seeking to assert its authority, the civic role of the poet announced in Akhmatova's poems of the First World War acquires a more prominent position. This is reflected in the new structure of *Anno Domini*, which is arranged along chronological lines. While the relationship between hero and heroine is still important, the private and public spheres are no longer seen as distinct, so that, for example, poems in which the heroine bemoans her failure in the sphere of love can easily be read as allegories of the political situation.

In the reduced cultural circumstances of Stalinism, Akhmatova's poetry of the 1930s and 1940s, after a period of silence, resumes with renewed vigour its political agenda. The love theme is pushed into the background, and in order to document the threat to Russian society and culture represented by the Terror, Akhmatova has recourse to two particular modes of discourse. On the one hand she writes overtly oppositional poems designed for circulation among a small group of friends, and on the other she develops the allusive extratextuality which characterises even her earliest poems into a sophisticated form of Aesopian language. Not surprisingly, the role of poetry itself remains a central concern. The most sustained example of Akhmatova's Aesopian style is *Poem Without a Hero*, which constitutes a memorial to the victims of Stalinism and a defence of humane cultural values presented under cover of a literary masquerade and a celebration of the city of St Petersburg.

Akhmatova's poetry of the 1950s and 1960s, written during the thaw, when the condemnation of Stalinism was no longer as urgent as it had been earlier, continues to use a highly allusive and even cryptic style. However, Akhmatova's writing undergoes another gradual change in purpose. In particular the love theme reasserts itself in a new form. The competitive edge which characterised the earlier relationship between heroine and hero is dispelled, and the two figures, though ordained by the exigencies of time and fate to a permanent state of 'non-meeting', triumph over this on a higher level by the intensity and durability of their love. The evolutionary pattern here can easily be identified by comparing the 1940s versions of *Poem Without a Hero* and especially *Prologue* with the revised form which they were given in the 1960s. In Akhmatova's post-war poetry the political component is not by any means lost; it becomes, however, one strand among many, each of which sustains and is supported by the others.

Thus on one level Akhmatova's poetry passes through a progression from a solipsistic concern with the figure of the heroine in the early books, through an increasingly political orientation in the poems of the middle period, towards the philosophical abstraction of the cycles of the 1960s. Yet superimposed on this pattern of evolution is a stylistic and conceptual continuity which links Akhmatova's poetry through all its periods. Her work in general is characterised by a simplicity of vocabulary and syntax which contrasts beguilingly with the complexity of her themes. Certain images and motifs are repeated persistently: the idea of the 'non-meeting', for example, which is central to the late cycles, has its origins in the early heroine's constantly failing quest for an ideal companion. The figures of the Muse and the double recur with some regularity as does the evocation of St Petersburg and the presiding genius of Pushkin. The role and function of poetry is a constant theme through all periods. Continuity is assured too by Akhmatova's technique of self-consciously referring back to her own earlier work, using it to characterise a historical epoch, to highlight changes in perspective or simply to develop its ideas further.

Above all, Akhmatova's poetry of different periods is united by the principle of extratextuality through which she encourages her readers to look for an elucidation of her poems outside her individual texts. What started above all as a rhetorical position designed to focus attention on the elusive figure of the heroine and increase the aura of mystery surrounding her began very early to develop in other directions as well. Reference, direct or indirect, to a wide range of other discursive systems is consistently used to expand the meaning of Akhmatova's texts. Literary, historical, religious, musical and visual associations are thus employed first of all to reinforce the sentiments expressed by the lyric heroine, then to locate the heroine within a broad social, cultural and historical context. From the 1920s they become at once a defence of a culture under threat and a vehicle for Aesopian expression. In the poetry of Akhmatova's last years these functions are supplemented by an increased mythologisation in which multiple associative paths intersect.

Akhmatova's use of the principle of extratextuality to serve the interrelated aims of preserving the cultural tradition and memorialising the victims of oppression is perhaps her most immediate legacy to the poets who succeeded her. The young writers whom she encouraged in the 1960s – Iosif Brodskii, Evgenii Rein and Aleksandr Kushner, for example – saw themselves as continuators and preservers of the modernist tradition which Akhmatova represented. This project assumed a clearly dissident character in that it sought to reassemble the fragments of the literary past and to return to the tradition at the point where it was cut off by the imposition of Socialist Realism. In the post-communist world, Akhmatova's protégés are now among the most prominent and influential of Russian poets, and Akhmatova's poetic ideas have found an ineradicable place in the Russian literary consciousness.

Select Bibliography

Akhmatova, A. A., *Vecher*, St Petersburg, 1912.
——, *Chetki*, St Petersburg, 1914.
——, *Belaya staya*, Petrograd, 1917.
——, *Podorozhnik*, Petrograd, 1921.
——, *U samogo morya*, Petrograd, 1921.
——, *Anno Domini MCMXXI*, Petrograd, 1921.
——, *Anno Domini*, 2nd edn, Petrograd, 1923.
——, *Iz shesti knig*, Leningrad, 1940.
——, *Izbrannoe*, Tashkent, 1943.
——, *Izbrannye stikhi*, Moscow, 1946 (edition not released to the public).
——, *Stikhotvoreniya 1909–1945*, Moscow, 1946 (edition not released to the public).
——, *Stikhotvoreniya*, Moscow, 1958.
——, *Stikhotvoreniya (1909–1960)*, Moscow, 1961.
——, *Beg vremeni*, Moscow, 1965.
——, 'Avtobiograficheskaya proza', *Literaturnoe obozrenie*, no. 5, 1989, pp. 3–17.
——, 'Otryvok iz perevoda "Makbeta"', *Literaturnoe obozrenie*, no. 5, 1989, pp. 18–21.
Amert, S., 'Akhmatova's "Pushkin i nevskoe vzmor´e"', *Transactions of the Association of Russian-American Scholars in the U.S.A.*, vol. 23, 1990, pp. 193–211.
——, *In a Shattered Mirror: The Later Poetry of Anna Akhmatova*, Stanford, Calif., 1992.
Annenkov, Yu., *Dnevnik moikh vstrech: tsikl tragedii*, Leningrad, 2 vols, 1991.
Bazhenov, M. N., 'Anna Akhmatova – Osip Mandel´shtam: biobibliografiya', *Sovetskaya bibliografiya*, no. 2, 1991, pp. 86–100.
Berlin, I., *Personal Impressions*, London, 1980.
Bobyshev, D., 'Akhmatova i emigratsiya', *Zvezda*, no. 2, 1991, pp. 177–80.
Bowra, C. M., *Poetry and Politics, 1900–1960*, Cambridge, 1966.
Braun, E., *The Theatre of Meyerhold: Revolution on the Modern Stage*, London, 1979.

Brown, C., *Mandelstam*, Cambridge, 1973.

Childers, R. and A. L. Crone, 'The Mandel'štam Presence in the Dedications of Poèma bez geroja', *Russian Literature*, vol. 15, 1984, pp. 51–82.

Chukovskaya, L. K., *Zapiski ob Anne Akhmatovoi*, vol. 1, Paris, 1976; vol. 2, Paris, 1980.

Chukovskii, K., 'Chitaya Akhmatovu', *Moskva*, no. 5, 1964, pp. 200–3.

Chumakov, Yu. N., 'Ob avtorskikh primechaniyakh k "Evgeniyu Oneginu"', *Boldinskie chteniya*, Gor'kii, 1976, pp. 58–72.

Crone, A. L., 'Blok as Don Juan in Akhmatova's "Poema bez geroia"', *Russian Language Journal*, nos. 121–2, 1981, pp. 147–55.

Dedyulin, S., '"Maloizvestnoe interv'yu Anny Akhmatovoi', *Voprosy literatury*, no. 7, 1978, pp. 313–14.

Dedyulin S. and G. Superfin (eds), *Akhmatovskii sbornik*, vol. 1, Paris, 1989.

Dodero Costa, M. L. (ed.), *Anna Achmatova (1889–1966): Atti del Convegno nel centenario della nascita, Torino, Villa Gualino, 12–13 dicembre 1989*, Allessandria, 1992.

Doherty, J., *The Acmeist Movement in Russian Poetry: Culture and the Word*, Oxford, 1995.

Driver, S., '*Axmatova's Poèma bez geroja* and Blok's *Vozmezdie*', in W. N. Vickery (ed.), *Aleksandr Blok Centenary Conference*, Columbus, Ohio, 1984, pp. 89–99.

Dzhandzhakova, E. V., 'Smuglyi otrok brodil po alleyam', *Russkaya rech'*, no. 5, 1976, pp. 16–19.

Eikhenbaum, B., *Anna Akhmatova: opyt analiza*, Petrograd, 1922.

Ecker, N., 'Elemente der Volksdichtung in der Lyrik Anna Achmatovas', unpublished D.Phil. thesis, University of Vienna, 1973.

Erdmann-Pandžić, E. von, '*Poèma bez geroja' von Anna A. Achmatova: Varientenedition und Interpretation von Symbolstrukturen*, Cologne, 1987.

Etkind, E., 'Bessmertie pamyati. Poema Anny Akhmatovoi Rekviem', *Studia Slavica Finlandensia*, vol. 8, 1991, pp. 98–133.

Faryno, J., 'Kod Akhmatovoi', *Russian Literature*, vol. 7/8, 1974, pp. 83–102.

——, 'Akhmatova's *Poem Without a Hero* as a *Moneta* and as a Revelation', *Essays in Poetics*, vol. 16, no. 2, 1991, pp. 75–93.

Genin, L., 'Akhmatova i tsarskaya tsenzura', *Zvezda*, no. 4, 1967, pp. 203–4.

Gershtein, E. G., 'Memuary i fakty (ob osvobozhdenii L'va Gumileva)', *Russian Literary Triquarterly*, no. 13, 1975, pp. 645–57.

——, 'Posleslovie', in A. Akhmatova, *O Pushkine*, Leningrad, 1977, pp. 277–317.

——, *Novoe o Mandel'shtame*, Paris, 1986.

Ginzburg, L. Ya., *O starom i novom: stat'i i ocherki*, Leningrad, 1982.

Graf-Schneider, M., '"Musa" dans l'oeuvre d'Anna Akhmatova', *Slavica Helvetica*, vol. 16, 1981, pp. 187–203.

Haight, A., *Anna Akhmatova: A Poetic Pilgrimage*, New York, 1976.

Hartman, A., 'The Metrical Typology of Anna Akhmatova', in L. Leighton (ed.), *Studies in Honor of Xenia Gasiorowska*, Columbus, Ohio, 1982, pp. 112–23.

Ivanova, L. V., *Vospominaniya: kniga ob ottse*, Moscow, 1992.

Jovanović, M., 'K razboru "chuzhikh golosov" v *Rekvieme* Akhmatovoi', *Russian Literature*, vol. 15, 1984, pp. 169–81.

Kaji, S., 'O slavoslovii Anny Akhmatovoi', *Japanese Slavic and East European Studies*, vol. 12, 1991, pp. 45–60.

Karpiak, R., 'The Sequels to Pushkin's *Kamennyi gost'*: Russian Don Juan Versions by Nikolai Gumilev and Vladimir Korvin-Piotrovskii', in S.D. Cioran, W. Smyrniw, G. Thomas (eds), *Studies in Honour of Louis Shein*, Hamilton, Ont., 1983, pp. 79–92.

Kats, B. and R.D. Timenchik, *Anna Akhmatova i muzyka: issledovatel'skie ocherki*, Leningrad, 1989.

Kelly, C., *A History of Russian Women's Writing, 1820–1992*, Oxford, 1994.

Ketchian, S. I., 'Akhmatova's Civic Poem "Stansy" and its Pushkinian Antecedent', *Slavic and East European Journal*, vol. 37, no. 2, 1993, pp. 194–210.

—— (ed.), *Anna Akhmatova 1889–1989: Papers from the Akhmatova Centennial Conference, Bellagio Study and Conference Center, June 1989*, Oakland, Calif., 1993.

Kolmogorov, A. N. and A. V. Prokhorov, 'O dol'nike sovremennoi russkoi poezii', *Voprosy yazykoznaniya*, no. 6, 1963, pp. 84–95 and no. 1, 1964, pp. 75–94.

Kralin, M. M., 'Nekrasovskaya traditsiya u Anny Akhmatovoi', *Nekrasovskii sbornik*, no. 8, 1983, pp. 74–86.

—— (ed.), *Ob Anne Akhmatovoi: stikhi, esse, vospominaniya*, Leningrad, 1990.

Kushner, A., *Apollon v snegu: zametki na polyakh*, Leningrad, 1991.

Landsman, I. M. and E. B. Naumov, 'Iz nablyudenii nad yazykom A. Akhmatovoi', *Voprosy russkogo i obshchego yazykoznaniya* (Sbornik nauchnykh trudov (Tashkentskii un-t), 580), 1979, pp. 75–82.

Leiter, S., *Akhmatova's Petersburg*, Cambridge, 1983.

Lisnyanskaya, I., *Muzyka 'Poemy bez geroya' Anny Akhmatovoi*, Moscow, 1991.

Loseff, L. and B. Scherr (eds), *A Sense of Place: Tsarskoe Selo and its*

Poets: Papers from the 1989 Dartmouth Conference Dedicated to the Centennial of Anna Akhmatova, Columbus, Ohio, 1993.

Luknitskaya, V. K., *Nikolai Gumilev: zhizn' poeta po materialam domashnego arkhiva sem'i Luknitskikh*, Leningrad, 1990.

——, *Pered toboi – zemlya*, Leningrad, 1990.

—— (ed.), 'Rannie pushkinskie shtudii Anny Akhmatovoi (po materialam arkhiva P. Luknitskogo)', *Voprosy literatury*, no. 1, 1978, pp. 185–228.

Luknitskii, P. N., *Acumiana: vstrechi s Annoi Akhmatovoi*, vol. 1, Paris, 1991.

Maksimov, D. E., 'Akhmatova o Bloke', *Zvezda*, no. 12, 1967, pp. 187–91.

Mandel'shtam, N. Ya., *Vospominaniya*, 3rd edn, Paris, 1982.

——, *Vtoraya kniga*, 4th edn, Paris, 1987.

——, *Kniga tret'ya*, Paris, 1987.

Meilakh, M. B. and V. N. Toporov, 'Akhmatova i Dante', *International Journal of Slavic Linguistics and Poetics*, vol. 15, 1972, pp. 29–75.

Metcalf, A. and J. Neville, '1940: Not So Much a Thaw – More a Change in the Air', in M. Pavlyshyn (ed.), *Glasnost' in Context: On the Recurrence of Liberalizations in East European Literatures and Cultures*, New York, 1990, pp. 117–26.

Nabokov, V. (ed.), *Eugene Onegin*, 4 vols, rev. edn, London, 1975.

Naiman, A., *Rasskazy o Anne Akhmatovoi*, Moscow, 1989.

——, 'Uroki poeta', *Literaturnaya gazeta*, 14 June 1989, p. 8.

Panchenko, A. M. and N. V. Gumileva (eds), 'Perepiska A.A. Akhmatovoi s L.N. Gumilevym', *Zvezda*, no. 4, 1994, pp. 170–88.

Pavlovskii, A. I., *Anna Akhmatova: zhizn' i tvorchestvo*, Moscow, 1991.

Reeder, R. (ed.), *The Complete Poems of Anna Akhmatova*, trans. Judith Hemschemeyer, 2 vols, Somerville, Mass., 1990, pp. 21–183.

——, *Anna Akhmatova: Poet and Prophet*, New York, 1994.

Reeve, F. D., *Aleksandr Blok: Between Image and Idea*, New York, 1962.

Roskina, N., *Chetyre glavy: iz literaturnykh vospominanii*, Paris, 1980.

Rosslyn, W. A., *The Prince, the Fool and the Nunnery: The Religious Theme in the Early Poetry of Anna Akhmatova*, Amersham, 1984.

——, 'Don Juan Feminised', in A. McMillin (ed.), *Symbolism and After: Essays on Russian Poetry in Honour of Georgette Donchin*, London, 1992, pp. 102–21.

—— (ed.), *The Speech of Unknown Eyes: Akhmatova's Readers on her Poetry*, 2 vols, Nottingham, 1990.

Sandler, S., 'The Stone Guest: Akhmatova, Pushkin and Don Juan', *Stanford Slavic Studies*, vol. 4, no. 2, 1992, pp. 35–49.

Satin, M. R., 'Akhmatova's "Shipovnik Tsvetet": A study of Creative

Method', unpublished Ph.D. thesis, University of Pennsylvania, 1977.

Saulenko, L. L., 'Pushkinskaya traditsiya v "Poeme bez geroya" Anny Akhmatovoi', *Voprosy russkoi literatury* (L'vov), vol. 36, no. 2, 1980, pp. 42–50.

——, 'Imya knigi (o traditsii v poetike A. Akhmatovoi)', *Voprosy russkoi literatury* (L'vov), vol. 40, no. 1, 1984, pp. 89–94.

Shilov, L., *Anna Akhmatova (100 let so dnya rozhdeniya)*, Moscow, 1989.

Subbotin, A., 'Mayakovskii i Akhmatova', *Ural*, no. 6, 1983, pp. 177–84.

——, *Gorizonty poezii*, Sverdlovsk, 1984.

Sukhanova, M., 'Fuga temporum', *Russian Literature*, vol. 30, 1991, pp. 337–42.

Thompson, R. D. B., 'The Anapaestic Dol'nik in the Poetry of Axmatova and Gumilev', in D. Mickiewicz (ed.), *Toward a Definition of Acmeism (Russian Language Journal*, Supplementary Issue), East Lansing, Mich., 1975, pp. 42–58.

Timenchik, R. D., 'Akhmatova i Pushkin: razbor stikhotvoreniya "Smuglyi otrok brodil po alleyam"', *Pushkinskii sbornik*, Riga, 1968, pp. 124–31.

——, 'Akhmatova i Pushkin: zametki k teme', *Pushkinskii sbornik*, no. 2, Riga, 1974, pp. 35–48.

——, 'Rizhskii epizod v "Poeme bez geroya" Anny Akhmatovoi', *Daugava*, no. 80, 1984, pp. 113–21.

—— (ed.), *Anna Akhmatova: Desyatye gody*, Moscow, 1989.

—— (ed.), *Anna Akhmatova: Requiem*, Moscow, 1989.

Timenchik, R. D., V. N. Toporov and T. V. Tsiv'yan, 'Akhmatova i Kuzmin', *Russian Literature*, vol. 6, 1978, pp. 213–305.

Tlusty, I. A., 'Anna Akhmatova and the Composition of her Poema bez geroya 1940–1962', unpublished D.Phil. thesis, University of Oxford, 1984.

Toporov, V. N., *Akhmatova i Blok (k probleme postroeniya poeticheskogo dialoga: 'blokovskii' tekst Akhmatovoi)*, Berkekey, 1981.

——, 'Ob istorizme Akhmatovoi', *Russian Literature*, vol. 28, 1990, pp. 277–418.

Toporov, V. N. and T. V. Tsiv'yan, 'O nervalianskom podtekste v russkom akmeizme (Akhmatova i Mandel'shtam)', *Russian Literature*, vol. 15, 1984, pp. 29–50.

Tsiv'yan, T. V., 'Zametki k deshirovke "Poemy bez geroya"', *Trudy po znakovym sistemam*, no. 5, 1971, pp. 255–77.

Verheul, K., *The Theme of Time in the Poetry of Anna Axmatova*, The Hague, 1971.

——, 'Public Themes in the Poetry of Anna Axmatova', in J. van der Eng-Liedmeier and K. Verheul (eds), *Tale Without a Hero and Twenty-Two Poems by Anna Axmatova*, The Hague, 1973, pp. 9–46.

Vilenkin, V. Ya., *V sto pervom zerkale*, 2nd edn, Moscow, 1990.

——, 'Obraz "teni" v poetike Anny Akhmatovoi', *Voprosy literatury*, no. 1, 1994, pp. 57–76.

Vinogradov, V., *O poezii Anny Akhmatovoi (stilisticheskie nabroski)*, Leningrad, 1925.

Wells, D. N., 'Folk Ritual in Anna Akhmatova's *Poema bez geroya'*, *Scottish Slavonic Review*, no. 7, 1986, pp. 69–88.

——, 'Akhmatova and Pushkin: The Genres of Elegy and Ballad', *Slavonic and East European Review*, vol. 71, no. 4, 1993, pp. 631–45.

——, *Akhmatova and Pushkin: The Pushkin Contexts of Akhmatova's Poetry*, Birmingham, 1994.

Zhirmunskii, V. M., *Voprosy teorii literatury*, Leningrad, 1928.

——, *Tvorchestvo Anny Akhmatovoi*, Leningrad, 1973.

Zykov, L., 'Nikolai Punin – adresat i geroi liriki Anny Akhmatovoi', *Zvezda*, no. 1, 1995, pp. 77–114.

Index

Index

Index

147, 154
Stikhotvoreniya (1958), 21
'Szhala ruki pod temnoi vual'yu', 48

'Tainy remesla', 65–6, 147
'Tak vot on – tot osennii peizazh'
  (*Severnye elegii*), 149–50
'Tebe pokorno? Ty soshel s uma', 56
'Techet reka nespeshno po doline', 60
'Ten'' ('V sorokovom godu'), 101–2
'Tot avgust, kak zheltoe plamya', 57, 60,
  62
'Tot golos, s tishinoi velikoi sporya', 53
'Tot gorod, mnoi lyubimyi s detstva',
  83–4
'Trinadtsat' strochek' ('Polnochnye
  stikhi'), 170, 173
'Tri raza pytat' prikhodila', 50–1
'Tumanom legkim park napolnilsya', 51
'Tvorchestvo' ('Tainy remesla'), 65
'Ty pover', ne zmeinoe ostroe zhalo',
  33–4, 49–50
'Ty vsegda tainstvennyi i novyi', 62
'Ty vydumal menya, takoi na svete net'
  ('Shipovnik tsvetet'), 155–7

'Umiraya, tomlyus' o bessmert'i', 47
'U menya est' ulybka odna', 35
U samogo morya, 7, 35, 38–9, 52, 55, 84

Vecher, 8, 24–5, 33, 36, 45, 175
  Lyric heroine, 27–8
  Structure, 47–51, 55
'Vecherom', 34–5
'Venok mertvym', 147
'Vmesto poslesloviya' ('Polnochnye
  stikhi'), 169
'Vospominanie' ('Shipovnik tsvetet'),
  155–7
'Vo sne' ('Shipovnik tsvetet'), 154
'Vnov' podaren mne dremotoi', 32
'Voronezh', 80–1
'Vse obeshchalo mne ego', 53–4
'Vse raskhishcheno, predano, prodano',
  56
'Vse ushli i nikto ne vernulsya', 131,
  172–3
'V pionerlagere', 138–9
'V sorokovom godu', 90, 102–3
'V zazerkal'e' ('Polnochnye stikhi'), 168

'Ya prishla tebya smenit', sestra', 34
'Ya soshla s uma, o mal'chik strannyi',
  31
'Ya ulybat'sya perestala', 52

'Ya znayu, c mesta ne sdvinut'sya', 68

'Zaplakannaya osen', kak vdova', 32
'Za ozerom luna ostanovilas'', 61
'Za takuyu skomoroshinu', 67–8
'Zdravstvui! Legkii shelest slyshish'',
  29, 46
'Zhdala ego naprasno mnogo let', 28

English titles

8 November 1913', 25, 41
'And it's impossible to take away from
  them', 165
'And Last' ('Midnight Verses'), 170–1,
  173–4
'And my heart needed nothing', 125
'And so in defiance', 67
'And there my marble double' ('In
  Tsarskoe Selo'), 39–40, 48
'And this will come to seem' ('The Wild
  Rose Blooms'), 162
Anno Domini, 12, 24, 33, 45, 78, 175
  Structure, 55–63
'Asleep' ('The Wild Rose Blooms'), 154
'As if on the edge of a cloud' ('Cinque'),
  151–2
'Awake' ('The Wild Rose Blooms'),
  154–5

'Believe me, it is not the sharp sting of a
  snake', 33–4, 49–50
'Benjamin Constant's *Adolphe* in
  Pushkin's Work', 14
'Betrayal', 48–9
'Bezhetsk', 59–60
'Biblical Poems', 36, 42
'A Burnt Notebook' ('The Wild Rose
  Blooms'), 158–61, 166–7
'Bury me, bury me, wind!', 49
By the Sea Shore, 7, 35, 38–9, 52, 55, 84

'The Cellar of Memory', 85–6
'The Children Speak', 136
'Cinque', 130, 151–4, 166, 174
  Relationship with other cycles, 143–4,
  156, 163
'Cleopatra', 82–3
'Coastal Victory Park', 136–8
'Courage', 130
'Creativity' ('The Secrets of the Craft'),
  65

'Dante', 78–80

Index

General Index

Acmeism, 8, 44, 127
Aesopian writing, 22, 78–83, 96, 142,
    176–7
    And Pushkin, 82–3, 132, 137–8
Akhmatova, Praskov'ya Fedoseevna
    (Akhmatova's great-grandmother), 6
Andronikova, Salomeya Nikolaevna,
    101–2
Annenskii, Innokentii Fedorovich, 40,
    153
    Kiparisovyi larets (*The Cypress
    Chest*), 6
    'Pace', 39–40
    'Peterburg' ('Petersburg'), 119
Anrep, Boris Vasil'evich, 11
Apollon (*Apollo*), 7–8
Arens, Anna Evgen'evna, 13

Baratynskii, Evgenii Abramovich, 125,
    134
Baudelaire, Charles, 14
    'Une Martyre' ('A Martyr'), 153–4
Belyaev, Yurii, 102
Blok, Aleksandr Aleksandrovich, 8, 10,
    98, 104, 110–11
    'Balaganchik' ('The Fairground
    Booth'), 105
    Death of, 12, 55, 58
    Dvenadtsat' (*The Twelve*), 126
    'Shagi komandora' ('The Steps of the
    Commendatore'), 102, 115
    Vozmezdie (*Retribution*), 125–7
Berlin, Sir Isaiah, 20, 23, 151, 156, 161,
    163
Bobyshev, Dmitrii, 23
Brodskii, Iosif Aleksandrovich, 23, 177
Brodyachaya sobaka (Stray Dog)
    cabaret, 9, 85
Bryusov, Valerii Yakovlevich, 5
Bulgakov, Mikhail Afanas'evich, 66, 156

Chaliapin, Fedor Ivanovich 109–10
Chenier, Andre, 14, 77
Civil War reflected in Akhmatova's
    work, 58
Cleopatra, 82–3

Constant, Benjamin, 14
Czapski, Jozef, 18, 20

Dante Alighieri, 64, 76, 78–80, 82, 163
Decembrist movement, 62, 76, 108,
    135–6, 138, 161
Derzhavin, Gavriil Romanovich, 37, 148
Dostoevskii, Fedor Mikhailovich, 14, 20,
    87–90, 112

Ekster, Aleksandra Aleksandrovich, 40
Euripides, 76

Folklore in Akhmatova's work, 33–5, 38

Garshin, Vladimir Georgievich, 18,
    123–4, 151
Gofman, Viktor, 103–4
Golenishchev-Kutuzov, Vladimir, 5
Gorenko, Andrei Andreevich
    (Akhmatova's brother), 4, 12
Gorenko, Andrei Antonovich
    (Akhmatova's father), 3, 10
Gorenko, Inna Andreevna (Akhmatova's
    sister), 3–4
Gorenko, Inna Erazmovna (Akhmatova's
    mother), 3–4, 13, 89
Gorenko, Iya Andreevna (Akhmatova's
    sister), 12
Gorodetskii, Sergei Mitrofanovich, 8
Guild of Poets (Tsekh poetov), 8
Gumilev, Lev Nikolaevich (Akhmatova's
    son), 13, 15, 21, 23
Gumilev, Nikolai Stepanovich, 4–14
    passim., 46–7, 58, 77–8, 136, 138
    'Don Zhuan' ('Don Juan'), 135
    Don Zhuan v Egipte (*Don Juan in
    Egypt*), 135
    Gondla, 104
    In *Poem Without a Hero*, 111, 113
    'P'yanyi dervish' ('The Drunk
    Dervish'), 59, 62
    'Pyatistopnye iamby' ('Five Foot
    Iambs'), 135

Hamsun, Knut, 3

Index

CPSIA information can be obtained
at www.ICGtesting.com
Printed in the USA
LVOW13s0404141217
559668LV00008B/142/P

9 781859 730997